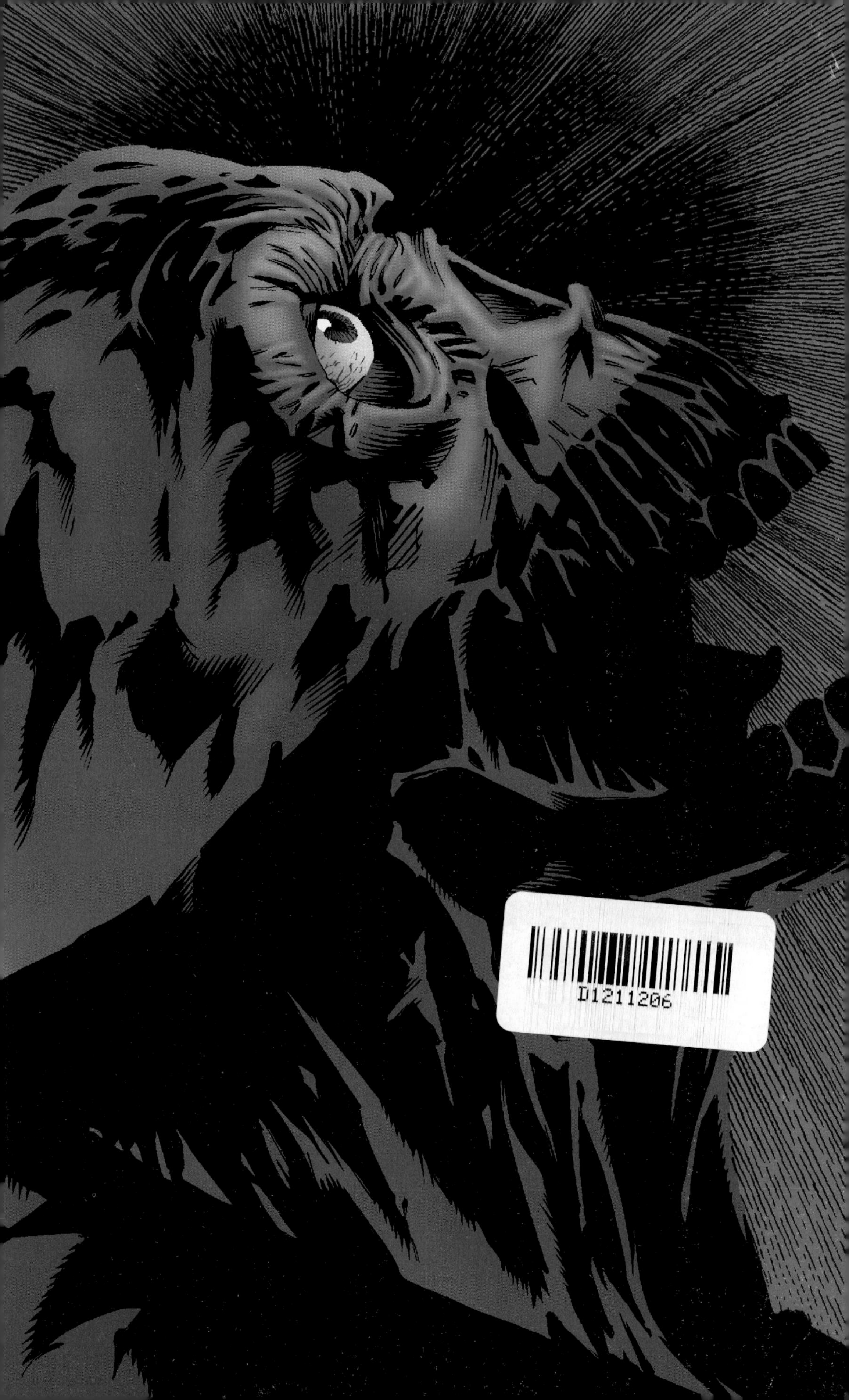

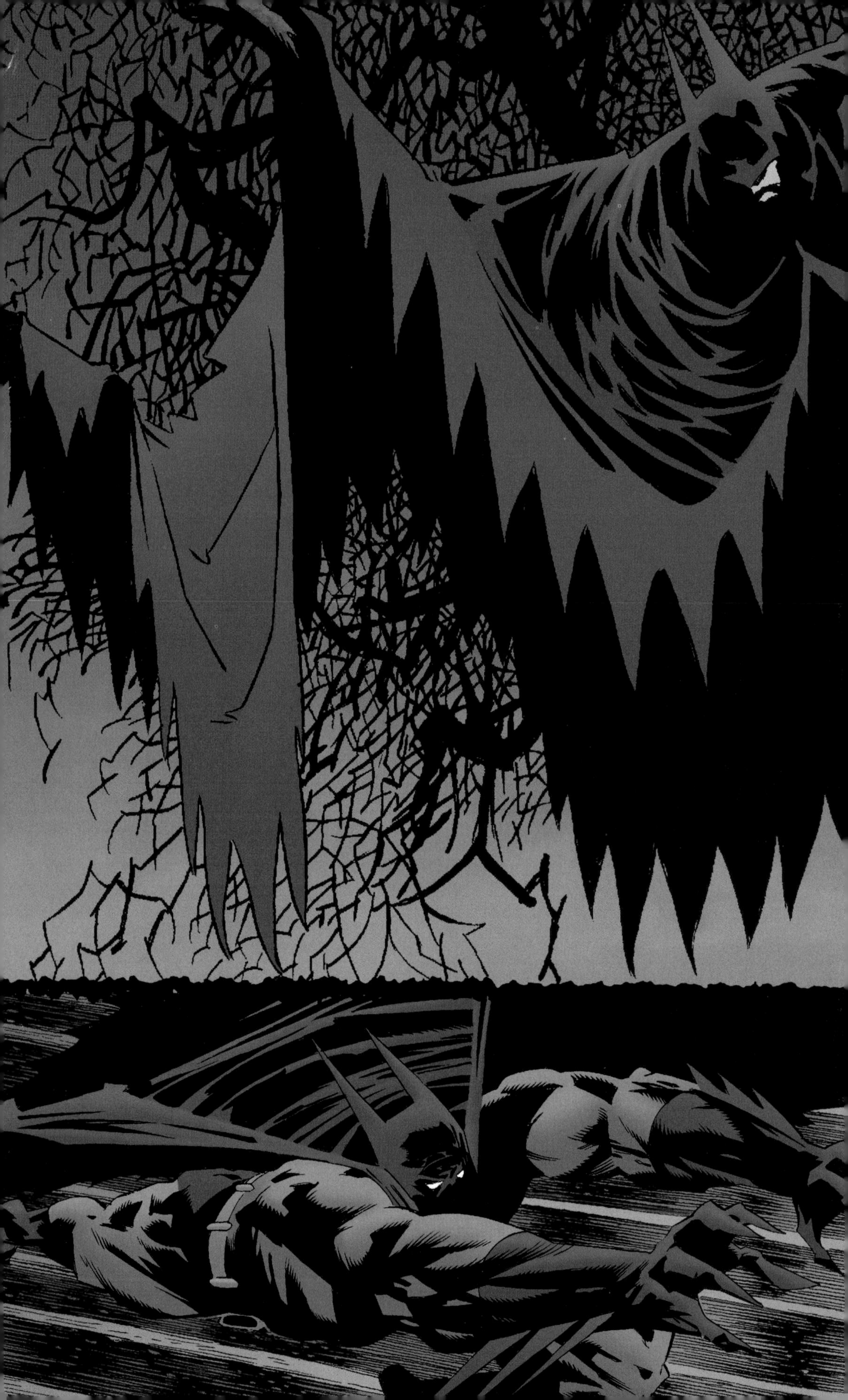

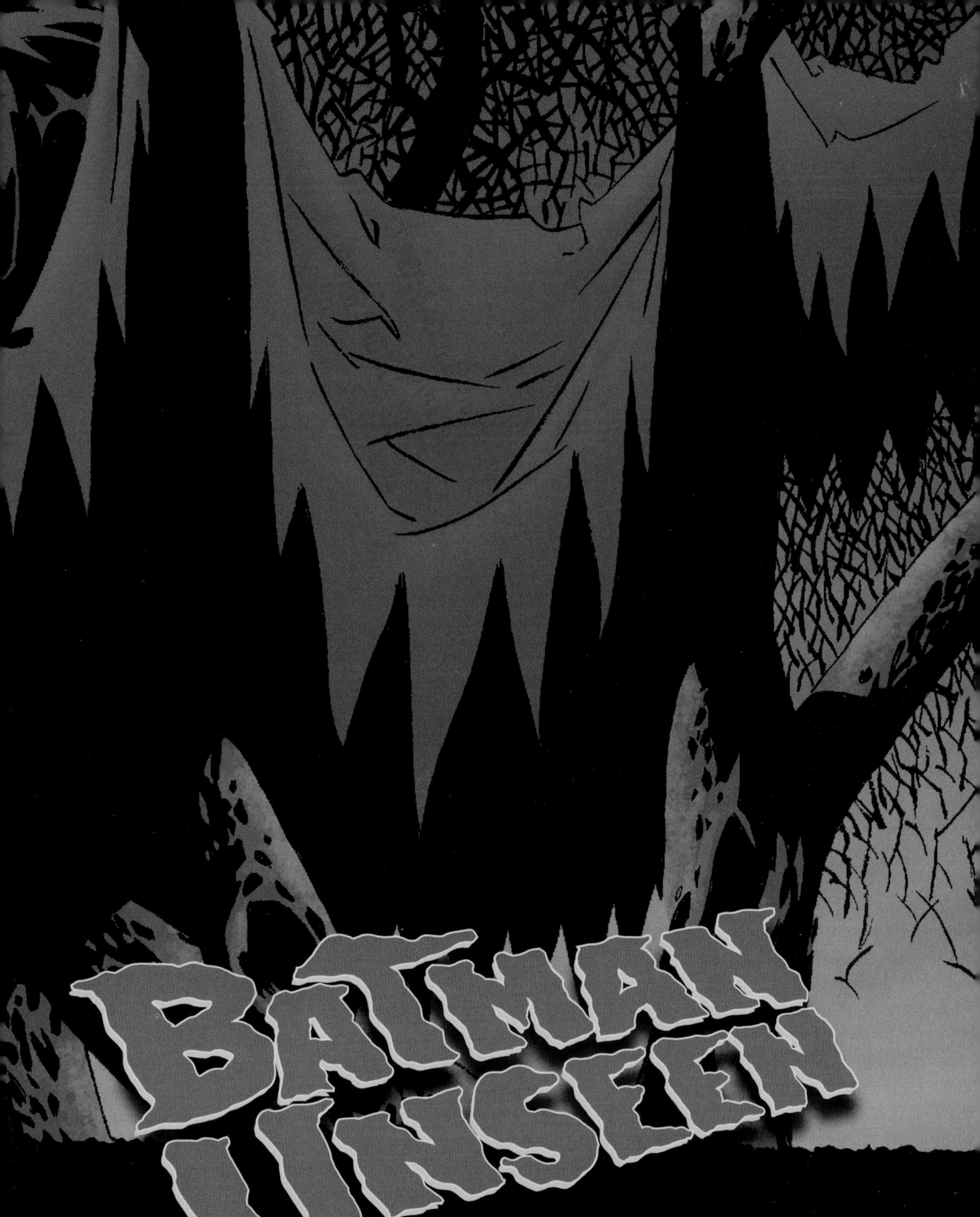
BATMAN
UNSEEN

DOUG MOENCH Writer

KELLEY JONES Artist & Covers

MICHELLE MADSEN Colorist

PAT BROSSEAU Letterer

BATMAN created by **BOB KANE**

BATMAN: UNSEEN
Published by DC Comics. Cover and compilation
Copyright © 2010 DC Comics. All Rights Reserved.

Originally published in single magazine form in
BATMAN: UNSEEN 1-5. Copyright © 2009, 2010 DC Comics.
All Rights Reserved. All characters, their distinctive
likenesses and related elements featured in this publication
are trademarks of DC Comics. The stories, characters and
incidents featured in this publication are entirely fictional.
DC Comics does not read or accept unsolicited submissions
of ideas, stories or artwork.

DC Comics, 1700 Broadway, New York, NY 10019
A Warner Bros. Entertainment Company
Printed by Quad/Graphics, Dubuque, IA, USA. 9/8/10.
First printing.
ISBN: 978-1-4012-2926-9

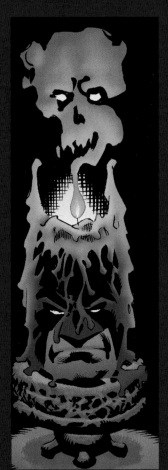

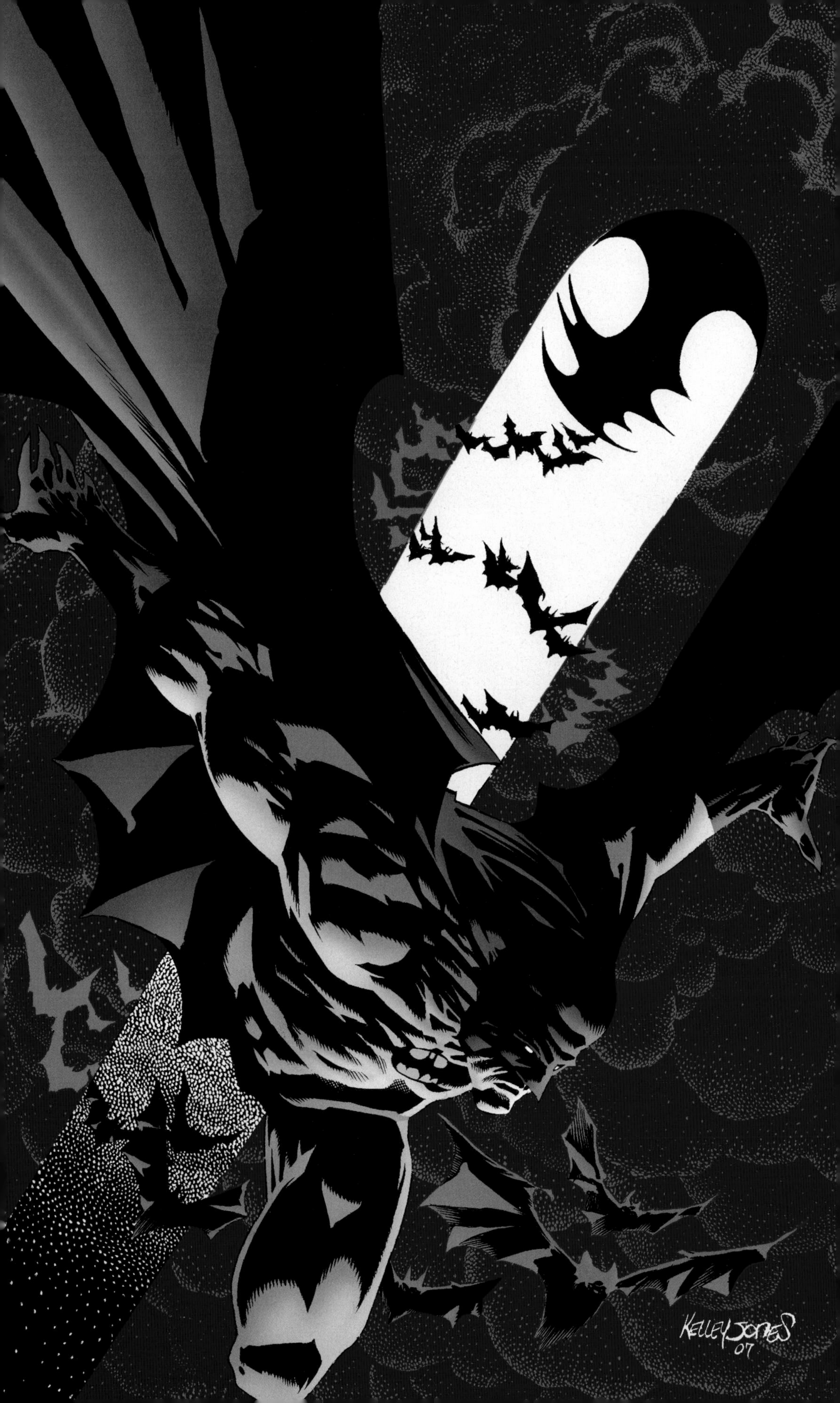
KELLEY JONES
07

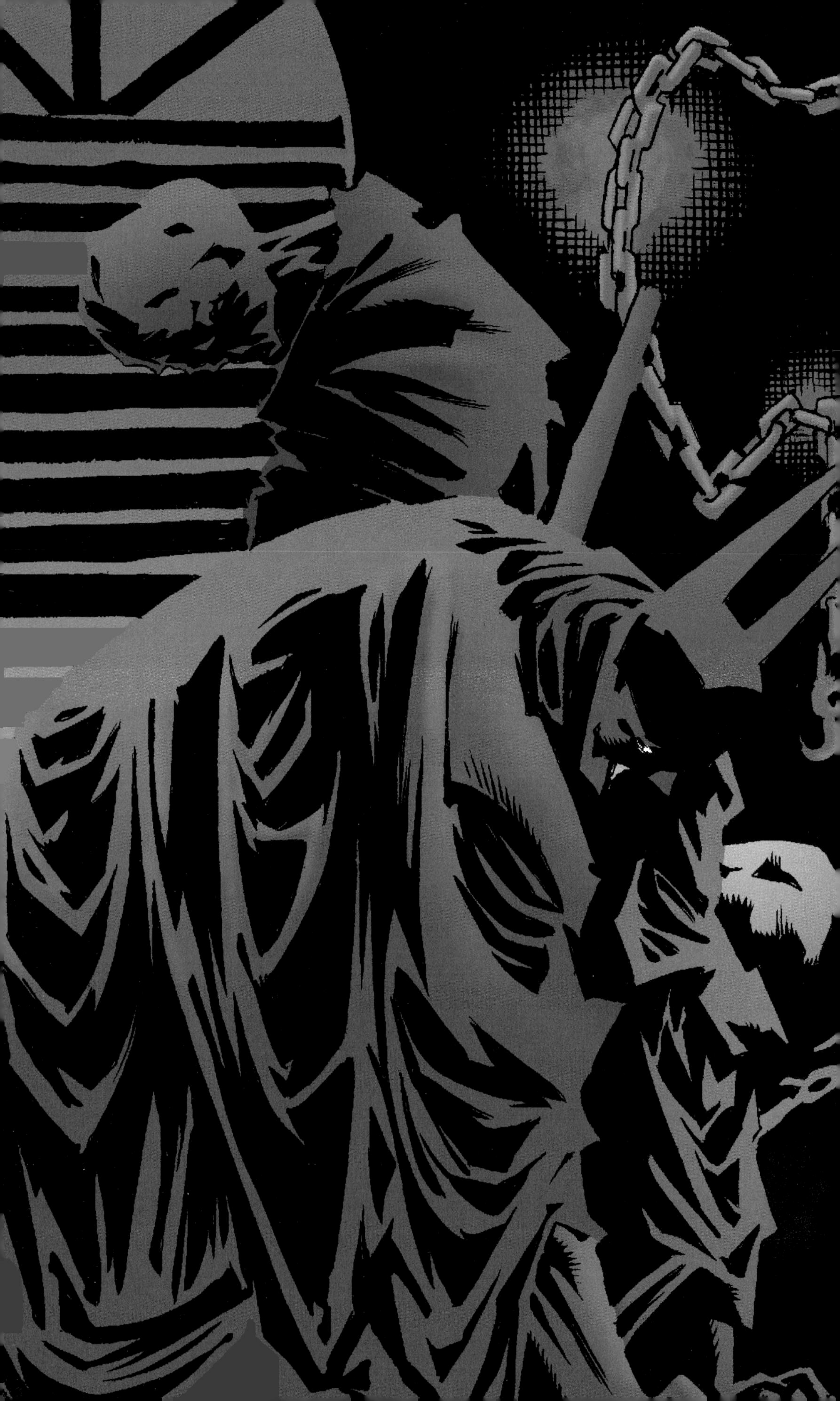

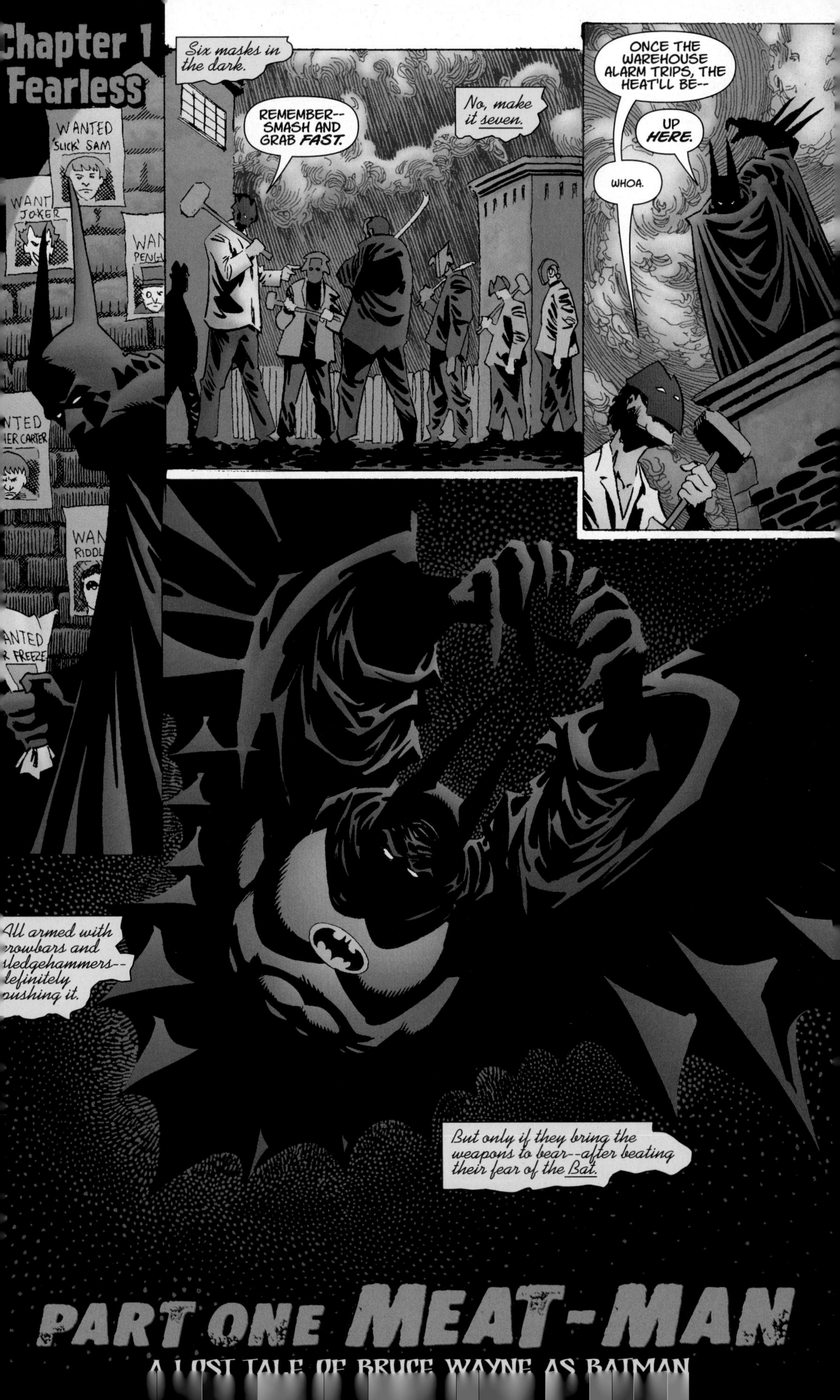

Chapter 1
Fearless
WANTED 'SLICK' SAM
WANT JOKER
WAN PENGU
NTED ER CARTER
WAN RIDDL
ANTED R FREEZE
Six masks in the dark.
REMEMBER-- SMASH AND GRAB FAST.
No, make it seven.
ONCE THE WAREHOUSE ALARM TRIPS, THE HEAT'LL BE--
UP HERE.
WHOA.
All armed with rowbars and ledgehammers-- efinitely ushing it.
But only if they bring the weapons to bear--after beating their fear of the Bat.
PART ONE MEAT-MAN
A LOST TALE OF BRUCE WAYNE AS BATMAN

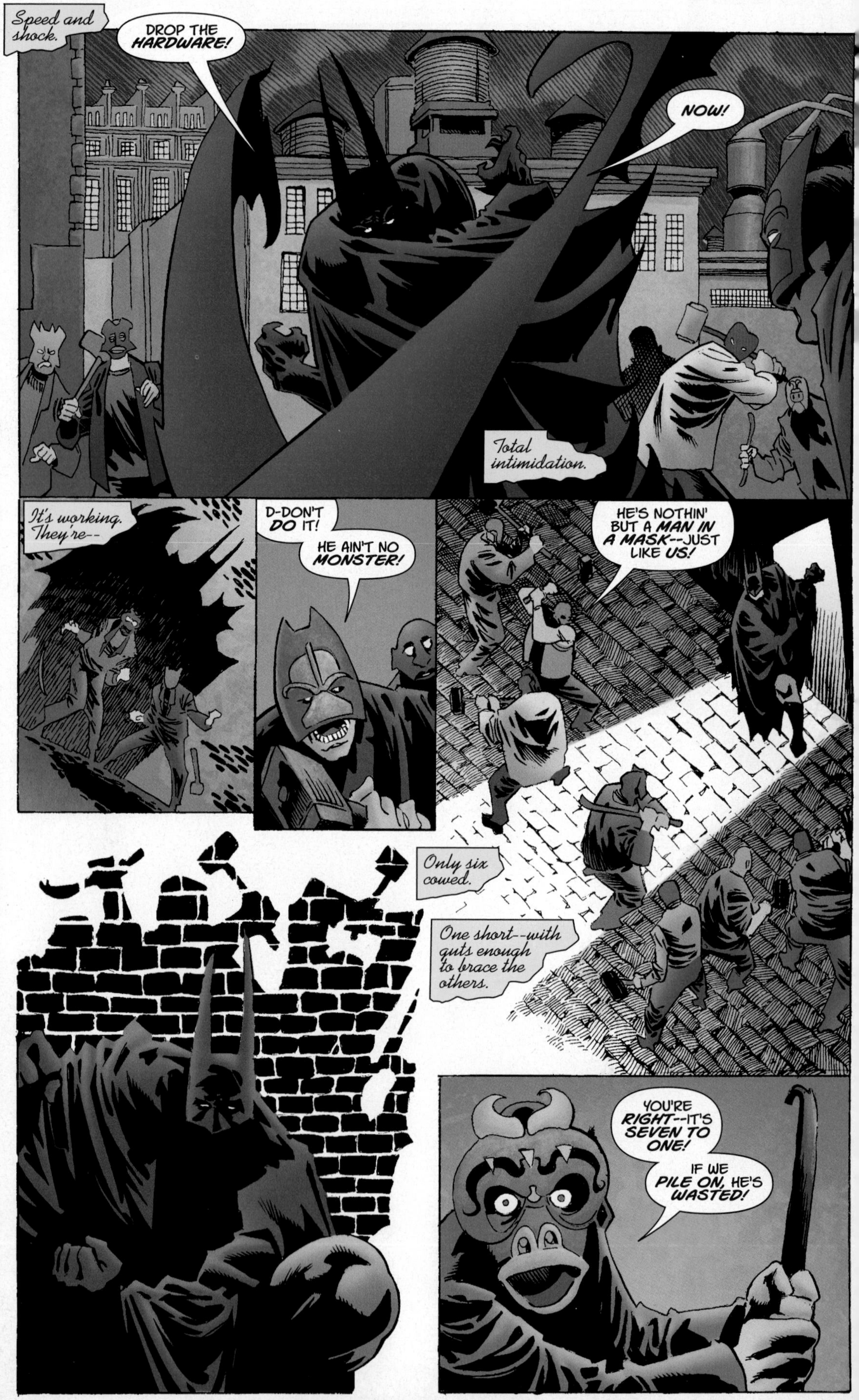

Speed and shock.
DROP THE HARDWARE!
NOW!
Total intimidation.
It's working. They're--
D-DON'T DO IT!
HE AIN'T NO MONSTER!
HE'S NOTHIN' BUT A MAN IN A MASK--JUST LIKE US!
Only six cowed.
One short--with guts enough to brace the others.
YOU'RE RIGHT--IT'S SEVEN TO ONE!
IF WE PILE ON, HE'S WASTED!

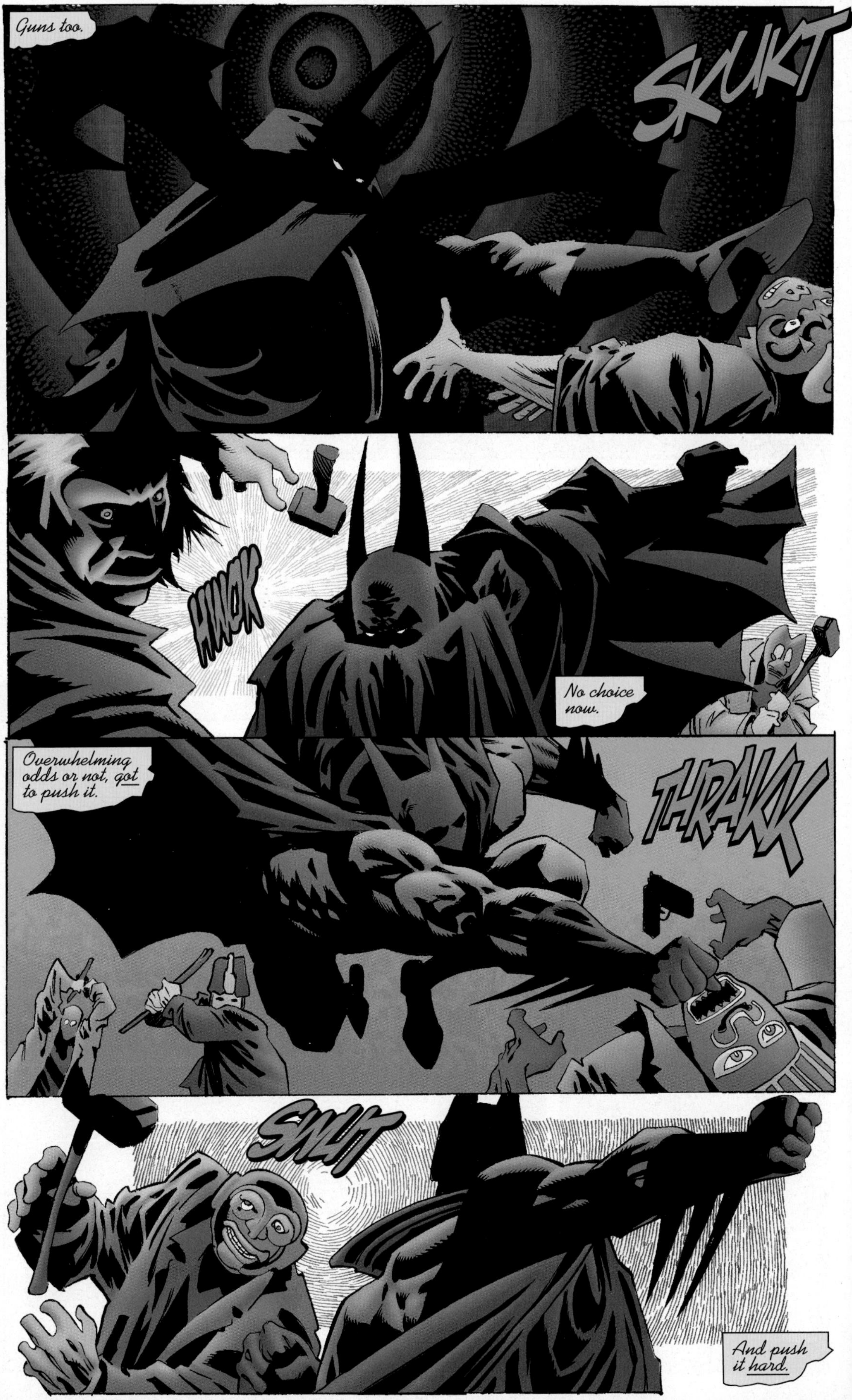
Guns too.
SKUKT
HWOK
No choice now.
Overwhelming odds or not, got to push it.
THRAKK
SNUT
And push it hard.

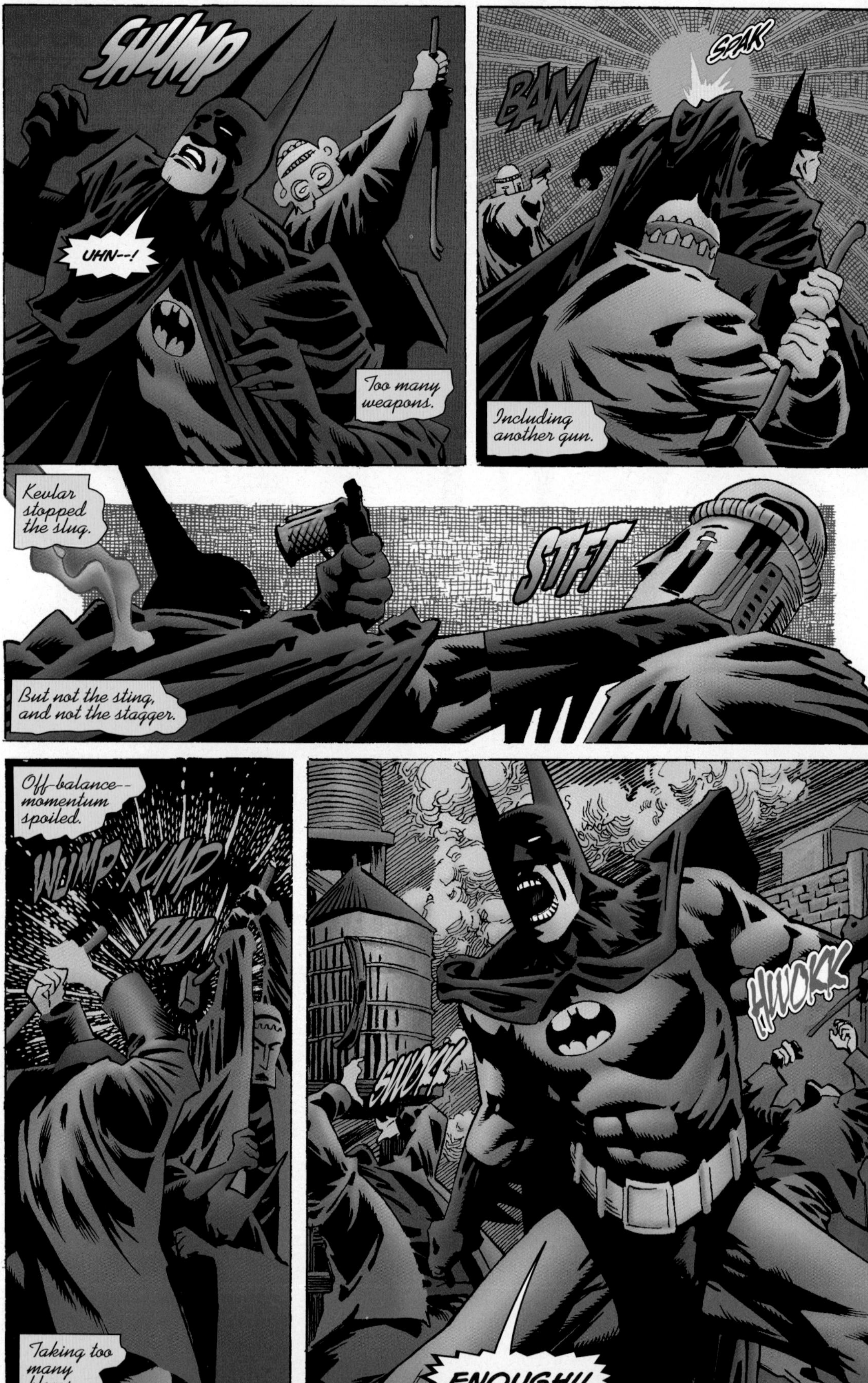
SHUMP
UHN--!
Too many weapons.
SPAK
BAM
Including another gun.
Kevlar stopped the slug.
STFT
But not the sting, and not the stagger.
Off-balance-- momentum spoiled.
WUMP KUMP
THD
Taking too many blows...
HWOKK
SNOKK
ENOUGH!!

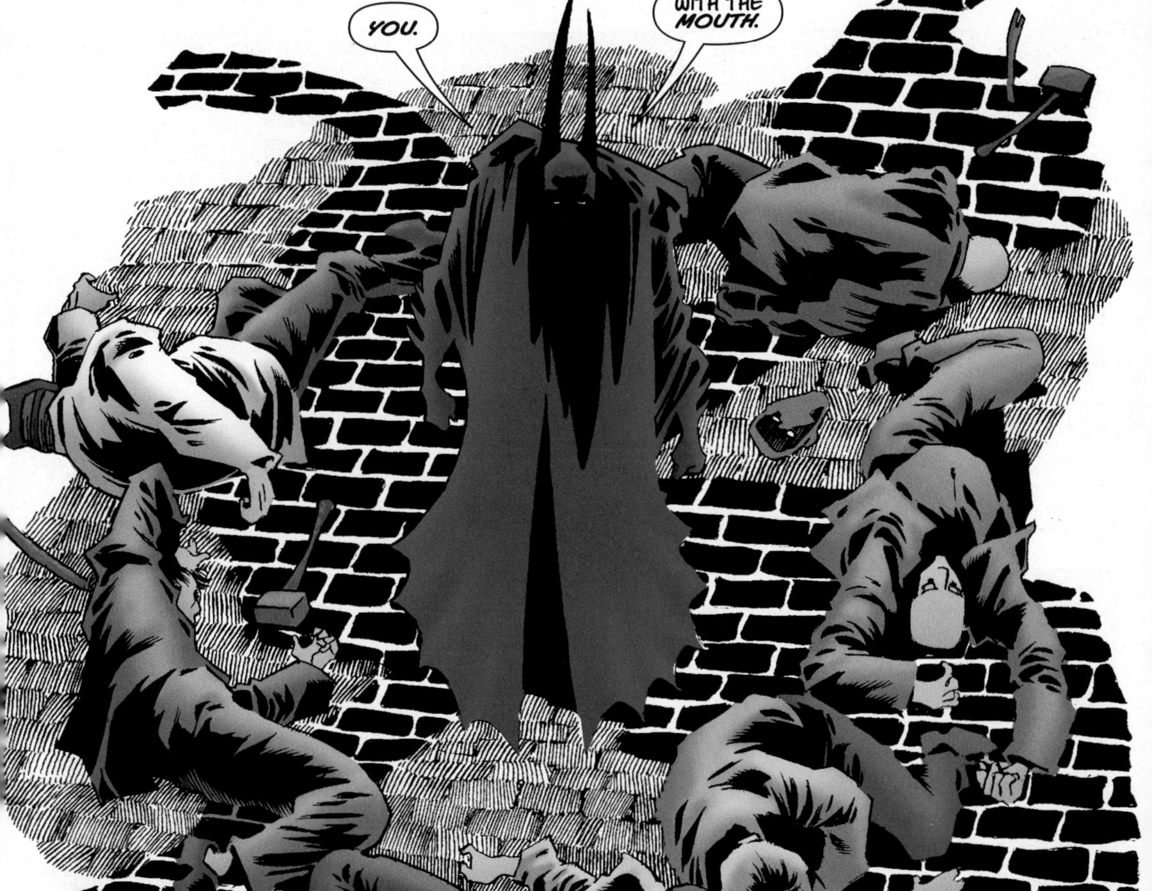
YOU.
WITH THE MOUTH.
NEARLY... D-DID IT...

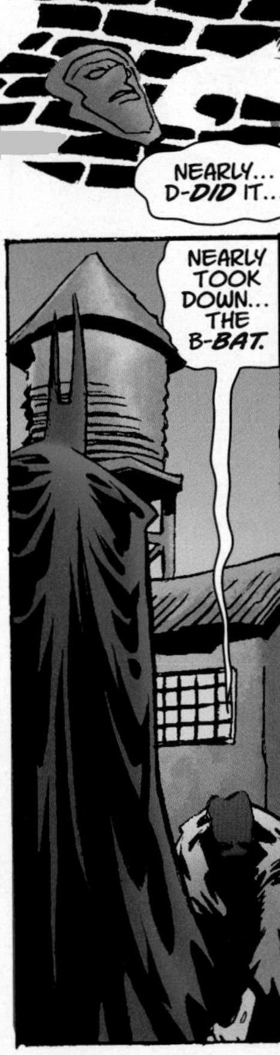
NEARLY TOOK DOWN... THE B-BAT.

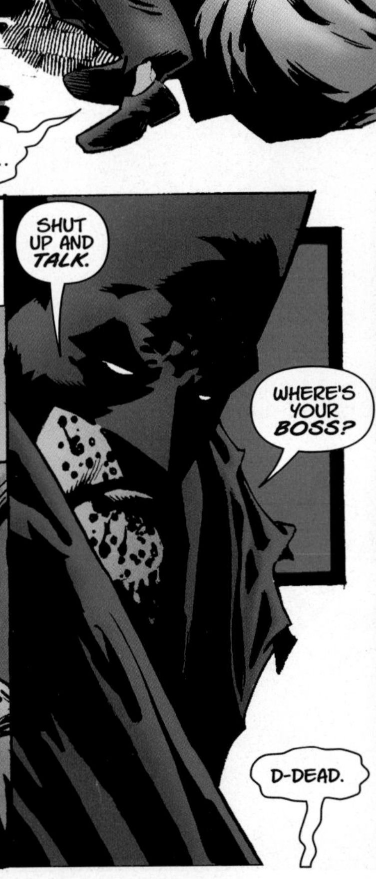
SHUT UP AND TALK.
WHERE'S YOUR BOSS?
D-DEAD.

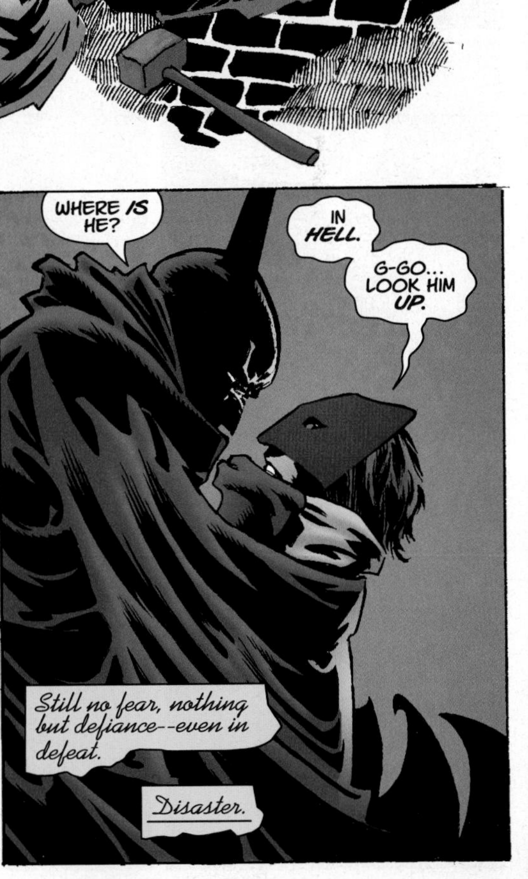
WHERE IS HE?
IN HELL.
G-GO... LOOK HIM UP.
Still no fear, nothing but defiance--even in defeat.
Disaster.

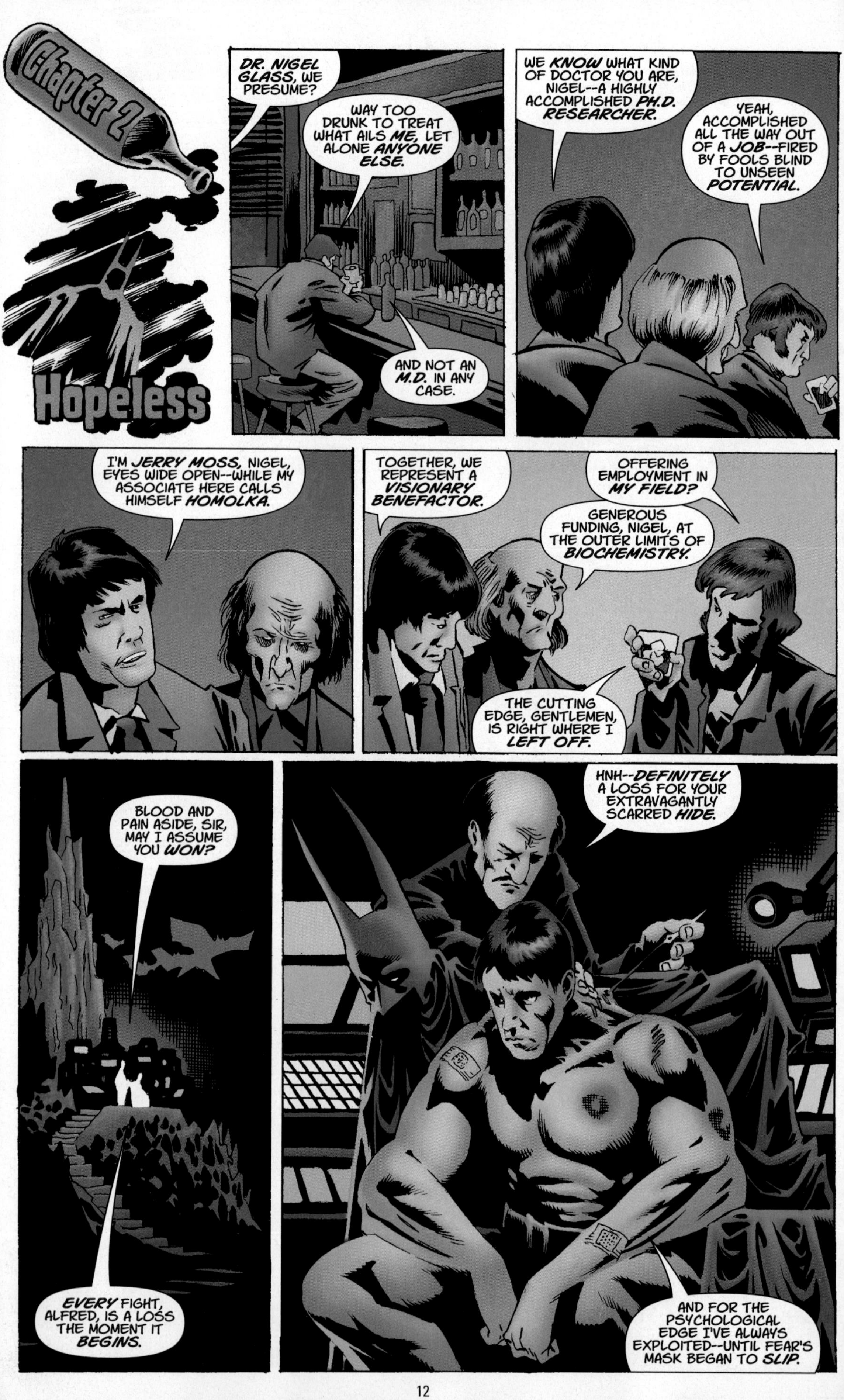
Chapter 2
Hopeless
DR. NIGEL GLASS, WE PRESUME?
WAY TOO DRUNK TO TREAT WHAT AILS ME, LET ALONE ANYONE ELSE.
AND NOT AN M.D. IN ANY CASE.
WE KNOW WHAT KIND OF DOCTOR YOU ARE, NIGEL--A HIGHLY ACCOMPLISHED PH.D. RESEARCHER.
YEAH, ACCOMPLISHED ALL THE WAY OUT OF A JOB--FIRED BY FOOLS BLIND TO UNSEEN POTENTIAL.
I'M JERRY MOSS, NIGEL, EYES WIDE OPEN--WHILE MY ASSOCIATE HERE CALLS HIMSELF HOMOLKA.
TOGETHER, WE REPRESENT A VISIONARY BENEFACTOR.
OFFERING EMPLOYMENT IN MY FIELD?
GENEROUS FUNDING, NIGEL, AT THE OUTER LIMITS OF BIOCHEMISTRY.
THE CUTTING EDGE, GENTLEMEN, IS RIGHT WHERE I LEFT OFF.
BLOOD AND PAIN ASIDE, SIR, MAY I ASSUME YOU WON?
EVERY FIGHT, ALFRED, IS A LOSS THE MOMENT IT BEGINS.
HNH--DEFINITELY A LOSS FOR YOUR EXTRAVAGANTLY SCARRED HIDE.
AND FOR THE PSYCHOLOGICAL EDGE I'VE ALWAYS EXPLOITED--UNTIL FEAR'S MASK BEGAN TO SLIP.

THEN YOU FIND THE TERMS *AGREEABLE,* DR. GLASS?

ANYTHING THAT PUTS ME BACK TO WORK, IT'S A *DEAL.*

EXCELLENT.

YOU'LL FORGIVE ME FOR NOT ENTERING THE LIGHT TO *SHAKE* ON IT, BUT MY BENEVOLENCE MUST REMAIN *ANONYMOUS.*

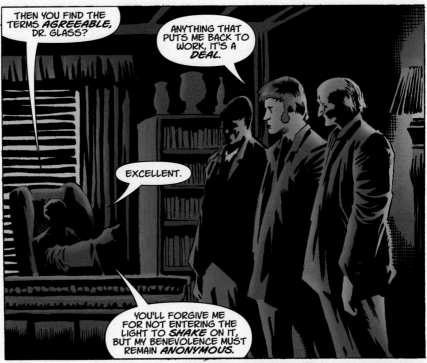

JUST SO LONG AS DEAD PRESIDENTS SHOW *THEIR* FACES IN SWEET GREEN.

THEN IF YOU'LL WAIT OUTSIDE WITH MR. HOMOLKA WHILE I FINALIZE THE DETAILS WITH MR. MOSS...

YOU *GOT* IT.

DETAILS, BOSS?

I WANT YOU TO PROVIDE NIGEL GLASS WITH A *RESEARCH LAB* AND WHATEVER ELSE HE WANTS--BUT DROP OUT OF SIGHT *BEFORE* DOING IT.

HOW *SO,* BOSS?

YOU WILL WITHDRAW TRANSFERRED FUNDS FROM YOUR BANK IN *CASH,* CLOSE YOUR *ACCOUNT,* AND NEVER RETURN TO THE BANK *AGAIN.*

YOU WILL THEN *MOVE--*LEAVING NO *FORWARDING ADDRESS*--TO A NEW PLACE LEASED UNDER A *DIFFERENT NAME...*

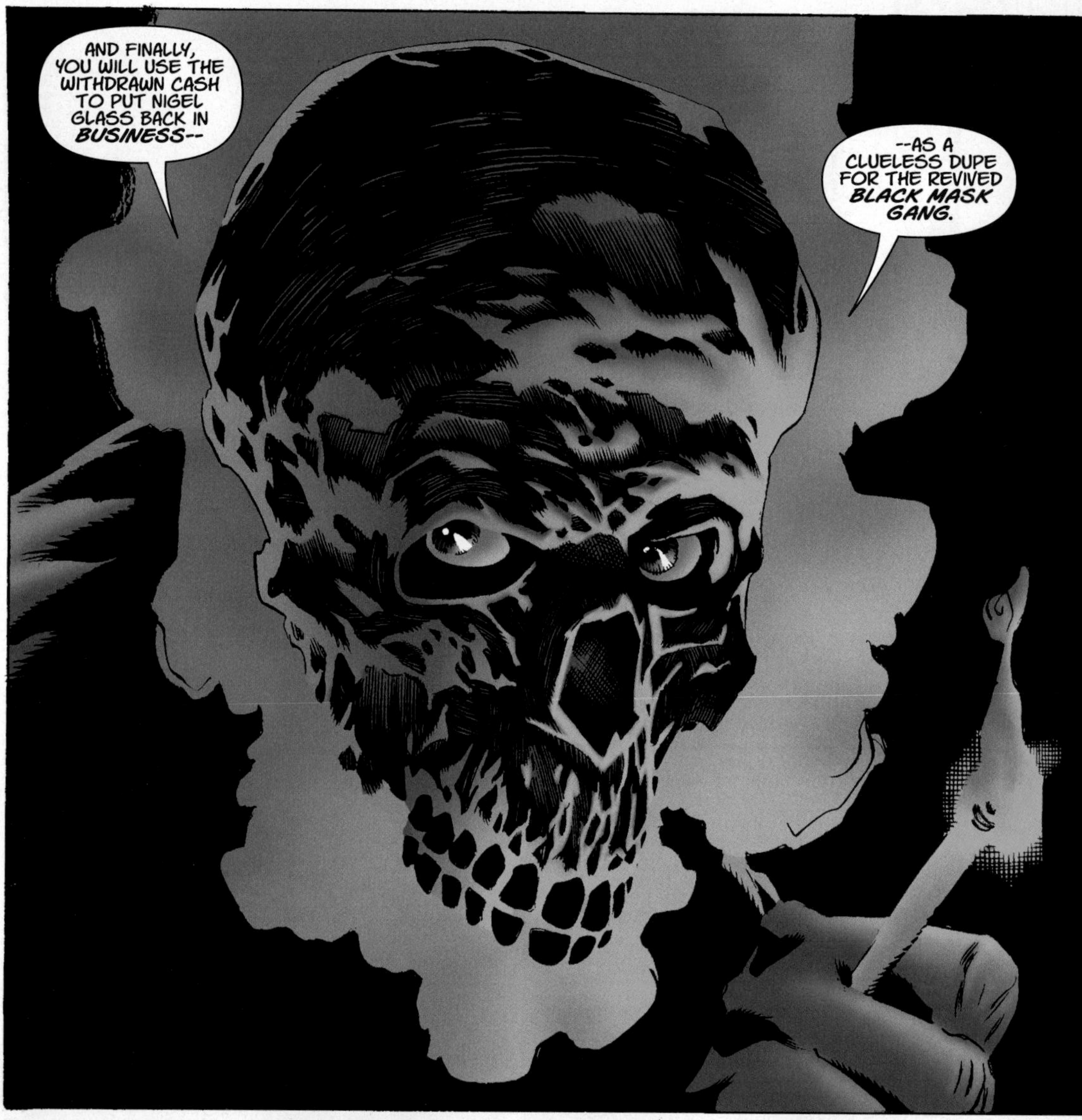
AND FINALLY, YOU WILL USE THE WITHDRAWN CASH TO PUT NIGEL GLASS BACK IN *BUSINESS*--
--AS A CLUELESS DUPE FOR THE REVIVED *BLACK MASK GANG*.

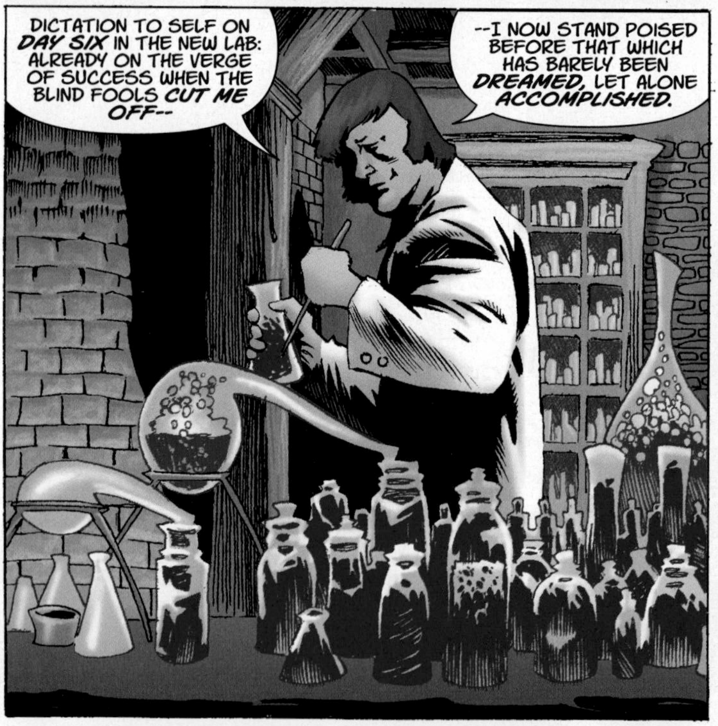
DICTATION TO SELF ON *DAY SIX* IN THE NEW LAB: ALREADY ON THE VERGE OF SUCCESS WHEN THE BLIND FOOLS *CUT ME OFF*--
--I NOW STAND POISED BEFORE THAT WHICH HAS BARELY BEEN *DREAMED*, LET ALONE *ACCOMPLISHED*.

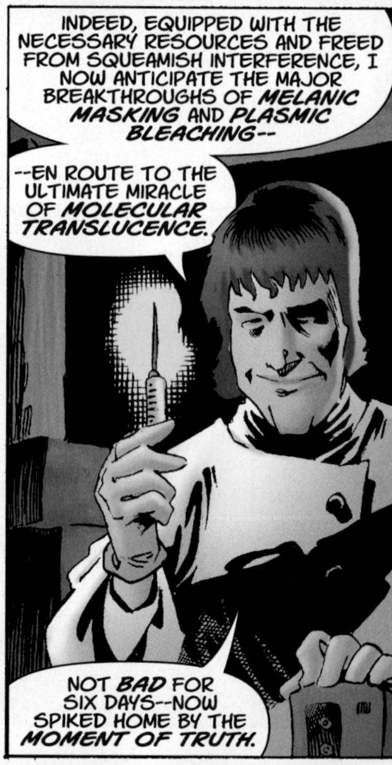
INDEED, EQUIPPED WITH THE NECESSARY RESOURCES AND FREED FROM SQUEAMISH INTERFERENCE, I NOW ANTICIPATE THE MAJOR BREAKTHROUGHS OF *MELANIC MASKING* AND *PLASMIC BLEACHING*--
--EN ROUTE TO THE ULTIMATE MIRACLE OF *MOLECULAR TRANSLUCENCE*.
NOT *BAD* FOR SIX DAYS--NOW SPIKED HOME BY THE *MOMENT OF TRUTH*.

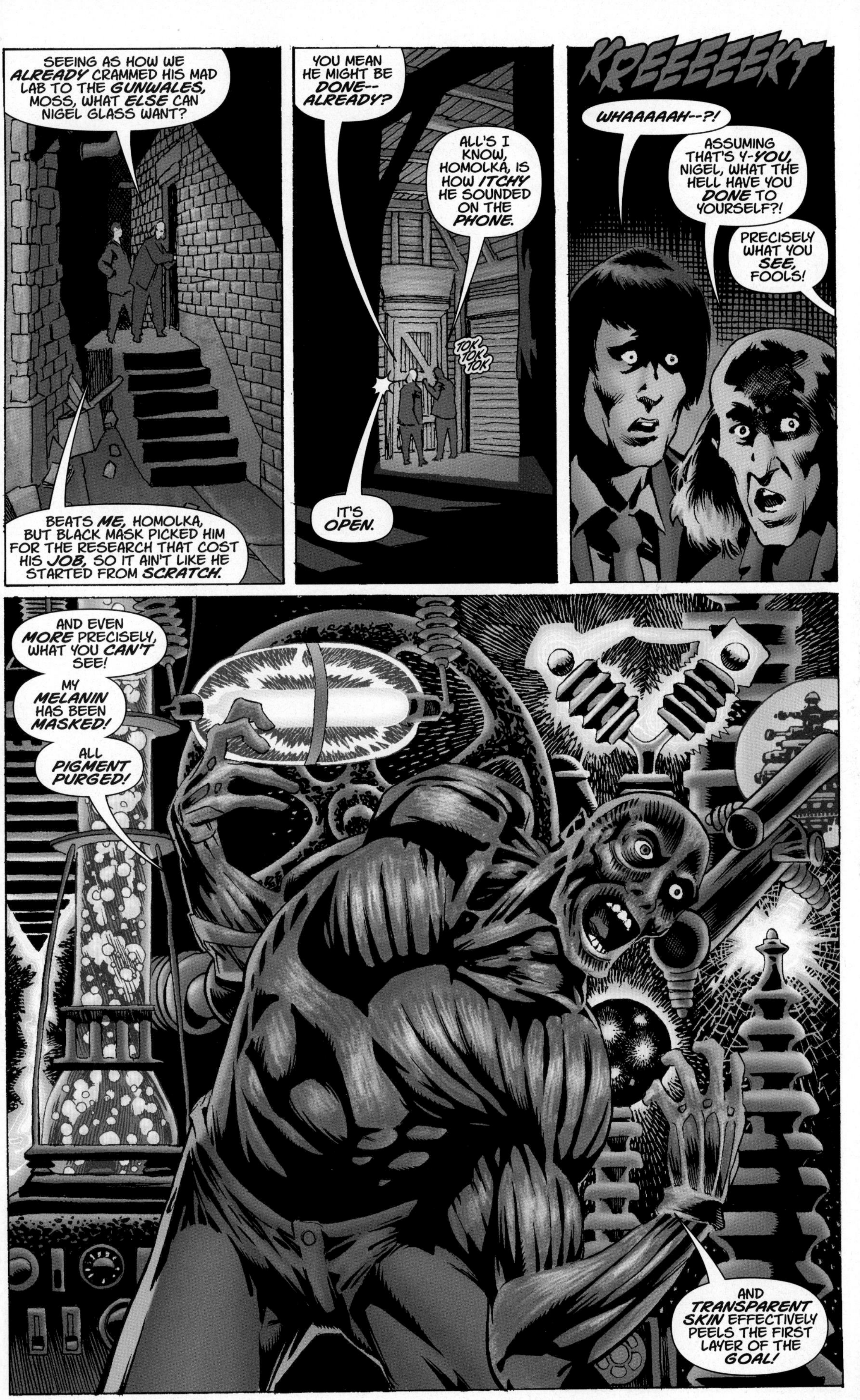
SEEING AS HOW WE ALREADY CRAMMED HIS MAD LAB TO THE GUNWALES, MOSS, WHAT ELSE CAN NIGEL GLASS WANT?
BEATS ME, HOMOLKA, BUT BLACK MASK PICKED HIM FOR THE RESEARCH THAT COST HIS JOB, SO IT AIN'T LIKE HE STARTED FROM SCRATCH.
YOU MEAN HE MIGHT BE DONE--ALREADY?
ALL'S I KNOW, HOMOLKA, IS HOW ITCHY HE SOUNDED ON THE PHONE.
TOK TOK TOK
IT'S OPEN.
KREEEEEKT
WHAAAAAH--?!
ASSUMING THAT'S Y-YOU, NIGEL, WHAT THE HELL HAVE YOU DONE TO YOURSELF?!
PRECISELY WHAT YOU SEE, FOOLS!
AND EVEN MORE PRECISELY, WHAT YOU CAN'T SEE!
MY MELANIN HAS BEEN MASKED!
ALL PIGMENT PURGED!
AND TRANSPARENT SKIN EFFECTIVELY PEELS THE FIRST LAYER OF THE GOAL!

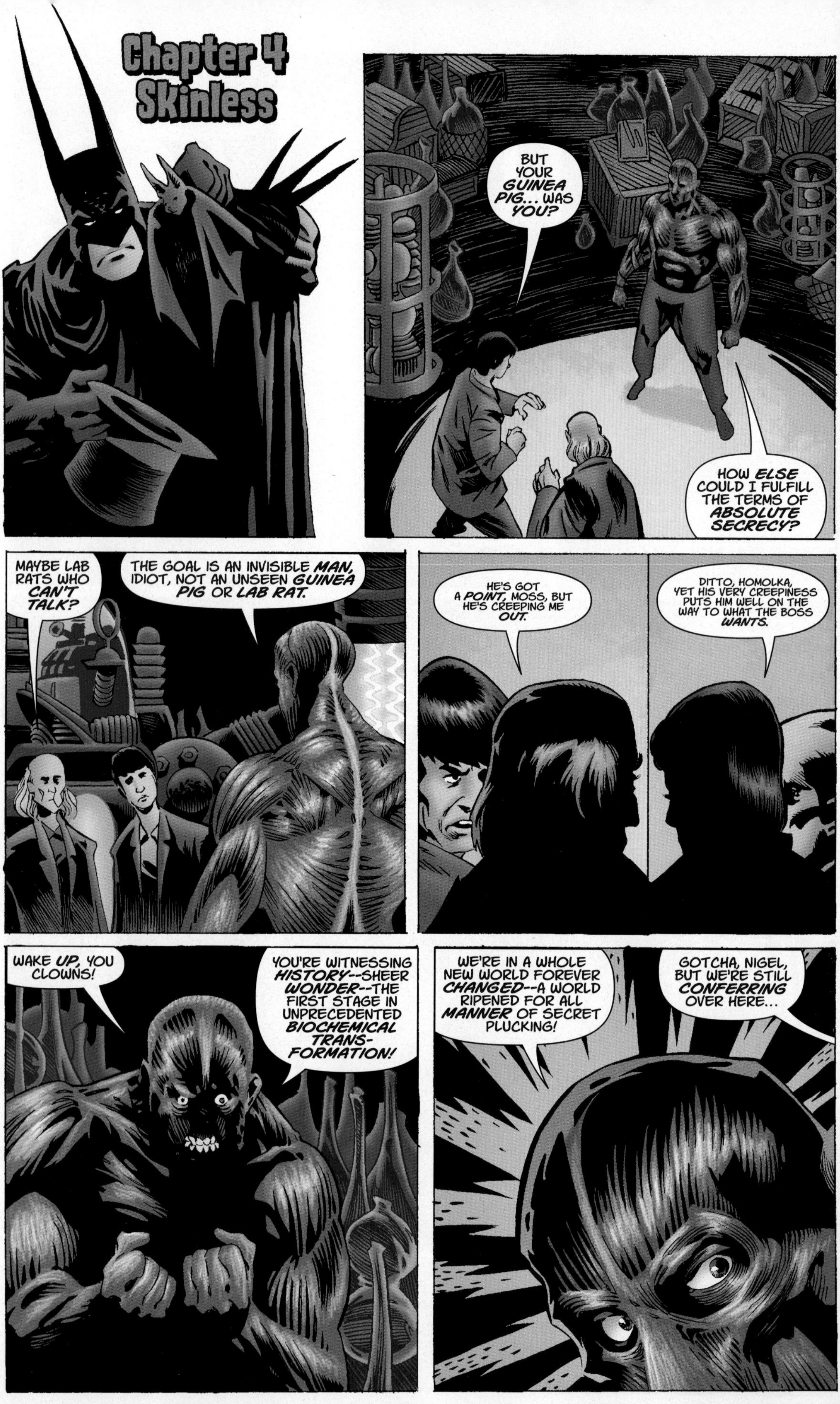
Chapter 4
Skinless
BUT YOUR GUINEA PIG... WAS YOU?
HOW ELSE COULD I FULFILL THE TERMS OF ABSOLUTE SECRECY?
MAYBE LAB RATS WHO CAN'T TALK?
THE GOAL IS AN INVISIBLE MAN, IDIOT, NOT AN UNSEEN GUINEA PIG OR LAB RAT.
HE'S GOT A POINT, MOSS, BUT HE'S CREEPING ME OUT.
DITTO, HOMOLKA, YET HIS VERY CREEPINESS PUTS HIM WELL ON THE WAY TO WHAT THE BOSS WANTS.
WAKE UP, YOU CLOWNS!
YOU'RE WITNESSING HISTORY--SHEER WONDER--THE FIRST STAGE IN UNPRECEDENTED BIOCHEMICAL TRANS-FORMATION!
WE'RE IN A WHOLE NEW WORLD FOREVER CHANGED--A WORLD RIPENED FOR ALL MANNER OF SECRET PLUCKING!
GOTCHA, NIGEL, BUT WE'RE STILL CONFERRING OVER HERE...

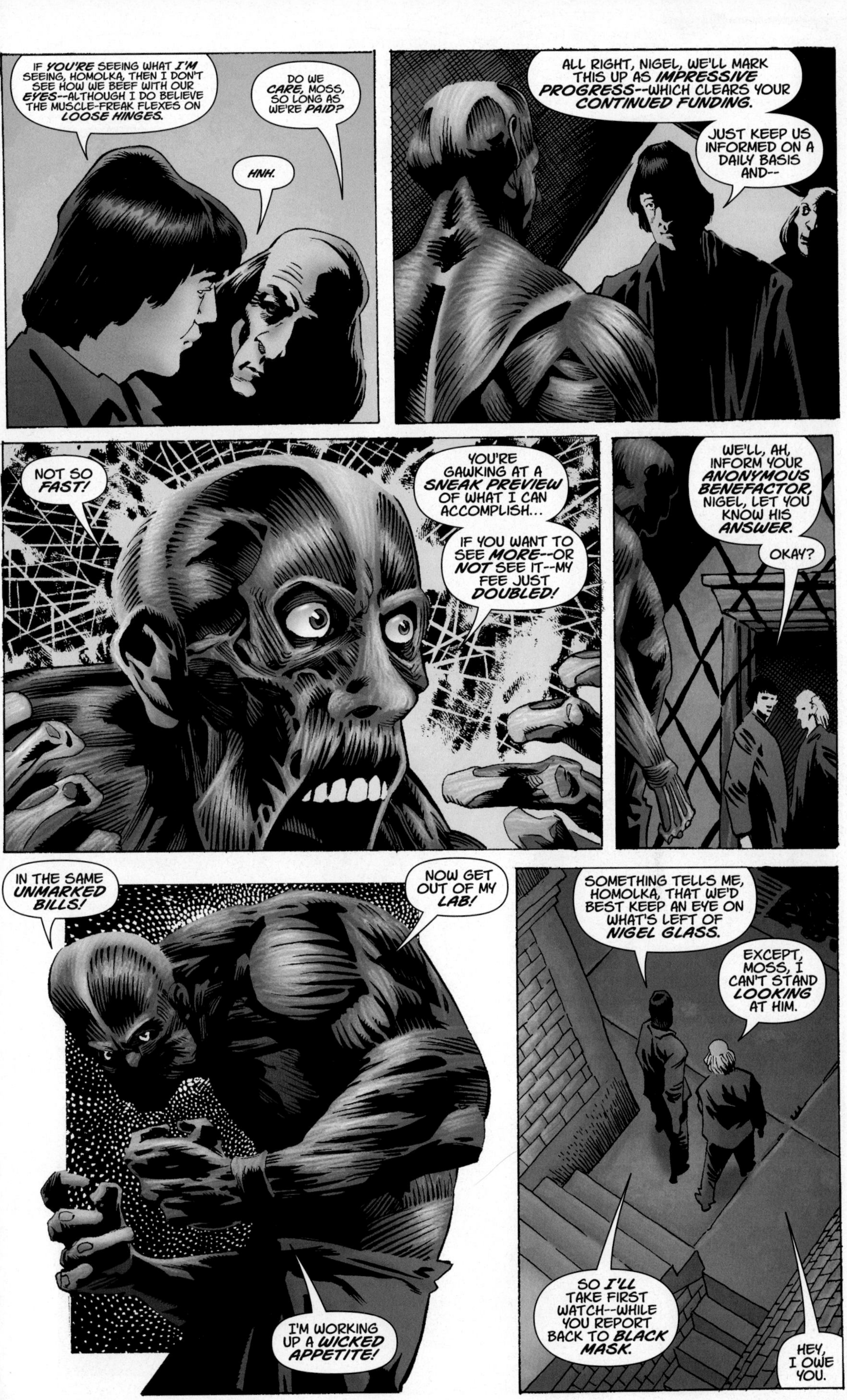
IF YOU'RE SEEING WHAT I'M SEEING, HOMOLKA, THEN I DON'T SEE HOW WE BEEF WITH OUR EYES--ALTHOUGH I DO BELIEVE THE MUSCLE-FREAK FLEXES ON LOOSE HINGES.
DO WE CARE, MOSS, SO LONG AS WE'RE PAID?
HNH.
ALL RIGHT, NIGEL, WE'LL MARK THIS UP AS IMPRESSIVE PROGRESS--WHICH CLEARS YOUR CONTINUED FUNDING.
JUST KEEP US INFORMED ON A DAILY BASIS AND--
NOT SO FAST!
YOU'RE GAWKING AT A SNEAK PREVIEW OF WHAT I CAN ACCOMPLISH...
IF YOU WANT TO SEE MORE--OR NOT SEE IT--MY FEE JUST DOUBLED!
WE'LL, AH, INFORM YOUR ANONYMOUS BENEFACTOR, NIGEL, LET YOU KNOW HIS ANSWER.
OKAY?
IN THE SAME UNMARKED BILLS!
NOW GET OUT OF MY LAB!
I'M WORKING UP A WICKED APPETITE!
SOMETHING TELLS ME, HOMOLKA, THAT WE'D BEST KEEP AN EYE ON WHAT'S LEFT OF NIGEL GLASS.
EXCEPT, MOSS, I CAN'T STAND LOOKING AT HIM.
SO I'LL TAKE FIRST WATCH--WHILE YOU REPORT BACK TO BLACK MASK.
HEY, I OWE YOU.

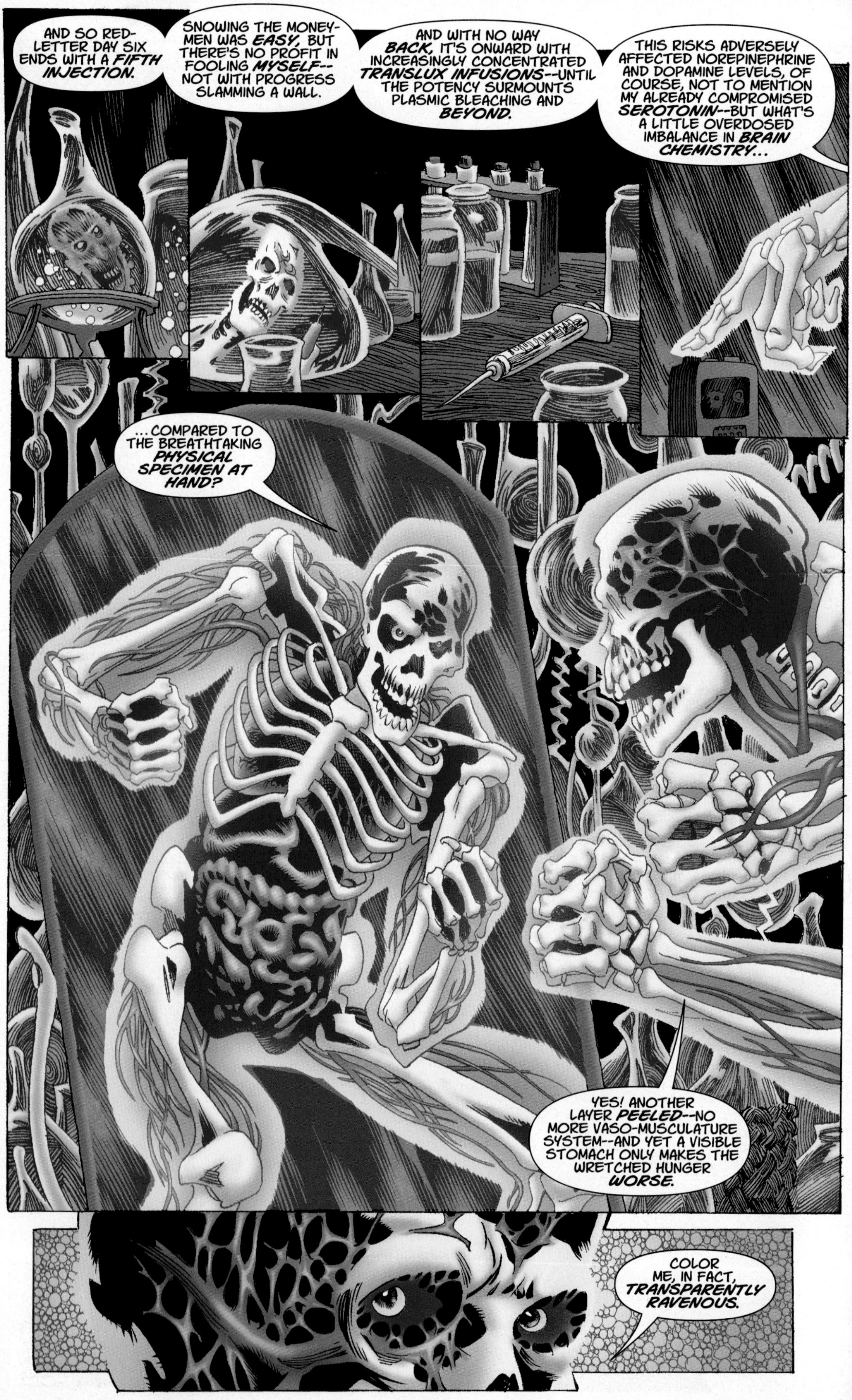
AND SO RED-LETTER DAY SIX ENDS WITH A FIFTH INJECTION.
SNOWING THE MONEY-MEN WAS EASY, BUT THERE'S NO PROFIT IN FOOLING MYSELF-- NOT WITH PROGRESS SLAMMING A WALL.
AND WITH NO WAY BACK, IT'S ONWARD WITH INCREASINGLY CONCENTRATED TRANSLUX INFUSIONS--UNTIL THE POTENCY SURMOUNTS PLASMIC BLEACHING AND BEYOND.
THIS RISKS ADVERSELY AFFECTED NOREPINEPHRINE AND DOPAMINE LEVELS, OF COURSE, NOT TO MENTION MY ALREADY COMPROMISED SEROTONIN--BUT WHAT'S A LITTLE OVERDOSED IMBALANCE IN BRAIN CHEMISTRY...
...COMPARED TO THE BREATHTAKING PHYSICAL SPECIMEN AT HAND?
YES! ANOTHER LAYER PEELED--NO MORE VASO-MUSCULATURE SYSTEM--AND YET A VISIBLE STOMACH ONLY MAKES THE WRETCHED HUNGER WORSE.
COLOR ME, IN FACT, TRANSPARENTLY RAVENOUS.

IT'S *HIM*.

BETTER *FOLLOW*.

BUT WHERE THE HELL IS HE HUSTLING AT *THIS* TIME OF NIGHT?

RING IT *UP*, CREEP, AND RING IT UP *FAST!* I'M *VORACIOUS* HERE!

IMPORT FOODS

NUMA'S GROCERY

MEAT FRESH VEGE

YEAH? AND WHO'RE YOU S'POSED TO *BE?* THE INCREDIBLE UNDERCOVER *JUNKFOOD MAN?*

WHO *AM* I? IS *THAT* YOUR QUESTION?

I'LL *SHOW* YOU WHO I AM!

WHUFUH--?

I AM THE ALMIGHTY FACE OF BIOLOGICAL *SHOCK AND AWE!*

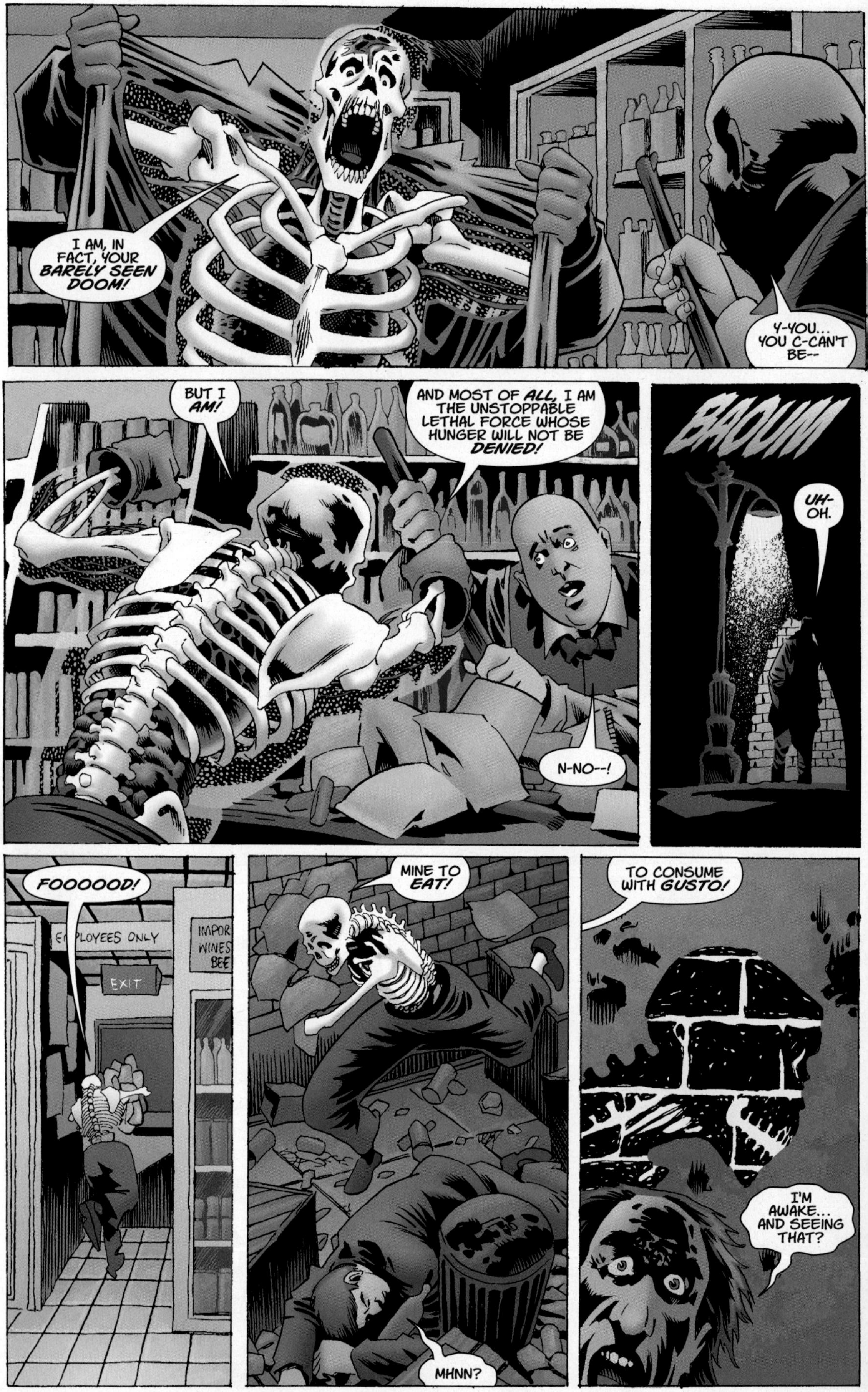
I AM, IN FACT, YOUR BARELY SEEN DOOM!
Y-YOU... YOU C-CAN'T BE--
BUT I AM!
AND MOST OF ALL, I AM THE UNSTOPPABLE LETHAL FORCE WHOSE HUNGER WILL NOT BE DENIED!
N-NO--!
BAOUM
UH-OH.
FOOOOOD!
EMPLOYEES ONLY
IMPOR WINES BEE
EXIT
MINE TO EAT!
MHNN?
TO CONSUME WITH GUSTO!
I'M AWAKE... AND SEEING THAT?

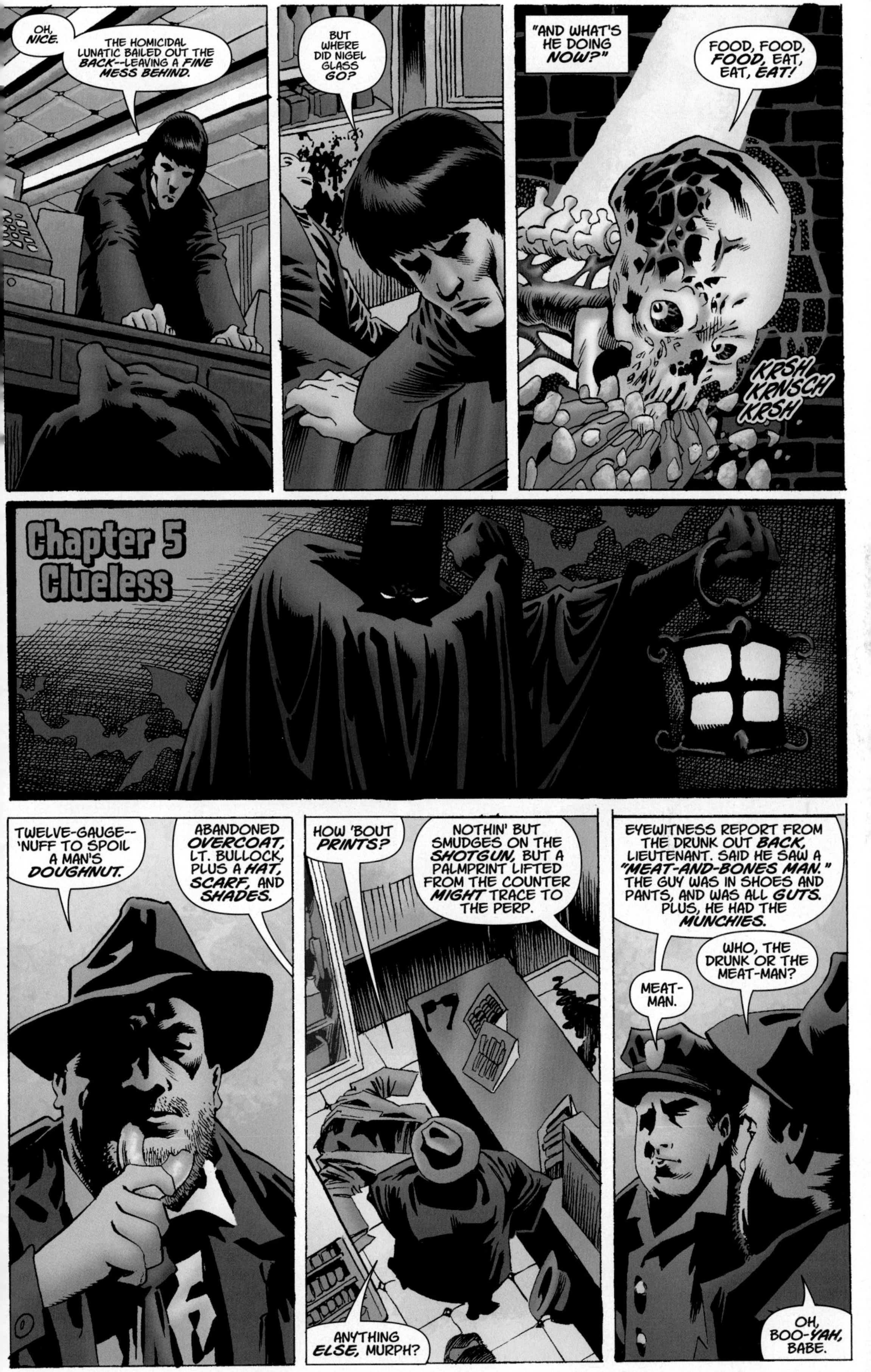
OH, NICE.
THE HOMICIDAL LUNATIC BAILED OUT THE BACK--LEAVING A FINE MESS BEHIND.
BUT WHERE DID NIGEL GLASS GO?
"AND WHAT'S HE DOING NOW?"
FOOD, FOOD, FOOD, EAT, EAT, EAT!
KRSH KRNSCH KRSH
Chapter 5 Clueless
TWELVE-GAUGE-- 'NUFF TO SPOIL A MAN'S DOUGHNUT.
ABANDONED OVERCOAT, LT. BULLOCK, PLUS A HAT, SCARF, AND SHADES.
HOW 'BOUT PRINTS?
NOTHIN' BUT SMUDGES ON THE SHOTGUN, BUT A PALMPRINT LIFTED FROM THE COUNTER MIGHT TRACE TO THE PERP.
ANYTHING ELSE, MURPH?
EYEWITNESS REPORT FROM THE DRUNK OUT BACK, LIEUTENANT. SAID HE SAW A "MEAT-AND-BONES MAN." THE GUY WAS IN SHOES AND PANTS, AND WAS ALL GUTS. PLUS, HE HAD THE MUNCHIES.
WHO, THE DRUNK OR THE MEAT-MAN?
MEAT-MAN.
OH, BOO-YAH, BABE.

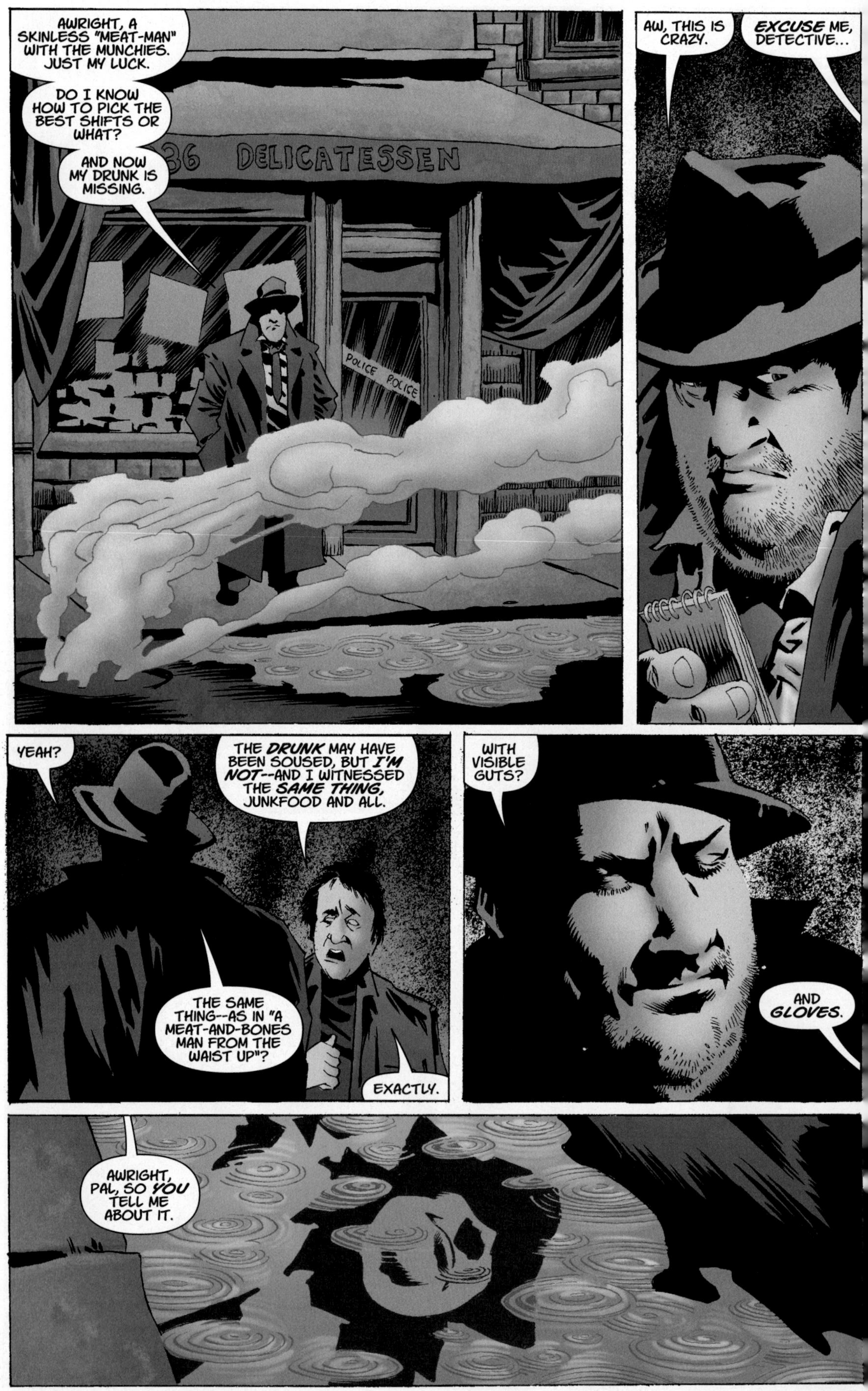
AWRIGHT, A SKINLESS "MEAT-MAN" WITH THE MUNCHIES. JUST MY LUCK.
DO I KNOW HOW TO PICK THE BEST SHIFTS OR WHAT?
AND NOW MY DRUNK IS MISSING.
36 DELICATESSEN
POLICE POLICE
AW, THIS IS CRAZY.
EXCUSE ME, DETECTIVE...
YEAH?
THE *DRUNK* MAY HAVE BEEN SOUSED, BUT *I'M NOT*--AND I WITNESSED THE *SAME THING,* JUNKFOOD AND ALL.
THE SAME THING--AS IN "A MEAT-AND-BONES MAN FROM THE WAIST UP"?
EXACTLY.
WITH VISIBLE GUTS?
AND *GLOVES.*
AWRIGHT, PAL, SO *YOU* TELL ME ABOUT IT.

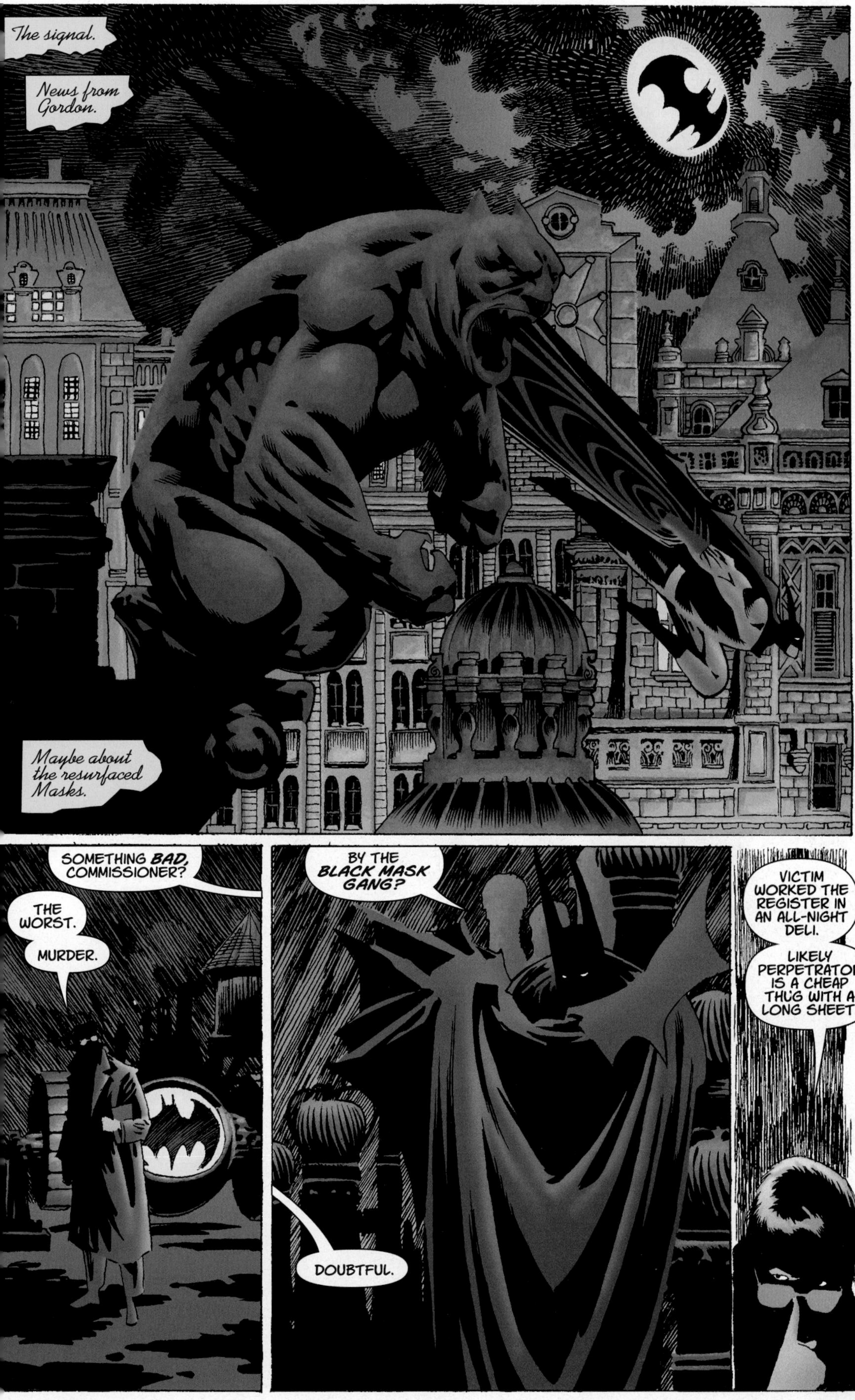
The signal.
News from Gordon.
Maybe about the resurfaced Masks.
SOMETHING BAD, COMMISSIONER?
THE WORST.
MURDER.
BY THE BLACK MASK GANG?
DOUBTFUL.
VICTIM WORKED THE REGISTER IN AN ALL-NIGHT DELI.
LIKELY PERPETRATOR IS A CHEAP THUG WITH A LONG SHEET.

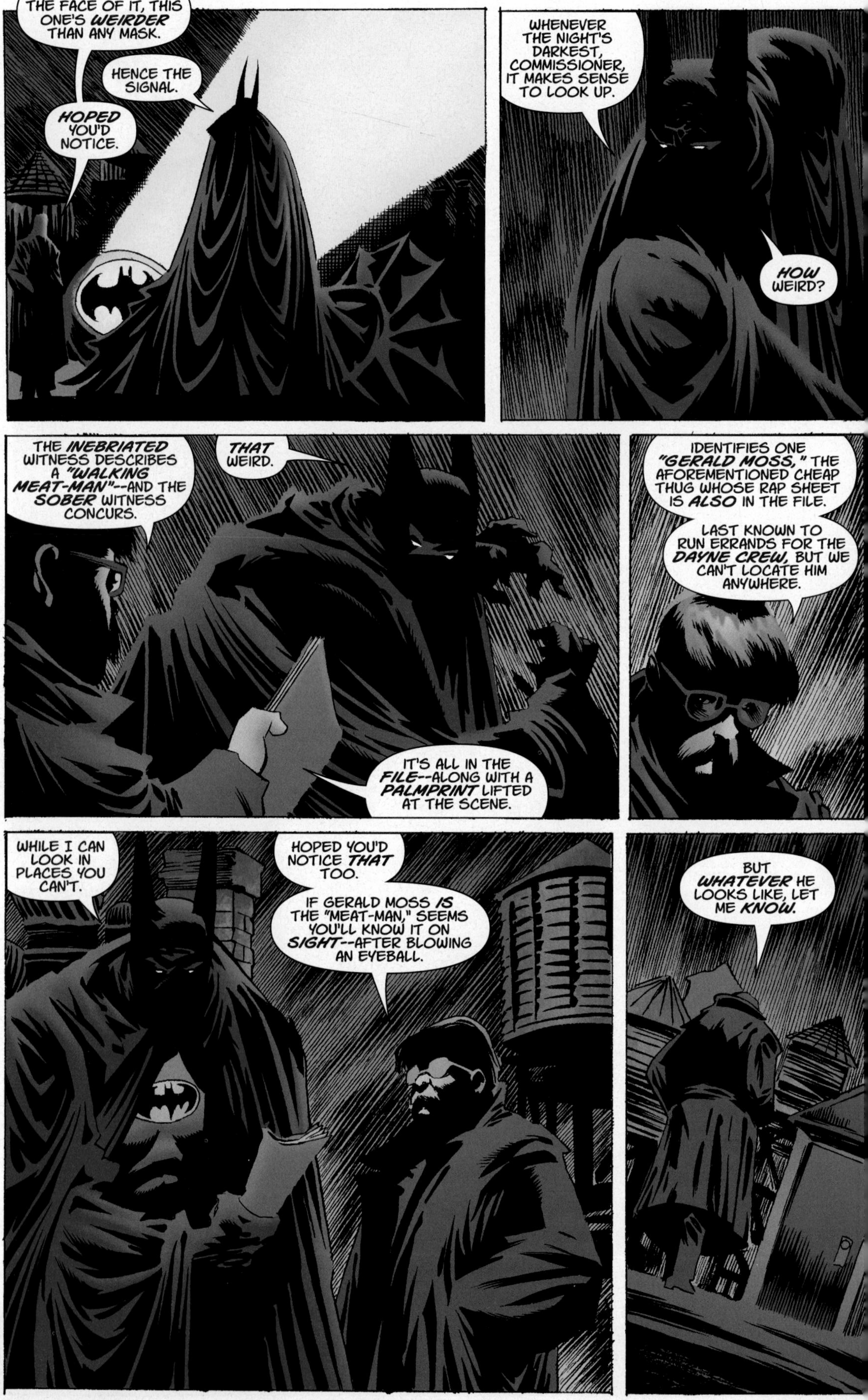
BUT JUST ON THE FACE OF IT, THIS ONE'S WEIRDER THAN ANY MASK.
HENCE THE SIGNAL.
HOPED YOU'D NOTICE.
WHENEVER THE NIGHT'S DARKEST, COMMISSIONER, IT MAKES SENSE TO LOOK UP.
HOW WEIRD?
THE INEBRIATED WITNESS DESCRIBES A "WALKING MEAT-MAN"--AND THE SOBER WITNESS CONCURS.
THAT WEIRD.
IT'S ALL IN THE FILE--ALONG WITH A PALMPRINT LIFTED AT THE SCENE.
IDENTIFIES ONE "GERALD MOSS," THE AFOREMENTIONED CHEAP THUG WHOSE RAP SHEET IS ALSO IN THE FILE.
LAST KNOWN TO RUN ERRANDS FOR THE DAYNE CREW, BUT WE CAN'T LOCATE HIM ANYWHERE.
WHILE I CAN LOOK IN PLACES YOU CAN'T.
HOPED YOU'D NOTICE THAT TOO.
IF GERALD MOSS IS THE "MEAT-MAN," SEEMS YOU'LL KNOW IT ON SIGHT--AFTER BLOWING AN EYEBALL.
BUT WHATEVER HE LOOKS LIKE, LET ME KNOW.

Chapter 6 Boneless

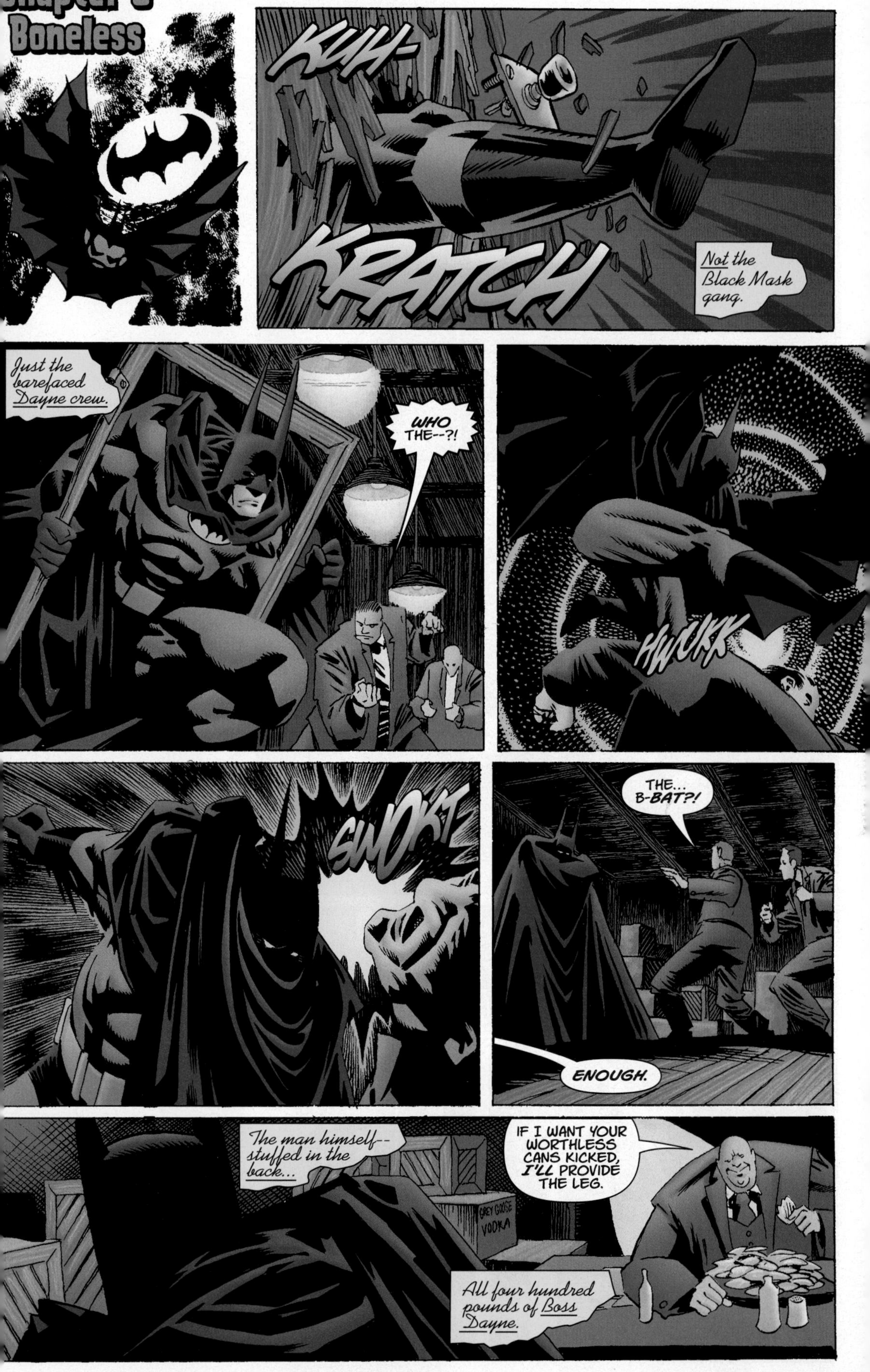
KUH-
KRATCH
Not the Black Mask gang.
Just the barefaced Dayne crew.
WHO THE--?!
HWUKK
SWOKT
THE... B-BAT?!
ENOUGH.
The man himself--stuffed in the back...
IF I WANT YOUR WORTHLESS CANS KICKED, I'LL PROVIDE THE LEG.
GREY GOOSE VODKA
All four hundred pounds of Boss Dayne.

NOW THEN, MR. EARS, YOU GOT NO PAPER ON ME AND YOU *KNOW* IT.

CALL ME A *WHISTLE*, I'M SO CLEAN.

UNLIKE *GERALD MOSS*.

TELL ME ABOUT HIM.

JERRY MOSS? SURE, *MAYBE* I KNEW THE SCREW-UP, AND MAYBE HE EVEN WORKED FOR ONE OF MY VARIOUS ENTERPRISES, ALL OF WHICH ARE STRICTLY STRAIGHT LIKE ME MYSELF.

IF MOSS MAYBE GOT *BENT*, IT'S NEWS TO ME INASMUCH AS I *FIRED* THE SCREW-UP MAYBE A YEAR AGO COME APRIL.

MAYBE.

FWAKK

GUH-H!

SO NOW I QUIVER IN MY TRIPLE-WIDE *SIZE TWELVES*?

IS *THAT* YOUR *DESIRED* SCENARIO?

Shllpt

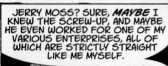

No fear again.

FNNT

GRAKK

FLTT

KLIZ

THUD THUD THUD

OKAY, NOW THAT WE'RE *BOTH* IN THE DARK, GLAD TO *HELP*.

BUT NEXT TIME, *KNOCK*.

Damn.

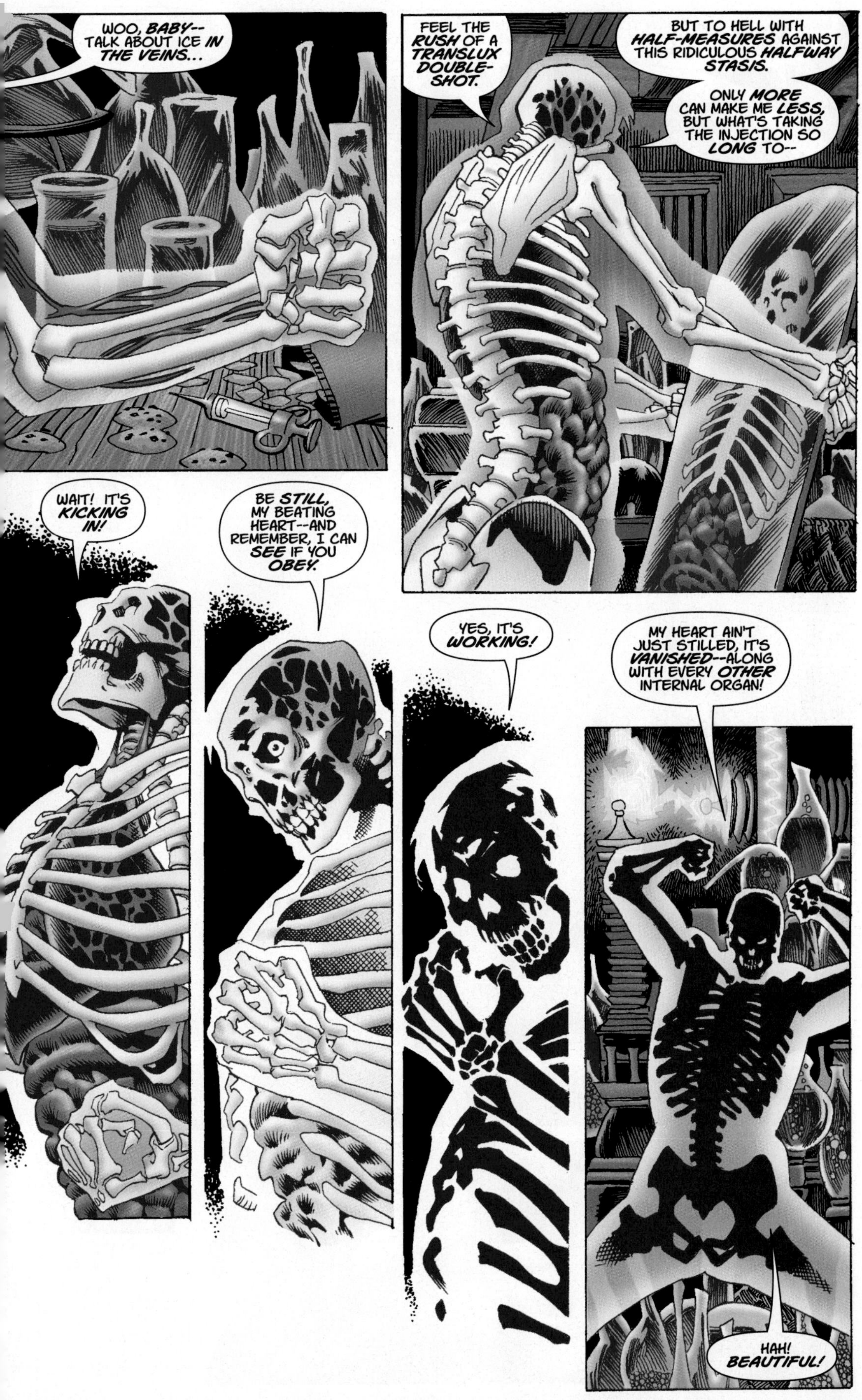
WOO, BABY--
TALK ABOUT ICE IN THE VEINS...
FEEL THE RUSH OF A TRANSLUX DOUBLE-SHOT.
BUT TO HELL WITH HALF-MEASURES AGAINST THIS RIDICULOUS HALFWAY STASIS.
ONLY MORE CAN MAKE ME LESS, BUT WHAT'S TAKING THE INJECTION SO LONG TO--
WAIT! IT'S KICKING IN!
BE STILL, MY BEATING HEART--AND REMEMBER, I CAN SEE IF YOU OBEY.
YES, IT'S WORKING!
MY HEART AIN'T JUST STILLED, IT'S VANISHED--ALONG WITH EVERY OTHER INTERNAL ORGAN!
HAH! BEAUTIFUL!

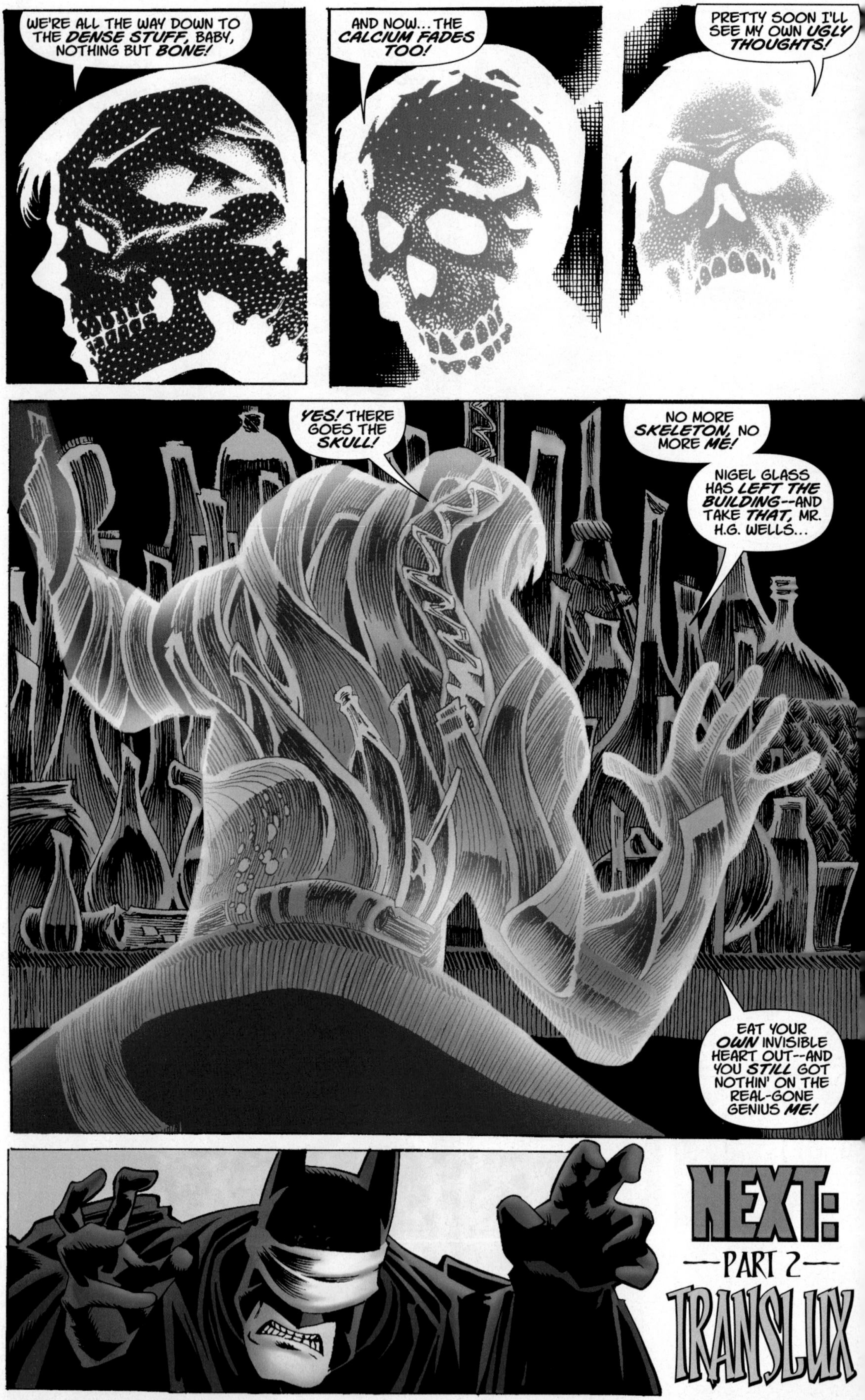
WE'RE ALL THE WAY DOWN TO THE DENSE STUFF, BABY, NOTHING BUT BONE!
AND NOW... THE CALCIUM FADES TOO!
PRETTY SOON I'LL SEE MY OWN UGLY THOUGHTS!
YES! THERE GOES THE SKULL!
NO MORE SKELETON, NO MORE ME!
NIGEL GLASS HAS LEFT THE BUILDING--AND TAKE THAT, MR. H.G. WELLS...
EAT YOUR OWN INVISIBLE HEART OUT--AND YOU STILL GOT NOTHIN' ON THE REAL-GONE GENIUS ME!
NEXT:
PART 2
TRANSLUX

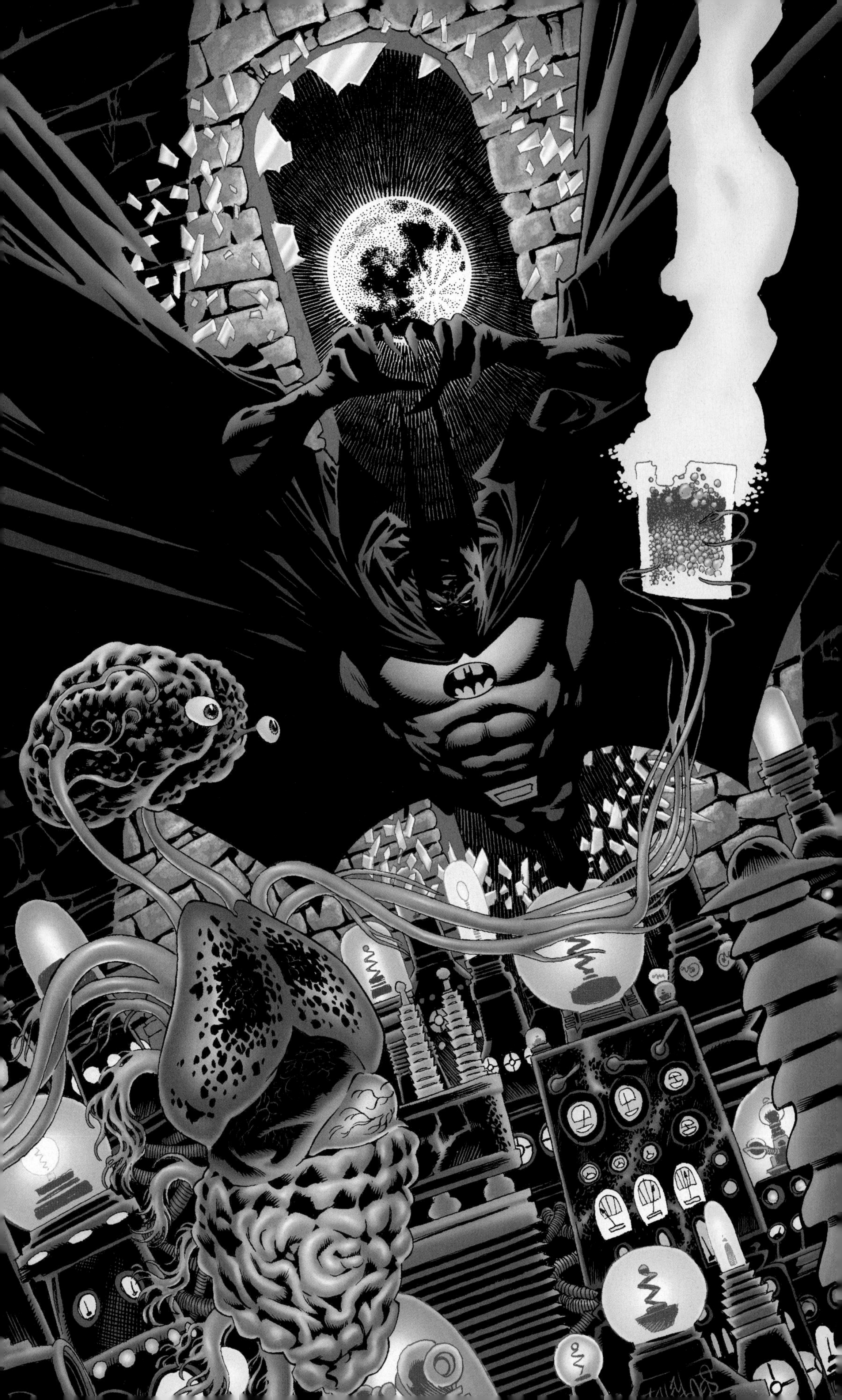

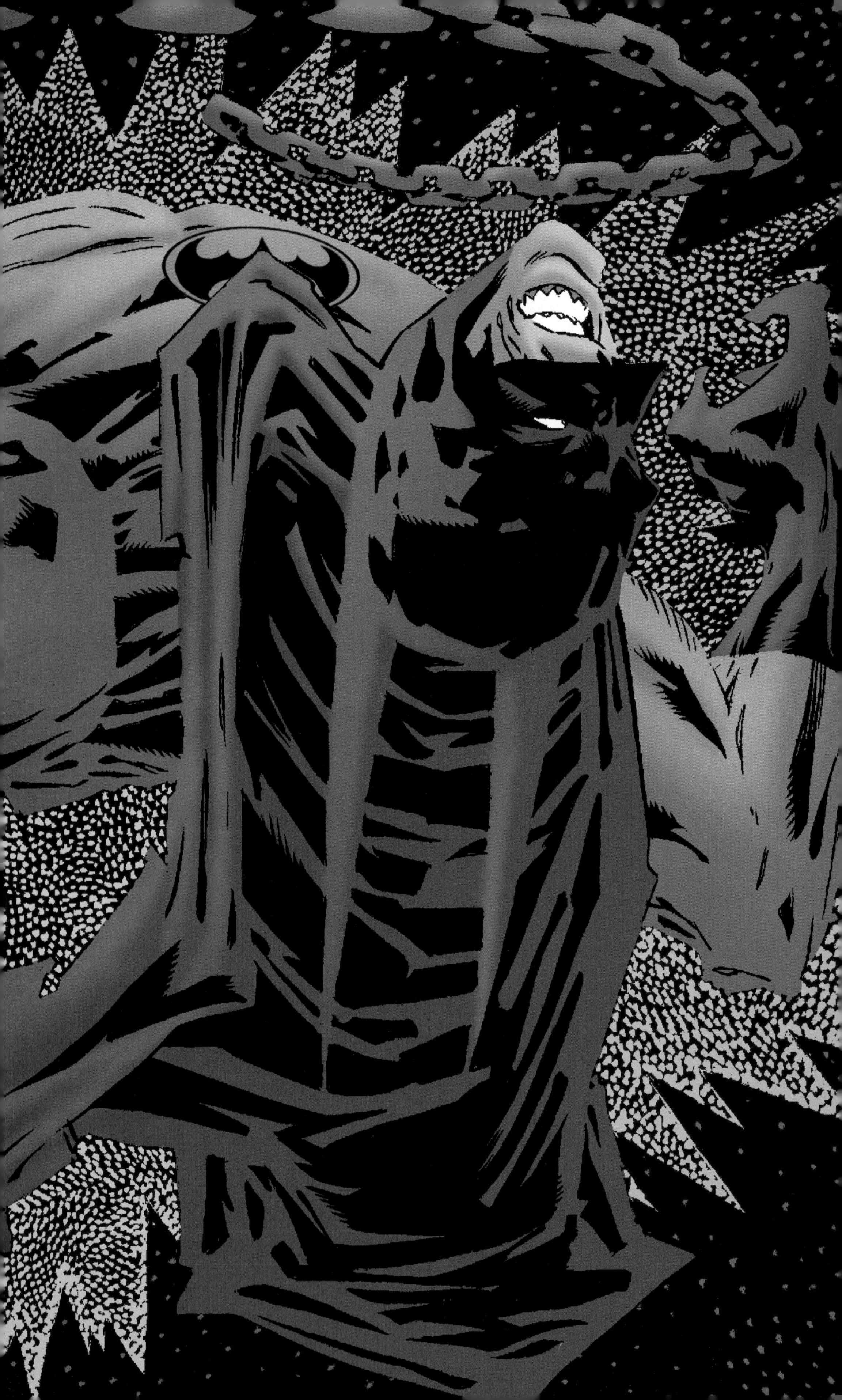

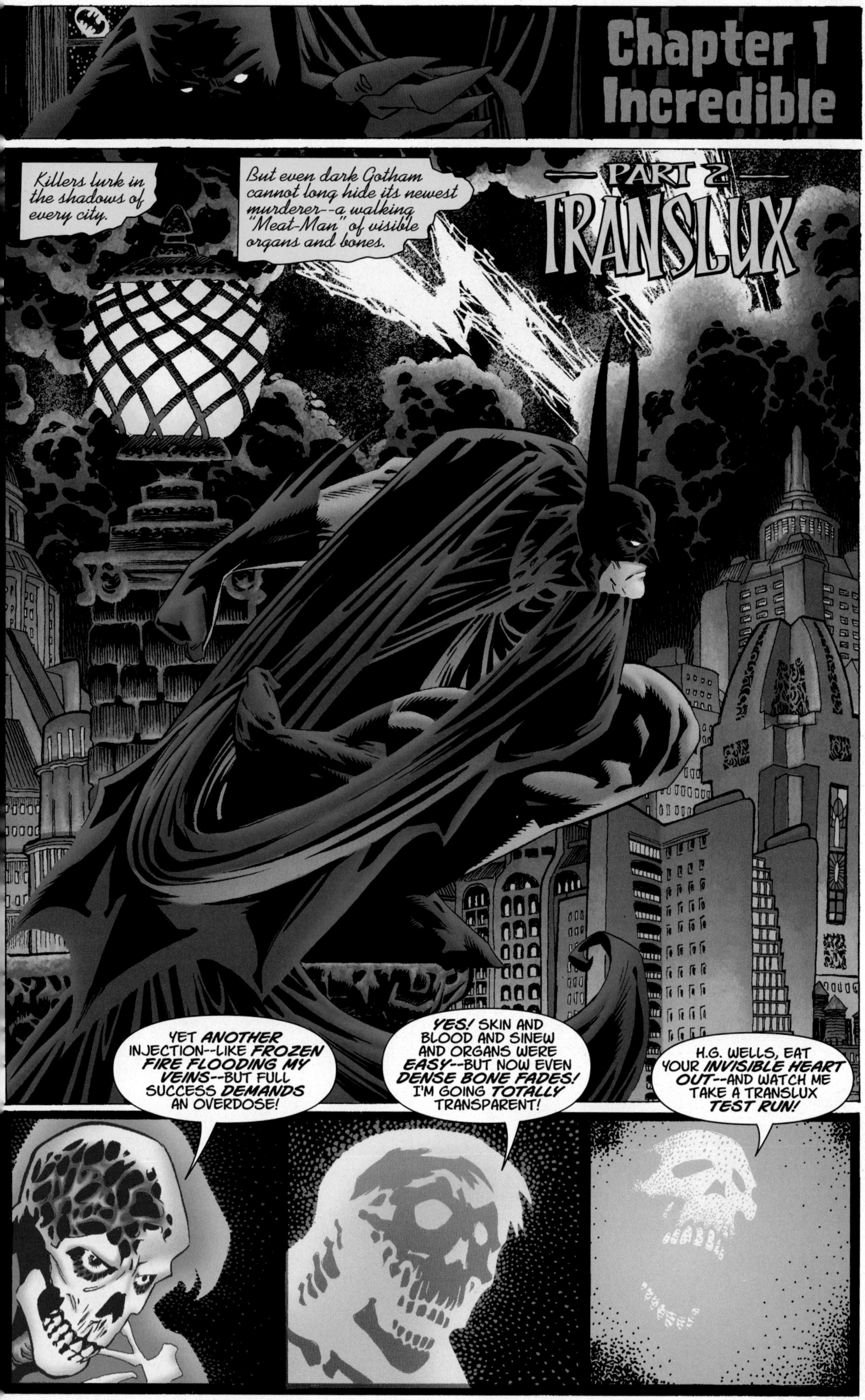
Chapter 1 Incredible
Killers lurk in the shadows of every city.
But even dark Gotham cannot long hide its newest murderer--a walking "Meat-Man" of visible organs and bones.
— PART 2 —
TRANSLUX
YET ANOTHER INJECTION--LIKE FROZEN FIRE FLOODING MY VEINS--BUT FULL SUCCESS DEMANDS AN OVERDOSE!
YES! SKIN AND BLOOD AND SINEW AND ORGANS WERE EASY--BUT NOW EVEN DENSE BONE FADES! I'M GOING TOTALLY TRANSPARENT!
H.G. WELLS, EAT YOUR INVISIBLE HEART OUT--AND WATCH ME TAKE A TRANSLUX TEST RUN!

Chapter 2 Invisible

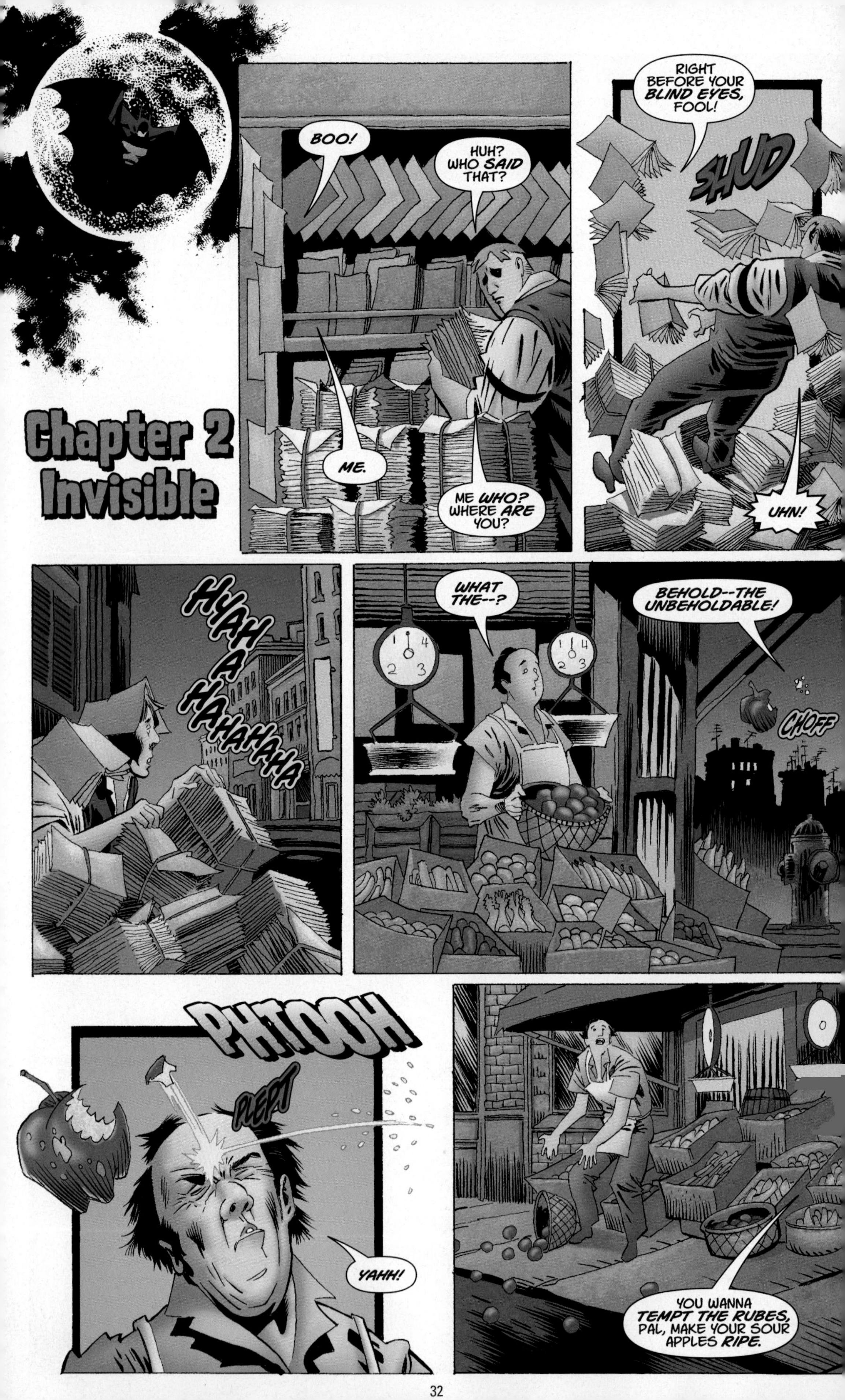
BOO!
HUH? WHO SAID THAT?
ME.
ME WHO? WHERE ARE YOU?
RIGHT BEFORE YOUR BLIND EYES, FOOL!
SHUD
UHN!
HYAH A HAHAHAHA
WHAT THE--?
BEHOLD--THE UNBEHOLDABLE!
CHOFF
PHTOOOH
PLEPT
YAHH!
YOU WANNA TEMPT THE RUBES, PAL, MAKE YOUR SOUR APPLES RIPE.

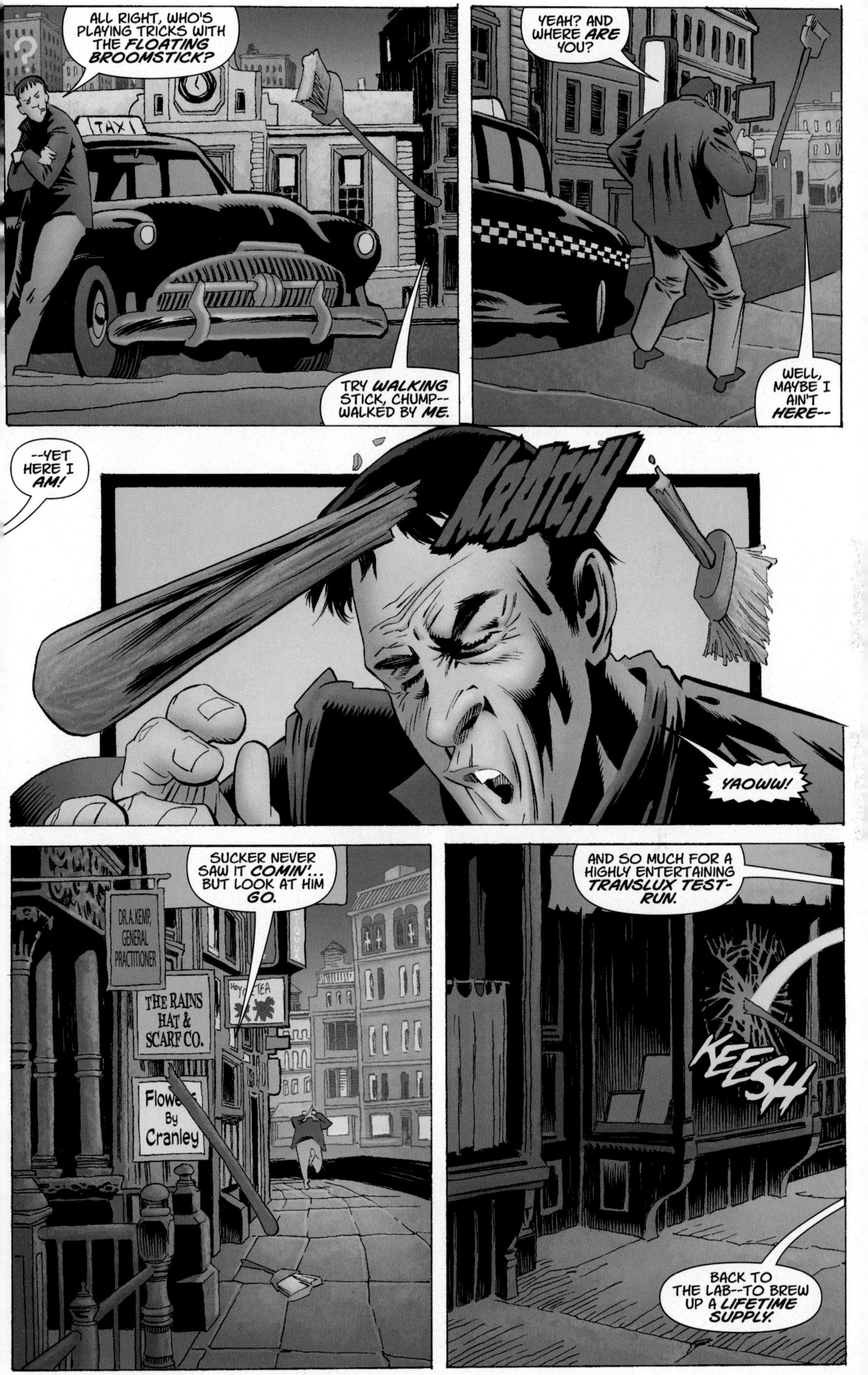

ALL RIGHT, WHO'S PLAYING TRICKS WITH THE FLOATING BROOMSTICK?
TAXI
TRY WALKING STICK, CHUMP-- WALKED BY ME.
YEAH? AND WHERE ARE YOU?
WELL, MAYBE I AIN'T HERE--
--YET HERE I AM!
KRATCH
YAOWW!
SUCKER NEVER SAW IT COMIN'... BUT LOOK AT HIM GO.
DR.A.KEMP, GENERAL PRACTITIONER
THE RAINS HAT & SCARF CO.
Flowe By Cranley
AND SO MUCH FOR A HIGHLY ENTERTAINING TRANSLUX TEST-RUN.
KEESH
BACK TO THE LAB--TO BREW UP A LIFETIME SUPPLY.

BAD NEWS, BLACK MASK--AS IN YOUR DR. NIGEL GLASS STOOGE HAS LURCHED MORE THAN LIKELY *LOOPY*.

LOOPY IN *WHAT* WAY, HOMOLKA?

IN THE WAY OF *UNSTABLE*, BOSS, PAST THE POINT OF *MANIACAL RAGE*.

RAGE ABOUT *WHAT*?

MOSTLY *MONEY*, BUT *HUNGER* TOO.

WANTS HIS *FEE DOUBLED*, WHICH AIN'T LOOPY IN AND OF ITSELF, BUT ANY GUY THRILLED BY *SHOWING OFF HIS INNARDS*, HE'S GOTTA BE--

INNARDS? HOMOLKA, ARE YOU TRYING TO TELL ME THAT NIGEL GLASS HAS ACHIEVED *VISIBLE PROGRESS* WITH HIS *TRANSLUX SERUM*?

WELL, "*PROGRESS*" AIN'T THE WORD *I'D* USE, BOSS, BUT--

SPIT IT *OUT*, HOMOLKA!

IS HE OR IS HE *NOT* TURNING HIMSELF *INVISIBLE*?

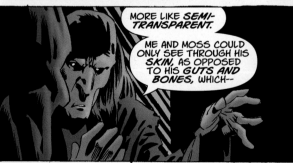

MORE LIKE *SEMI-TRANSPARENT*.

ME AND MOSS COULD ONLY SEE THROUGH HIS *SKIN*, AS OPPOSED TO HIS *GUTS AND BONES*, WHICH--

JUST MADE A MESS *WASTING* A GUY.

AND I MEAN A *SHOTGUNNED* MESS.

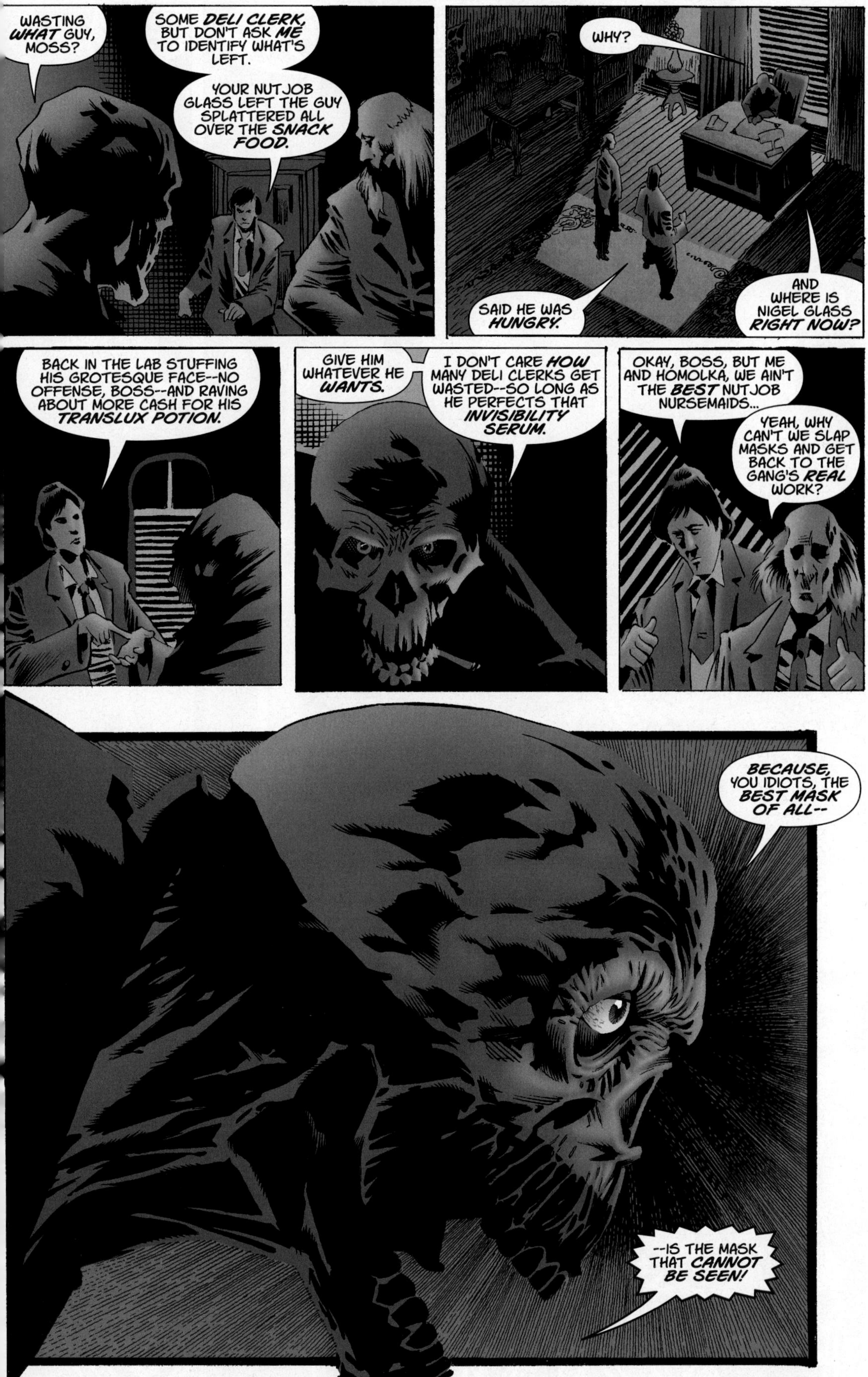
WASTING WHAT GUY, MOSS?
SOME DELI CLERK, BUT DON'T ASK ME TO IDENTIFY WHAT'S LEFT.
YOUR NUTJOB GLASS LEFT THE GUY SPLATTERED ALL OVER THE SNACK FOOD.
WHY?
SAID HE WAS HUNGRY.
AND WHERE IS NIGEL GLASS RIGHT NOW?
BACK IN THE LAB STUFFING HIS GROTESQUE FACE--NO OFFENSE, BOSS--AND RAVING ABOUT MORE CASH FOR HIS TRANSLUX POTION.
GIVE HIM WHATEVER HE WANTS.
I DON'T CARE HOW MANY DELI CLERKS GET WASTED--SO LONG AS HE PERFECTS THAT INVISIBILITY SERUM.
OKAY, BOSS, BUT ME AND HOMOLKA, WE AIN'T THE BEST NUTJOB NURSEMAIDS...
YEAH, WHY CAN'T WE SLAP MASKS AND GET BACK TO THE GANG'S REAL WORK?
BECAUSE, YOU IDIOTS, THE BEST MASK OF ALL--
--IS THE MASK THAT CANNOT BE SEEN!

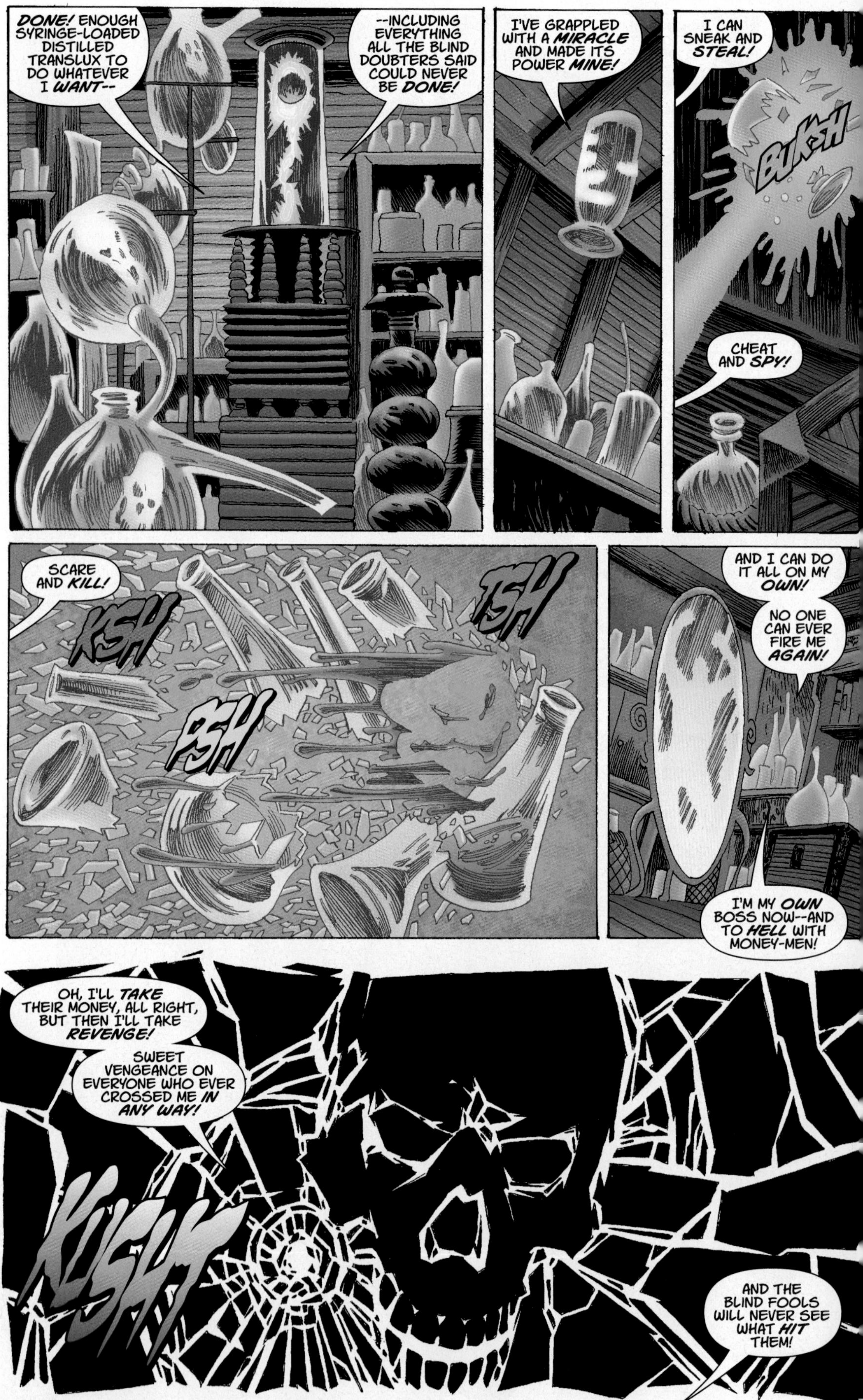
DONE! ENOUGH SYRINGE-LOADED DISTILLED TRANSLUX TO DO WHATEVER I WANT--
--INCLUDING EVERYTHING ALL THE BLIND DOUBTERS SAID COULD NEVER BE DONE!
I'VE GRAPPLED WITH A MIRACLE AND MADE ITS POWER MINE!
I CAN SNEAK AND STEAL!
BUKSH
CHEAT AND SPY!
SCARE AND KILL!
KSH
TSH
PSH
AND I CAN DO IT ALL ON MY OWN!
NO ONE CAN EVER FIRE ME AGAIN!
I'M MY OWN BOSS NOW--AND TO HELL WITH MONEY-MEN!
OH, I'LL TAKE THEIR MONEY, ALL RIGHT, BUT THEN I'LL TAKE REVENGE!
SWEET VENGEANCE ON EVERYONE WHO EVER CROSSED ME IN ANY WAY!
KUSH
AND THE BLIND FOOLS WILL NEVER SEE WHAT HIT THEM!

Chapter 3 Investigated

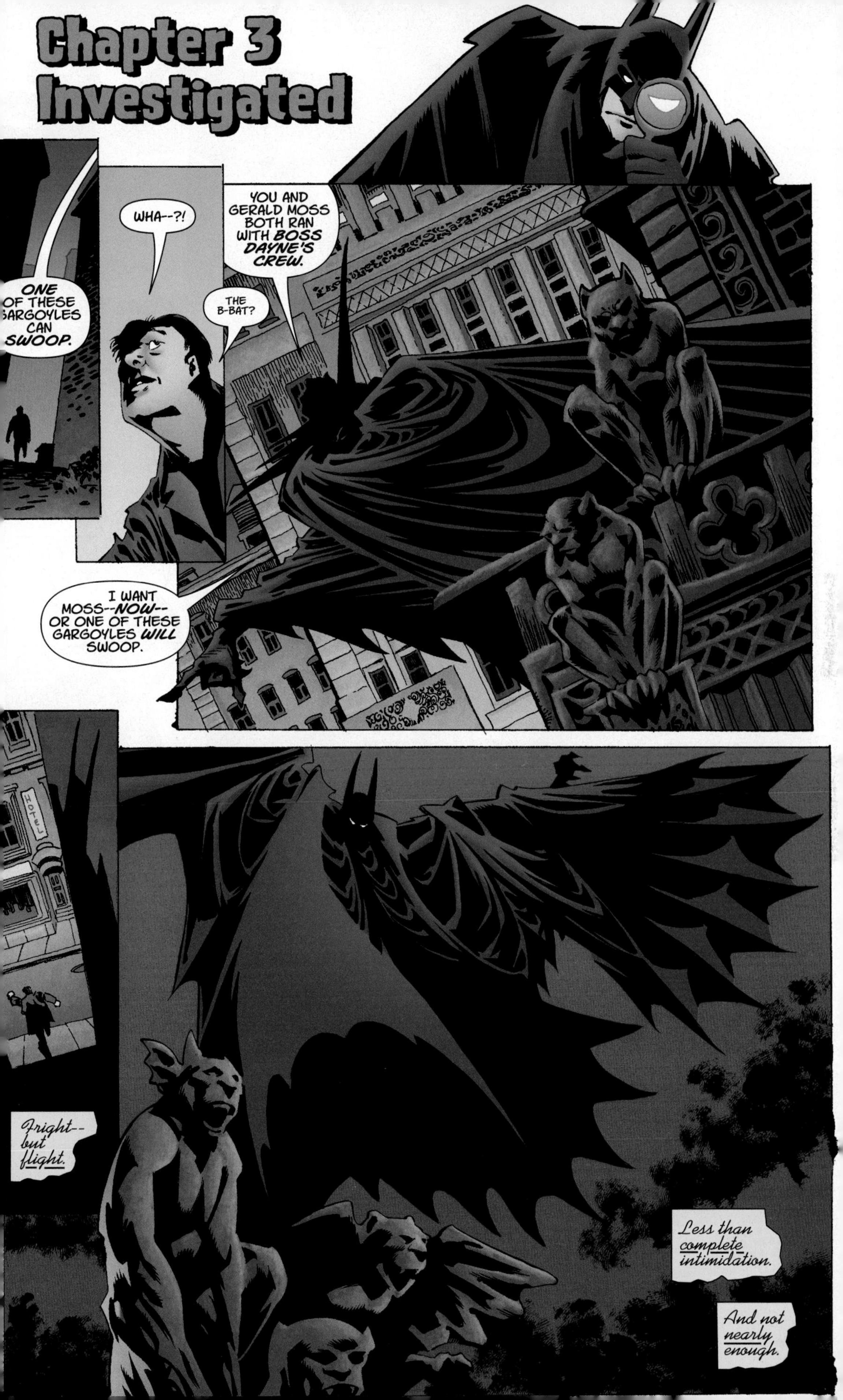

ONE OF THESE ARGOYLES CAN SWOOP.
WHA--?!
THE B-BAT?
YOU AND GERALD MOSS BOTH RAN WITH BOSS DAYNE'S CREW.
I WANT MOSS--NOW-- OR ONE OF THESE GARGOYLES WILL SWOOP.
HOTEL
Fright-- but flight.
Less than complete intimidation.
And not nearly enough.

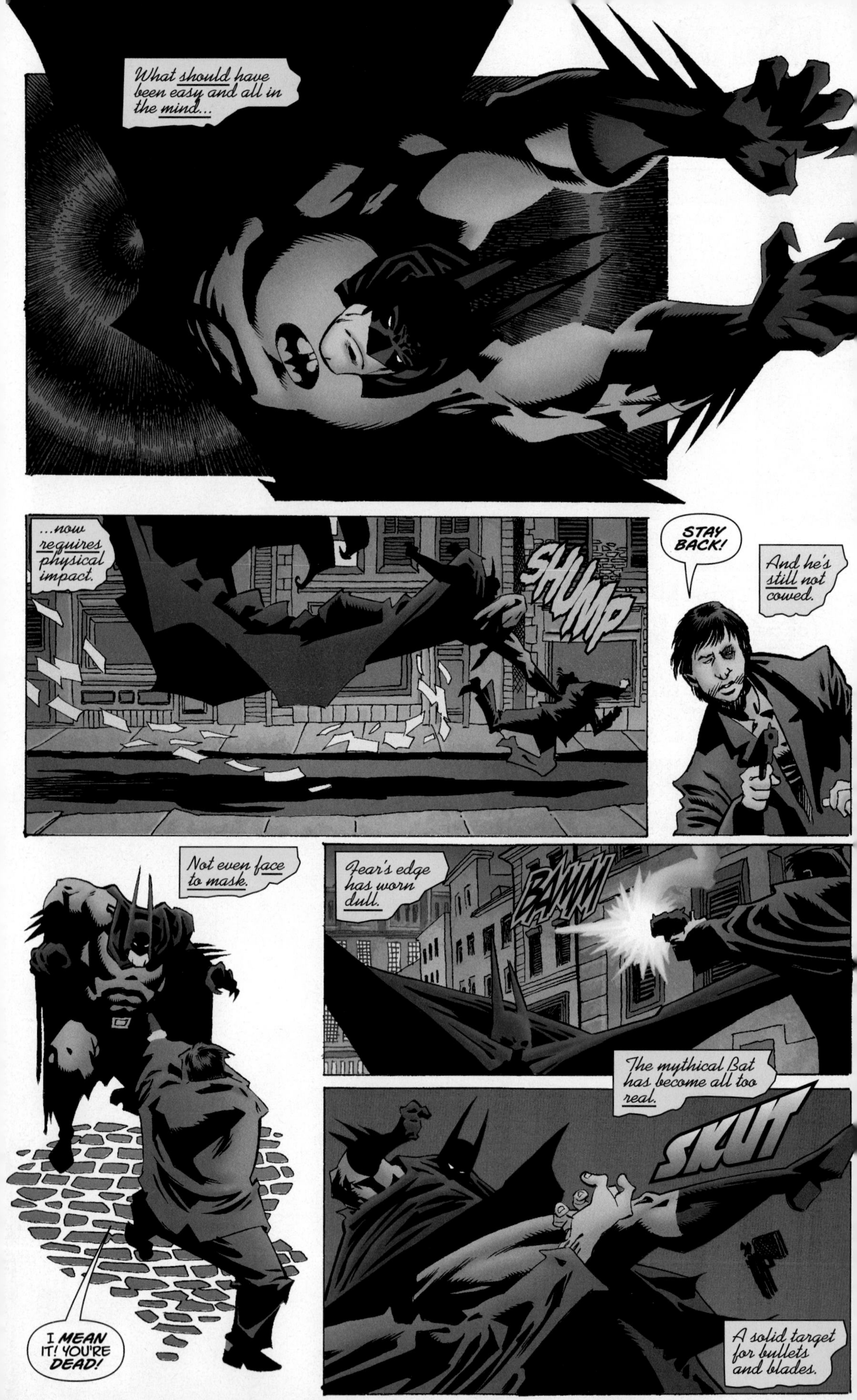
What should have been easy and all in the mind...
...now requires physical impact.
SHUMP
STAY BACK!
And he's still not cowed.
Not even face to mask.
I MEAN IT! YOU'RE DEAD!
Fear's edge has worn dull.
BAMM
The mythical Bat has become all too real.
SKUTT
A solid target for bullets and blades.

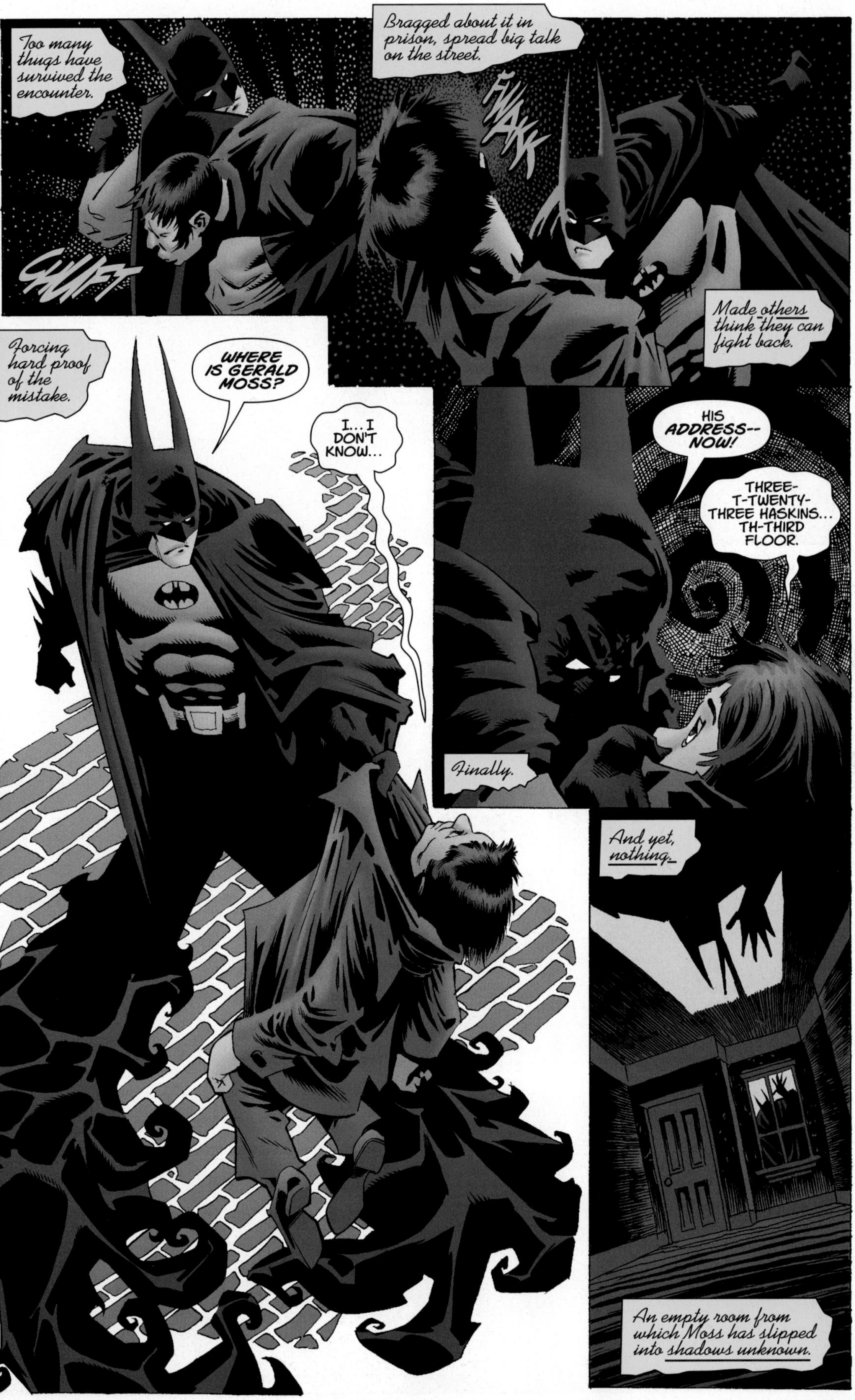
Too many thugs have survived the encounter.
Bragged about it in prison, spread big talk on the street.
FWAKK
Made others think they can fight back.
Forcing hard proof of the mistake.
WHERE IS GERALD MOSS?
I... I DON'T KNOW...
HIS ADDRESS-- NOW!
THREE- T-TWENTY- THREE HASKINS... TH-THIRD FLOOR.
Finally.
And yet, nothing.
An empty room from which Moss has slipped into shadows unknown.

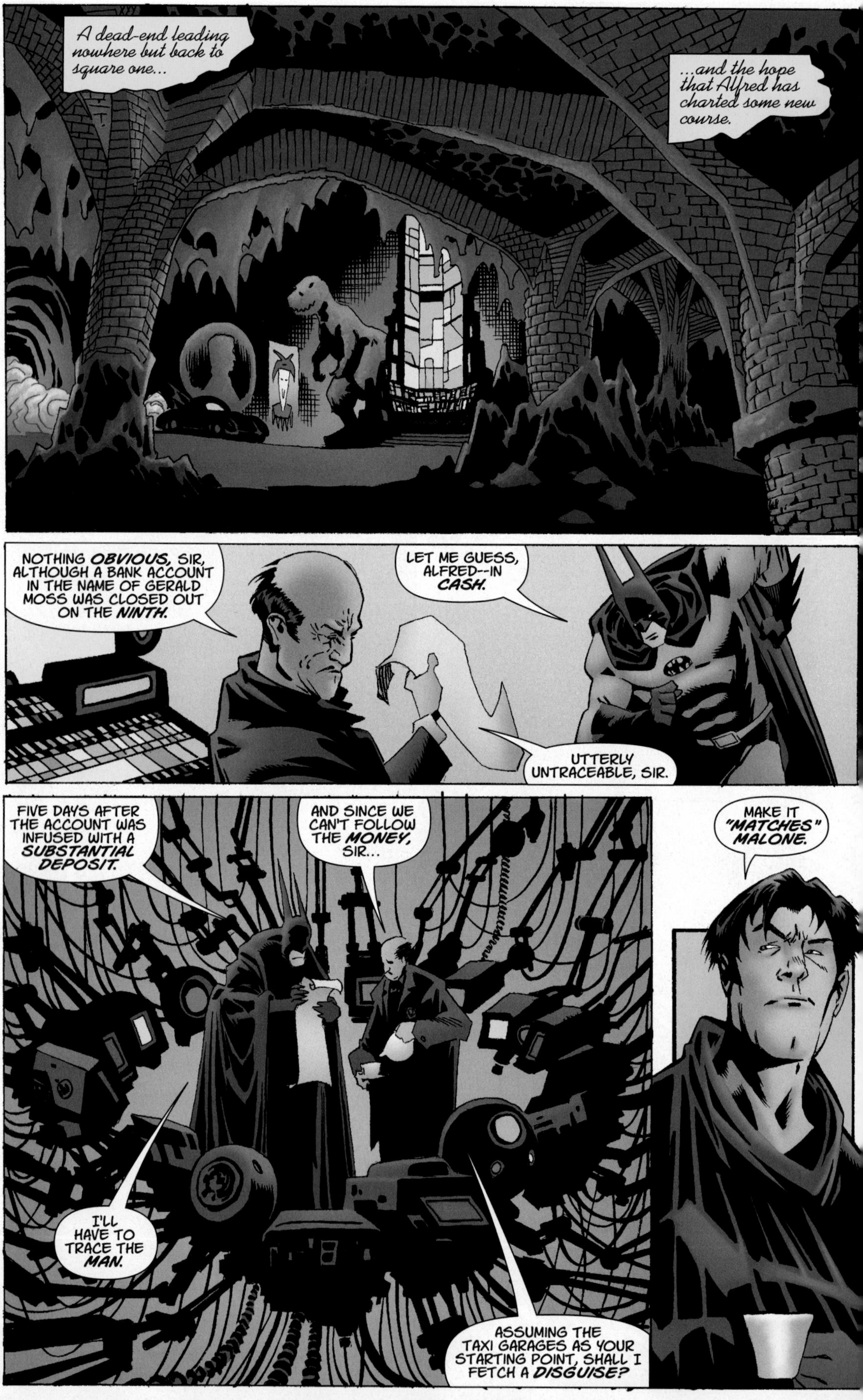
A dead-end leading nowhere but back to square one...
...and the hope that Alfred has charted some new course.
NOTHING OBVIOUS, SIR, ALTHOUGH A BANK ACCOUNT IN THE NAME OF GERALD MOSS WAS CLOSED OUT ON THE NINTH.
LET ME GUESS, ALFRED--IN CASH.
UTTERLY UNTRACEABLE, SIR.
FIVE DAYS AFTER THE ACCOUNT WAS INFUSED WITH A SUBSTANTIAL DEPOSIT.
AND SINCE WE CAN'T FOLLOW THE MONEY, SIR...
I'LL HAVE TO TRACE THE MAN.
ASSUMING THE TAXI GARAGES AS YOUR STARTING POINT, SHALL I FETCH A DISGUISE?
MAKE IT "MATCHES" MALONE.

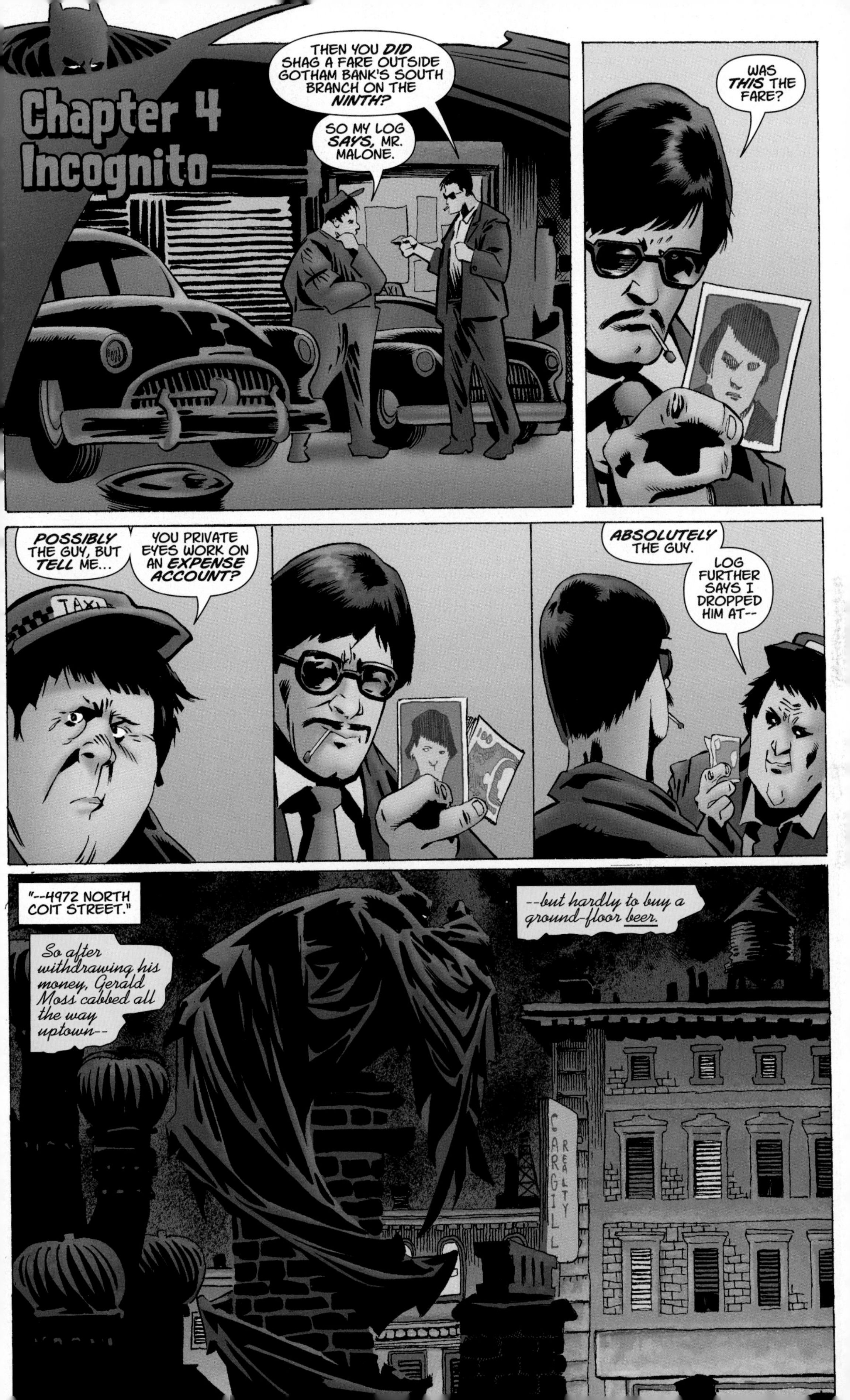

Chapter 4
Incognito
THEN YOU DID SHAG A FARE OUTSIDE GOTHAM BANK'S SOUTH BRANCH ON THE NINTH?
SO MY LOG SAYS, MR. MALONE.
TAXI
WAS THIS THE FARE?
POSSIBLY THE GUY, BUT TELL ME...
YOU PRIVATE EYES WORK ON AN EXPENSE ACCOUNT?
TAXI
ABSOLUTELY THE GUY.
LOG FURTHER SAYS I DROPPED HIM AT--
"--4972 NORTH COIT STREET."
So after withdrawing his money, Gerald Moss cabbed all the way uptown--
--but hardly to buy a ground-floor beer.
CARGILL REALTY

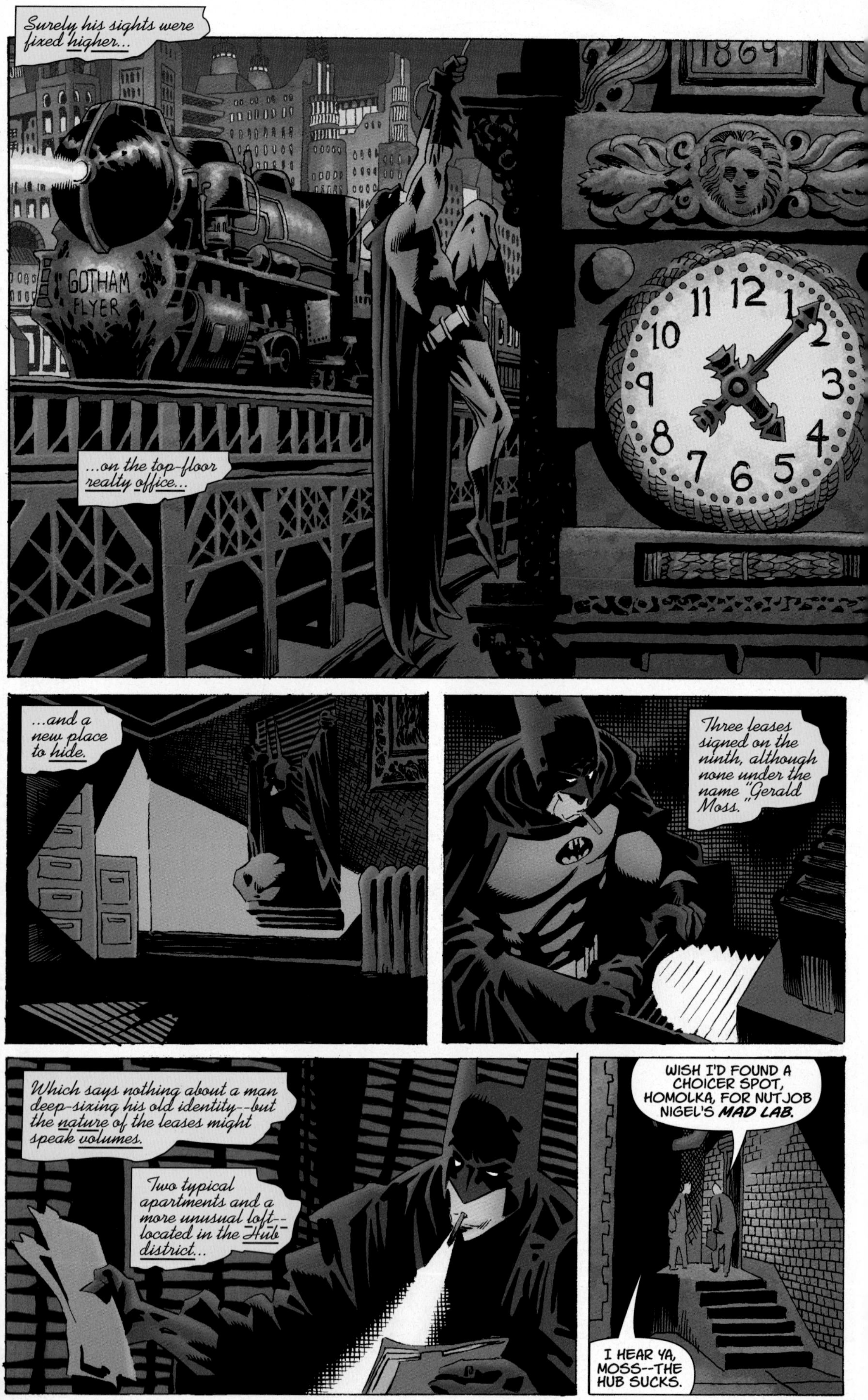
Surely his sights were fixed higher...
1869
GOTHAM FLYER
...on the top-floor realty office...
...and a new place to hide.
Three leases signed on the ninth, although none under the name "Gerald Moss."
Which says nothing about a man deep-sixing his old identity--but the nature of the leases might speak volumes.
Two typical apartments and a more unusual loft--located in the Hub district...
WISH I'D FOUND A CHOICER SPOT, HOMOLKA, FOR NUTJOB NIGEL'S MAD LAB.
I HEAR YA, MOSS--THE HUB SUCKS.

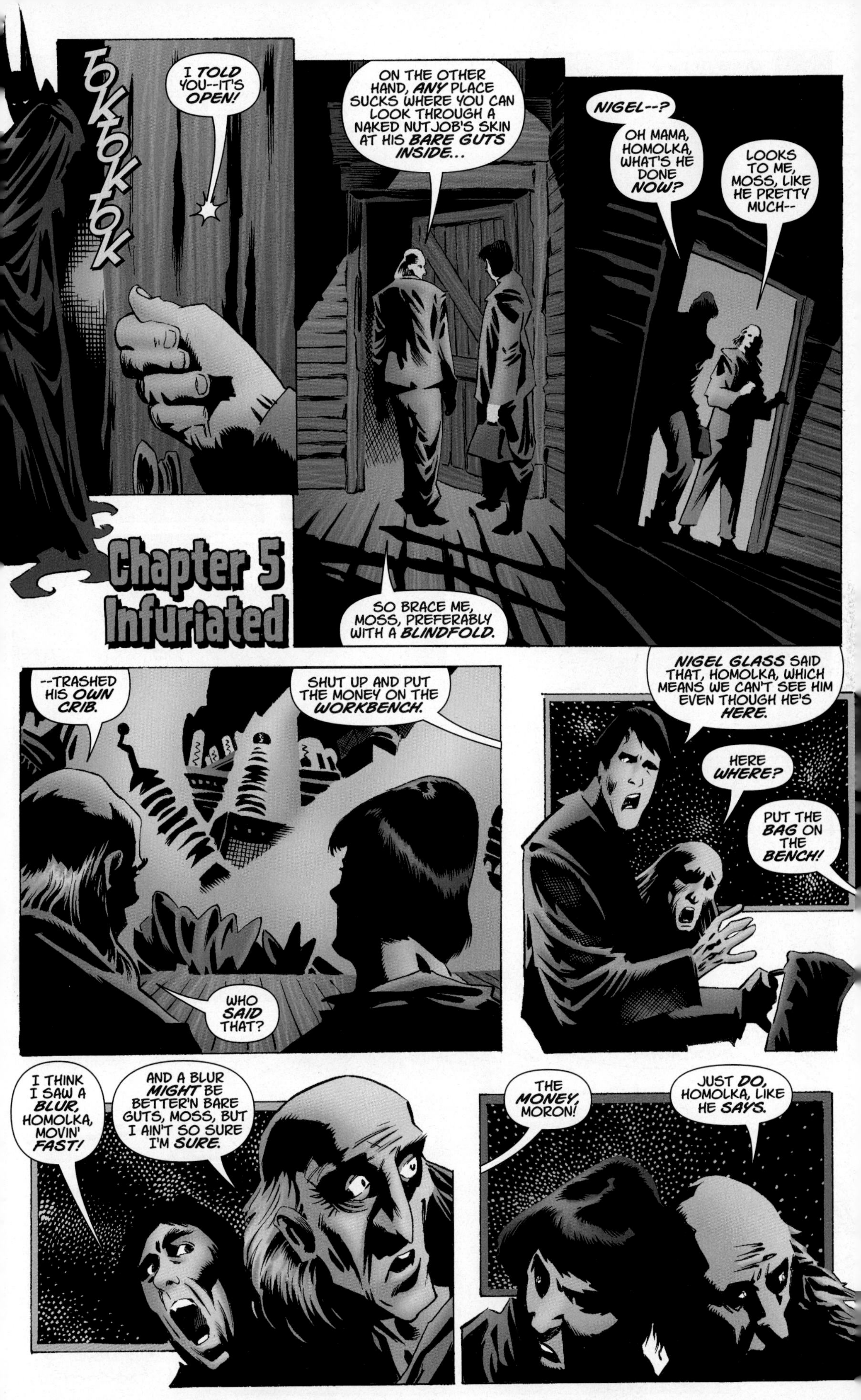
TOKTOKTOKTOK
I TOLD YOU--IT'S OPEN!
Chapter 5 Infuriated
ON THE OTHER HAND, ANY PLACE SUCKS WHERE YOU CAN LOOK THROUGH A NAKED NUTJOB'S SKIN AT HIS BARE GUTS INSIDE...
SO BRACE ME, MOSS, PREFERABLY WITH A BLINDFOLD.
NIGEL--?
OH MAMA, HOMOLKA, WHAT'S HE DONE NOW?
LOOKS TO ME, MOSS, LIKE HE PRETTY MUCH--
--TRASHED HIS OWN CRIB.
SHUT UP AND PUT THE MONEY ON THE WORKBENCH.
WHO SAID THAT?
NIGEL GLASS SAID THAT, HOMOLKA, WHICH MEANS WE CAN'T SEE HIM EVEN THOUGH HE'S HERE.
HERE WHERE?
PUT THE BAG ON THE BENCH!
I THINK I SAW A BLUR, HOMOLKA, MOVIN' FAST!
AND A BLUR MIGHT BE BETTER'N BARE GUTS, MOSS, BUT I AIN'T SO SURE I'M SURE.
THE MONEY, MORON!
JUST DO, HOMOLKA, LIKE HE SAYS.

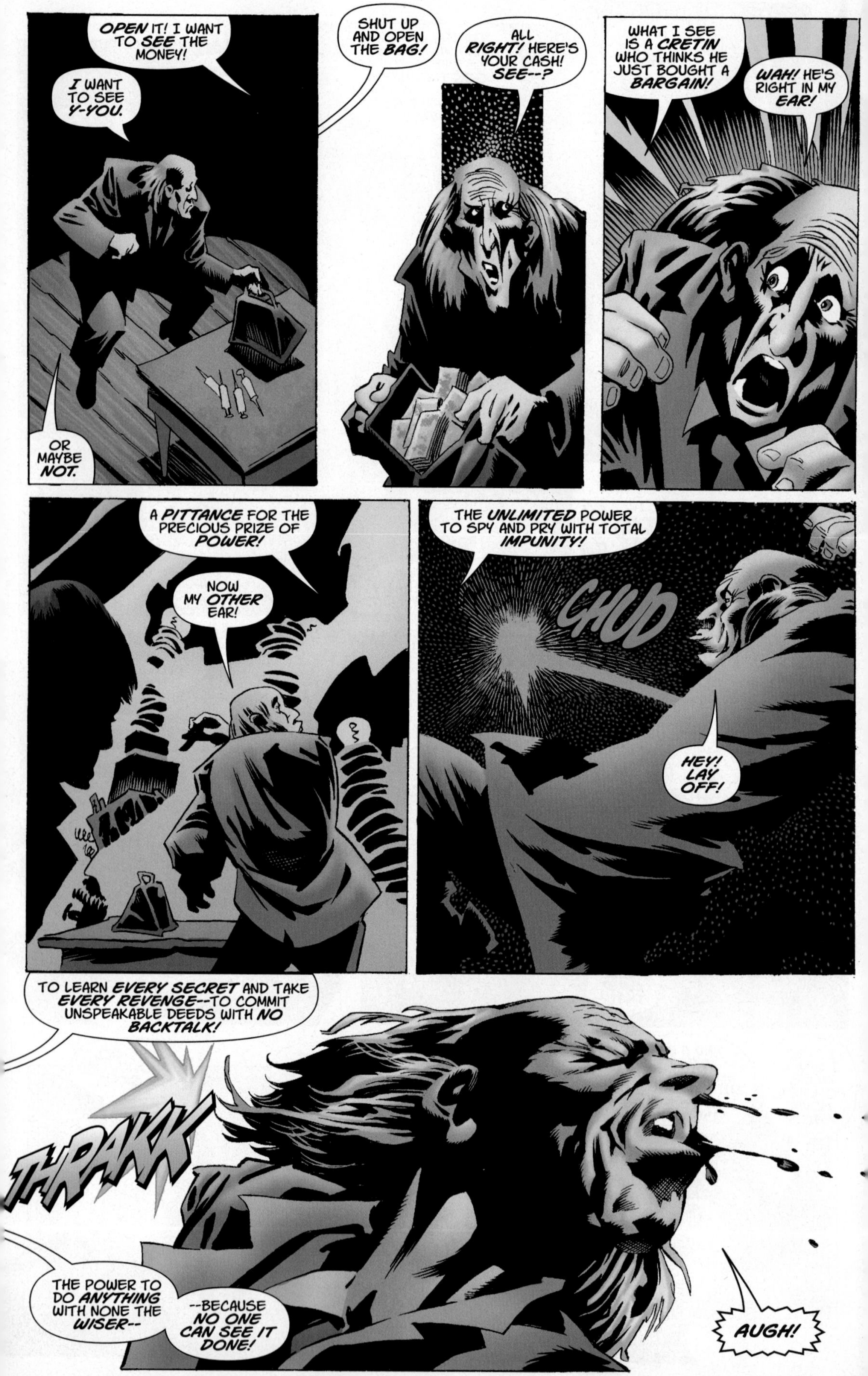
OPEN IT! I WANT TO SEE THE MONEY!
I WANT TO SEE Y-YOU.
OR MAYBE NOT.
SHUT UP AND OPEN THE BAG!
ALL RIGHT! HERE'S YOUR CASH! SEE--?
WHAT I SEE IS A CRETIN WHO THINKS HE JUST BOUGHT A BARGAIN!
WAH! HE'S RIGHT IN MY EAR!
A PITTANCE FOR THE PRECIOUS PRIZE OF POWER!
NOW MY OTHER EAR!
THE UNLIMITED POWER TO SPY AND PRY WITH TOTAL IMPUNITY!
CHUD
HEY! LAY OFF!
TO LEARN EVERY SECRET AND TAKE EVERY REVENGE--TO COMMIT UNSPEAKABLE DEEDS WITH NO BACKTALK!
THRAKK
THE POWER TO DO ANYTHING WITH NONE THE WISER--
--BECAUSE NO ONE CAN SEE IT DONE!
AUGH!

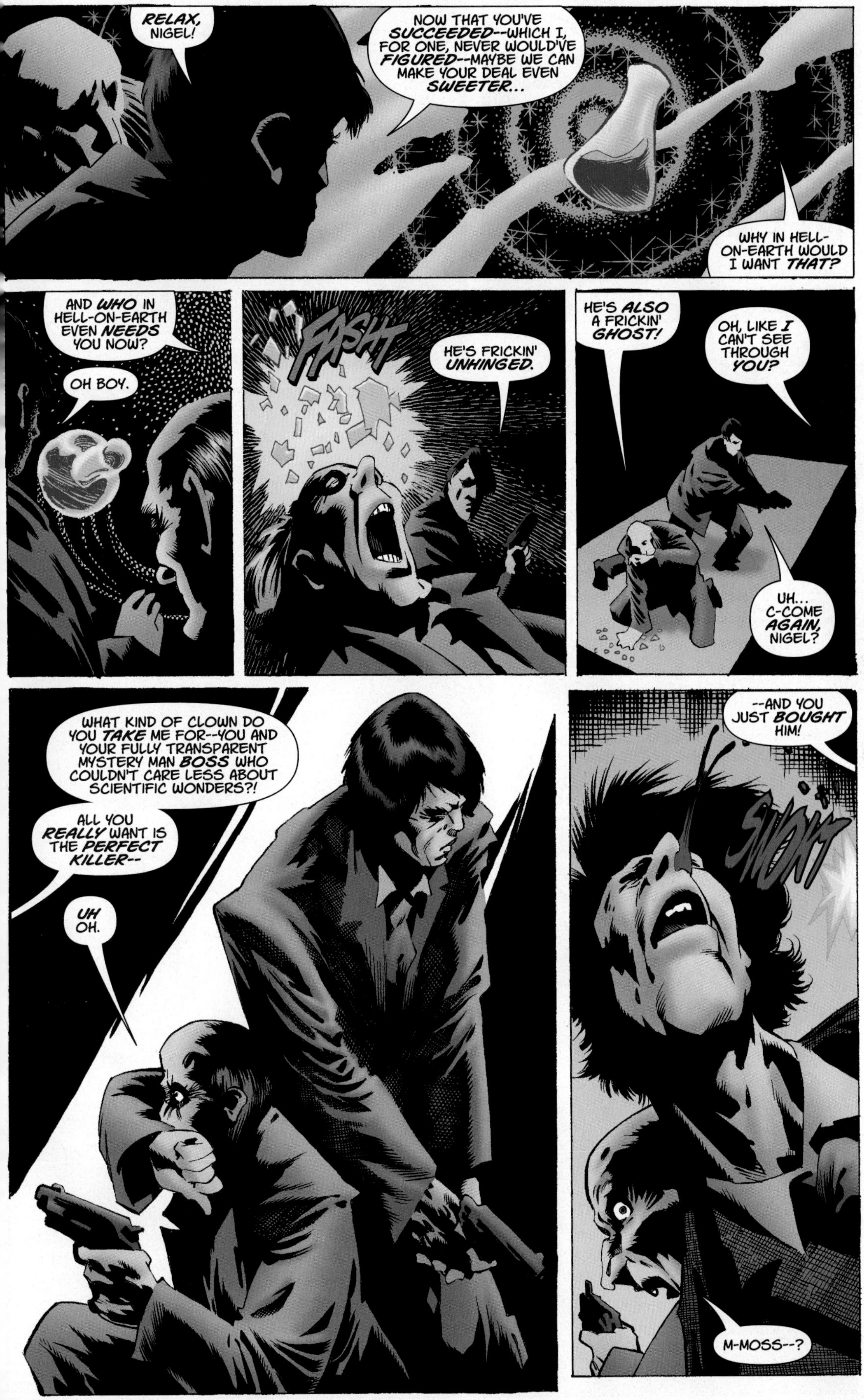
RELAX, NIGEL!
NOW THAT YOU'VE SUCCEEDED--WHICH I, FOR ONE, NEVER WOULD'VE FIGURED--MAYBE WE CAN MAKE YOUR DEAL EVEN SWEETER...
WHY IN HELL-ON-EARTH WOULD I WANT THAT?
AND WHO IN HELL-ON-EARTH EVEN NEEDS YOU NOW?
OH BOY.
FASH
HE'S FRICKIN' UNHINGED.
HE'S ALSO A FRICKIN' GHOST!
OH, LIKE I CAN'T SEE THROUGH YOU?
UH... C-COME AGAIN, NIGEL?
WHAT KIND OF CLOWN DO YOU TAKE ME FOR--YOU AND YOUR FULLY TRANSPARENT MYSTERY MAN BOSS WHO COULDN'T CARE LESS ABOUT SCIENTIFIC WONDERS?!
ALL YOU REALLY WANT IS THE PERFECT KILLER--
UH OH.
--AND YOU JUST BOUGHT HIM!
SNOKT
M-MOSS--?

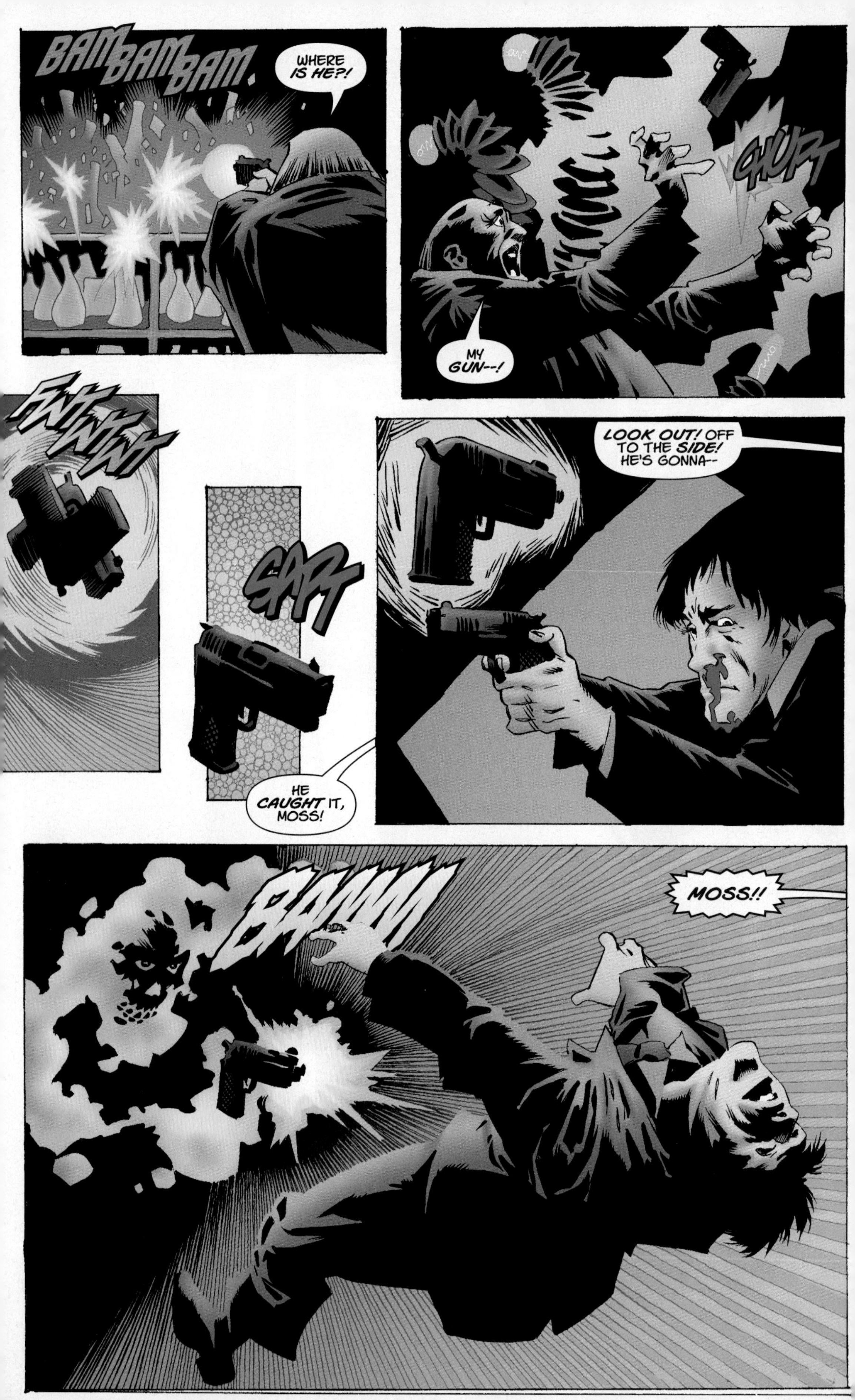
BAM BAM BAM
WHERE IS HE?!
CHUPT
MY GUN--!
SAPT
HE CAUGHT IT, MOSS!
LOOK OUT! OFF TO THE SIDE! HE'S GONNA--
BAMM
MOSS!!

Chapter 6
Insane

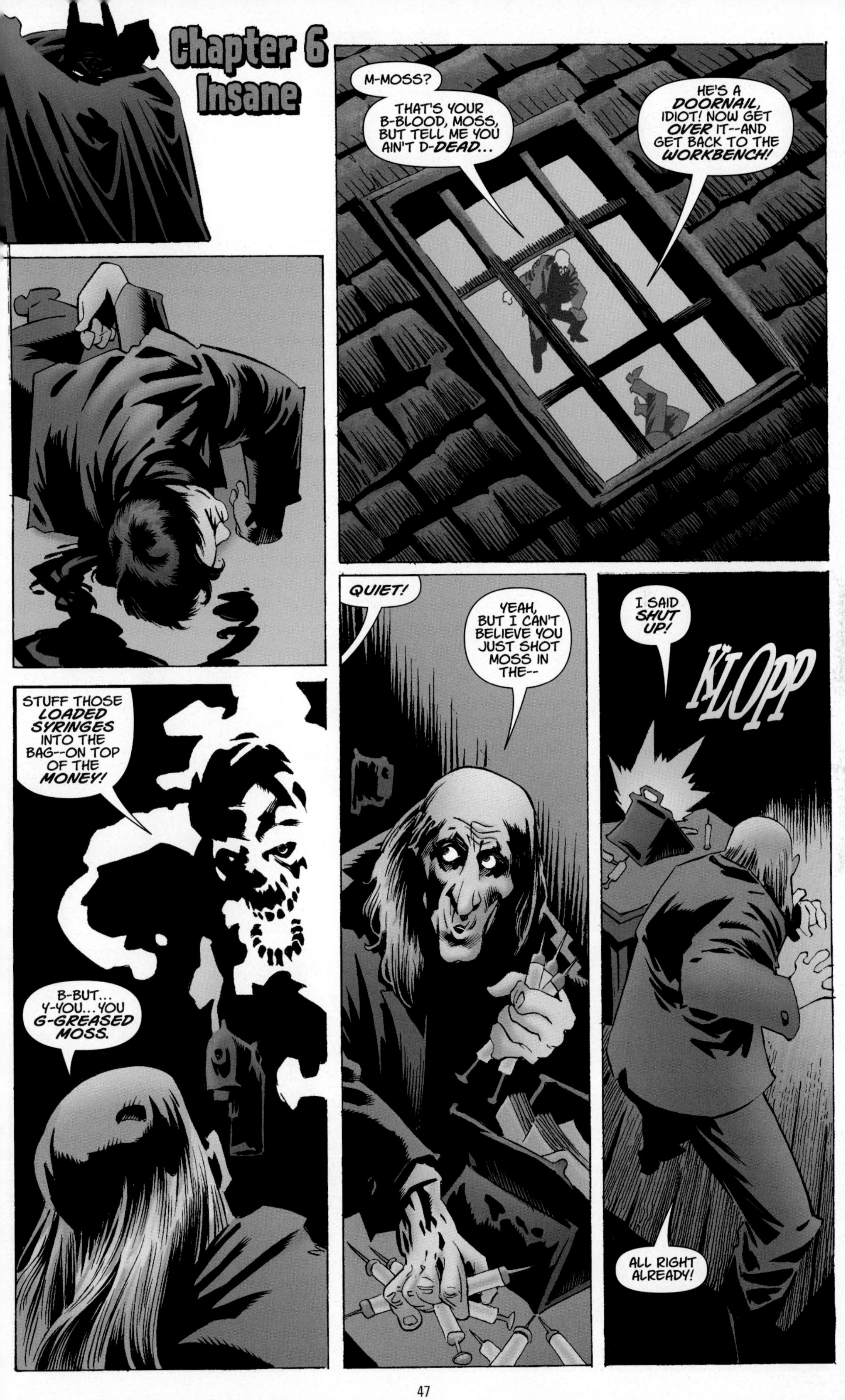

M-MOSS?
THAT'S YOUR B-BLOOD, MOSS, BUT TELL ME YOU AIN'T D-DEAD...
HE'S A DOORNAIL, IDIOT! NOW GET OVER IT--AND GET BACK TO THE WORKBENCH!
STUFF THOSE LOADED SYRINGES INTO THE BAG--ON TOP OF THE MONEY!
B-BUT... Y-YOU...YOU G-GREASED MOSS.
QUIET!
YEAH, BUT I CAN'T BELIEVE YOU JUST SHOT MOSS IN THE--
I SAID SHUT UP!
KLOPP
ALL RIGHT ALREADY!

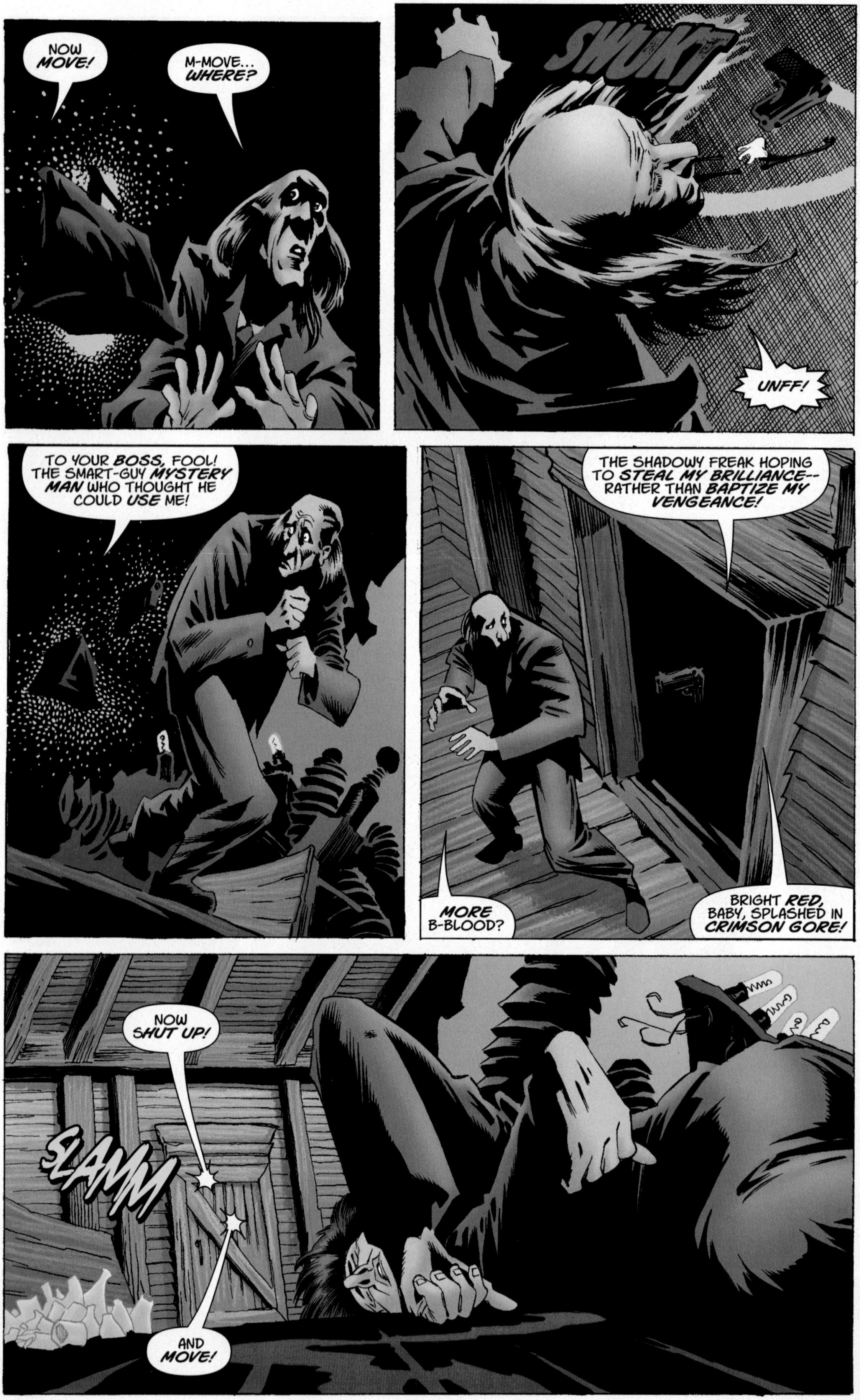
NOW MOVE!
M-MOVE... WHERE?
SMUK!
UNFF!
TO YOUR BOSS, FOOL! THE SMART-GUY MYSTERY MAN WHO THOUGHT HE COULD USE ME!
THE SHADOWY FREAK HOPING TO STEAL MY BRILLIANCE-- RATHER THAN BAPTIZE MY VENGEANCE!
MORE B-BLOOD?
BRIGHT RED, BABY, SPLASHED IN CRIMSON GORE!
NOW SHUT UP!
SLAMM
AND MOVE!

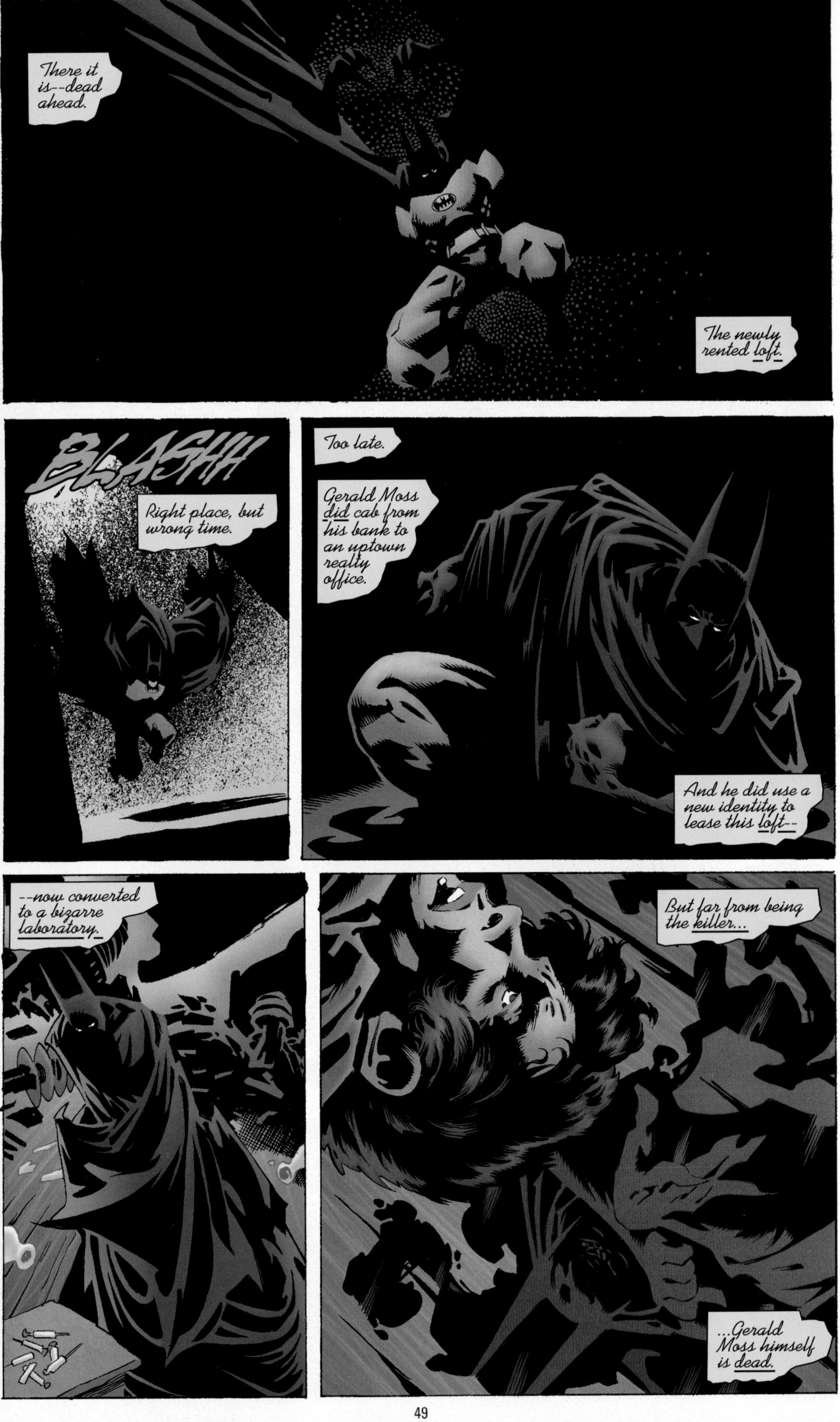
There it is--dead ahead.
The newly rented loft.
BLASHH
Right place, but wrong time.
Too late.
Gerald Moss did cab from his bank to an uptown realty office.
And he did use a new identity to lease this loft--
--now converted to a bizarre laboratory.
But far from being the killer...
...Gerald Moss himself is dead.

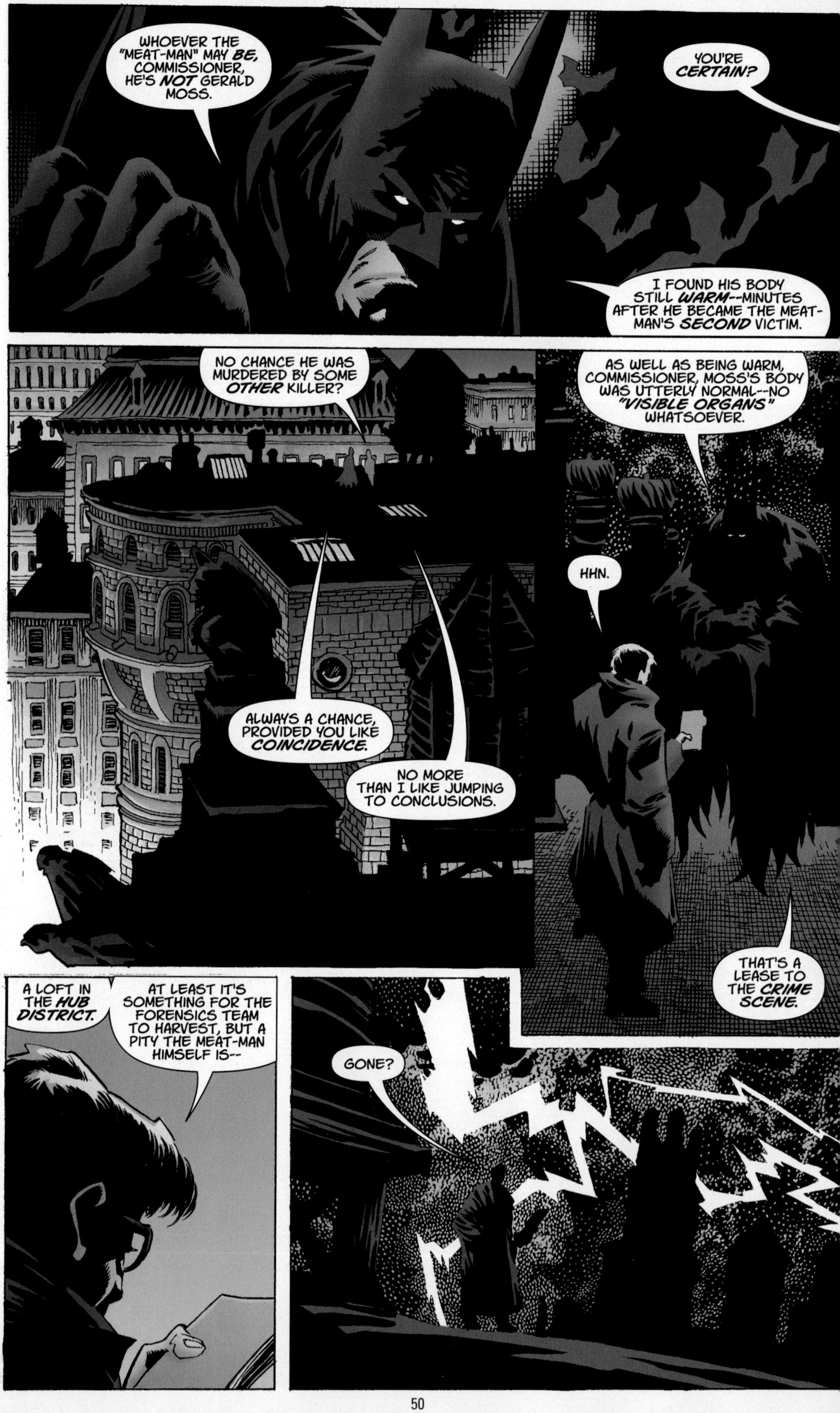
WHOEVER THE "MEAT-MAN" MAY *BE,* COMMISSIONER, HE'S *NOT* GERALD MOSS.
YOU'RE *CERTAIN?*
I FOUND HIS BODY STILL *WARM*--MINUTES AFTER HE BECAME THE MEAT-MAN'S *SECOND* VICTIM.
NO CHANCE HE WAS MURDERED BY SOME *OTHER* KILLER?
ALWAYS A CHANCE, PROVIDED YOU LIKE *COINCIDENCE.*
NO MORE THAN I LIKE JUMPING TO CONCLUSIONS.
AS WELL AS BEING WARM, COMMISSIONER, MOSS'S BODY WAS UTTERLY NORMAL--NO *"VISIBLE ORGANS"* WHATSOEVER.
HHN.
THAT'S A LEASE TO THE *CRIME SCENE.*
A LOFT IN THE *HUB DISTRICT.*
AT LEAST IT'S SOMETHING FOR THE FORENSICS TEAM TO HARVEST, BUT A PITY THE MEAT-MAN HIMSELF IS--
GONE?

Chapter 7
Invasion

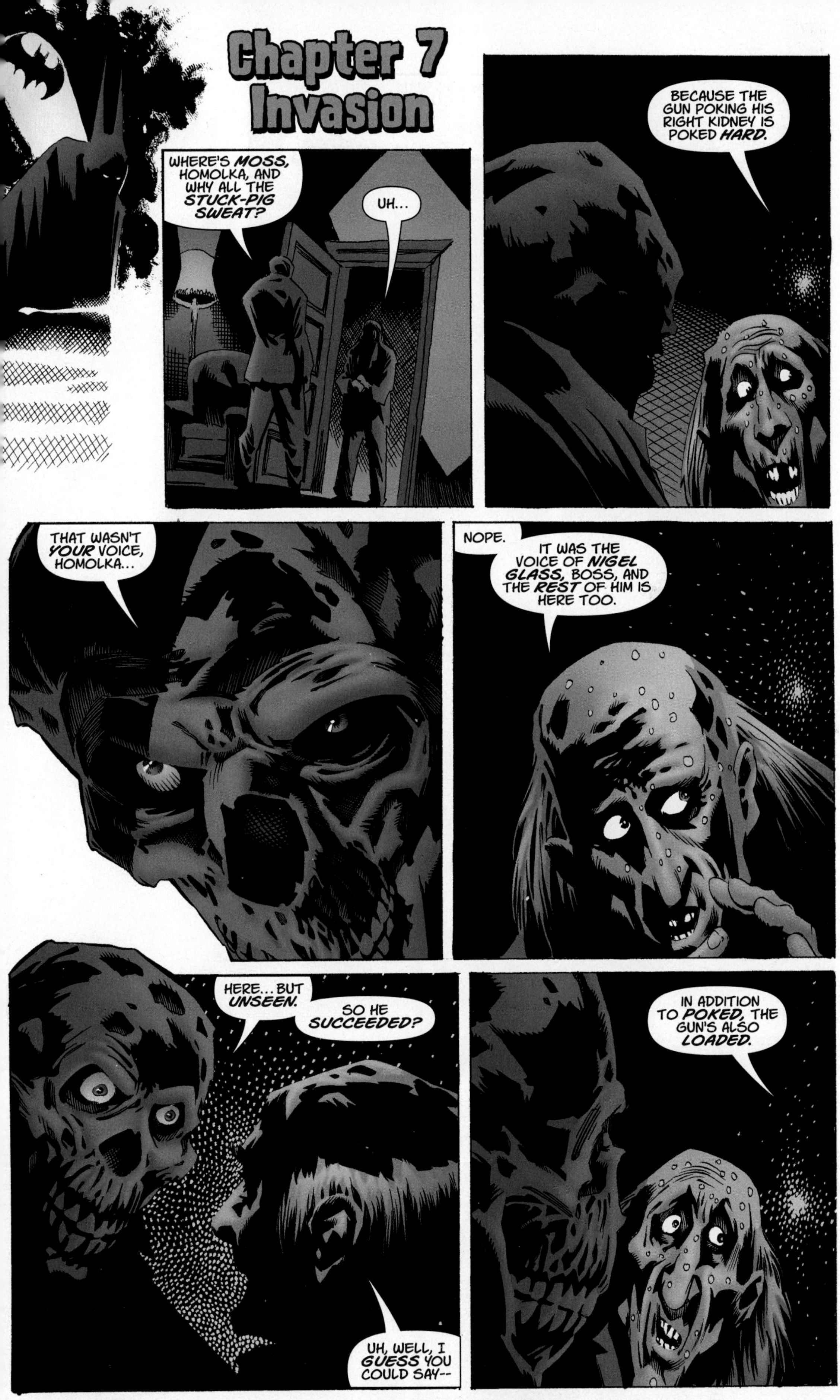
WHERE'S **MOSS**, HOMOLKA, AND WHY ALL THE **STUCK-PIG SWEAT?**
UH...
BECAUSE THE GUN POKING HIS RIGHT KIDNEY IS POKED **HARD**.
THAT WASN'T **YOUR** VOICE, HOMOLKA...
NOPE.
IT WAS THE VOICE OF **NIGEL GLASS**, BOSS, AND THE **REST** OF HIM IS HERE TOO.
HERE... BUT **UNSEEN**.
SO HE **SUCCEEDED?**
UH, WELL, I **GUESS** YOU COULD SAY--
IN ADDITION TO **POKED**, THE GUN'S ALSO **LOADED**.

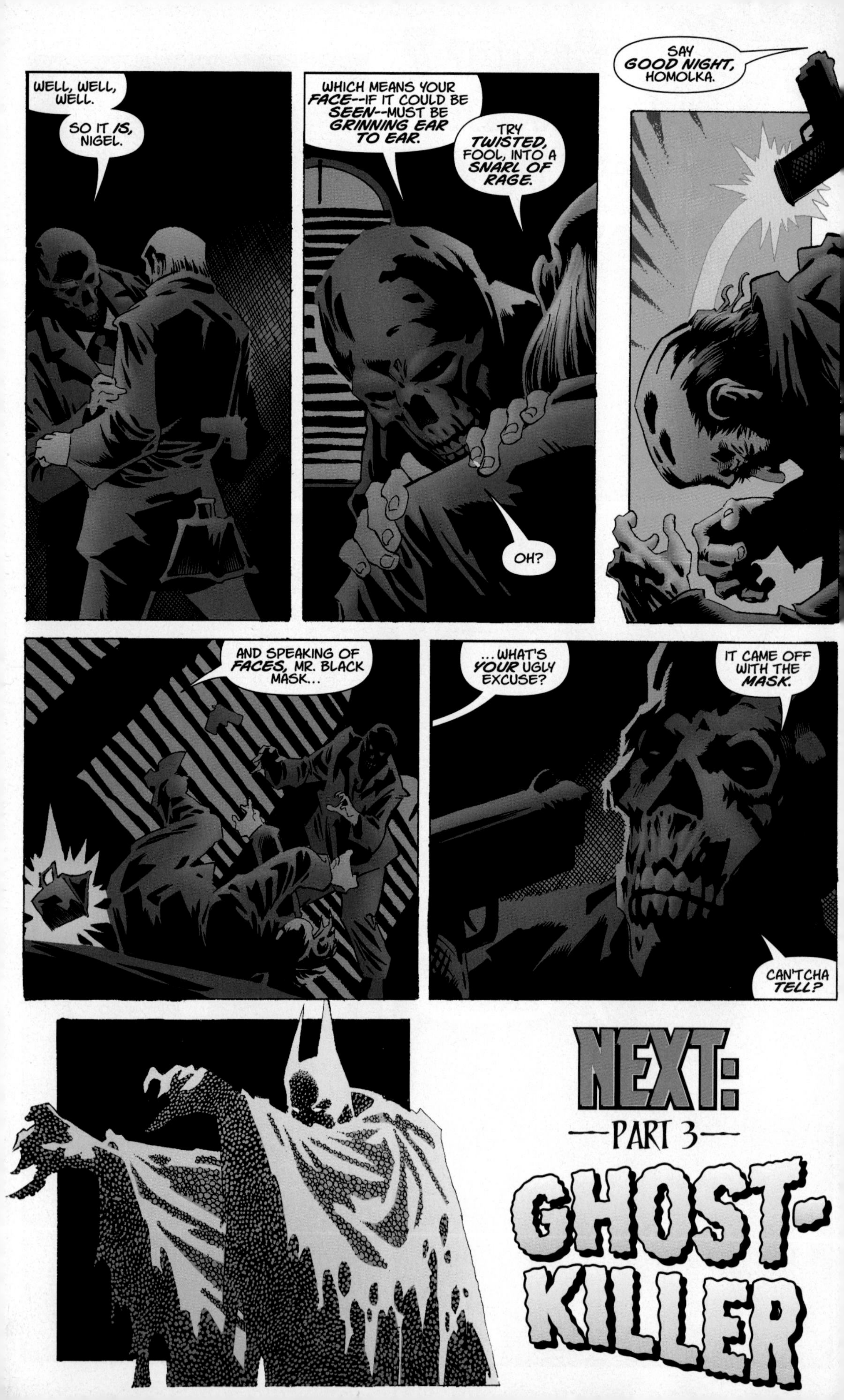
WELL, WELL, WELL.
SO IT IS, NIGEL.
WHICH MEANS YOUR FACE--IF IT COULD BE SEEN--MUST BE GRINNING EAR TO EAR.
TRY TWISTED, FOOL, INTO A SNARL OF RAGE.
OH?
SAY GOOD NIGHT, HOMOLKA.
AND SPEAKING OF FACES, MR. BLACK MASK...
...WHAT'S YOUR UGLY EXCUSE?
IT CAME OFF WITH THE MASK.
CAN'TCHA TELL?
NEXT:
—PART 3—
GHOST-KILLER

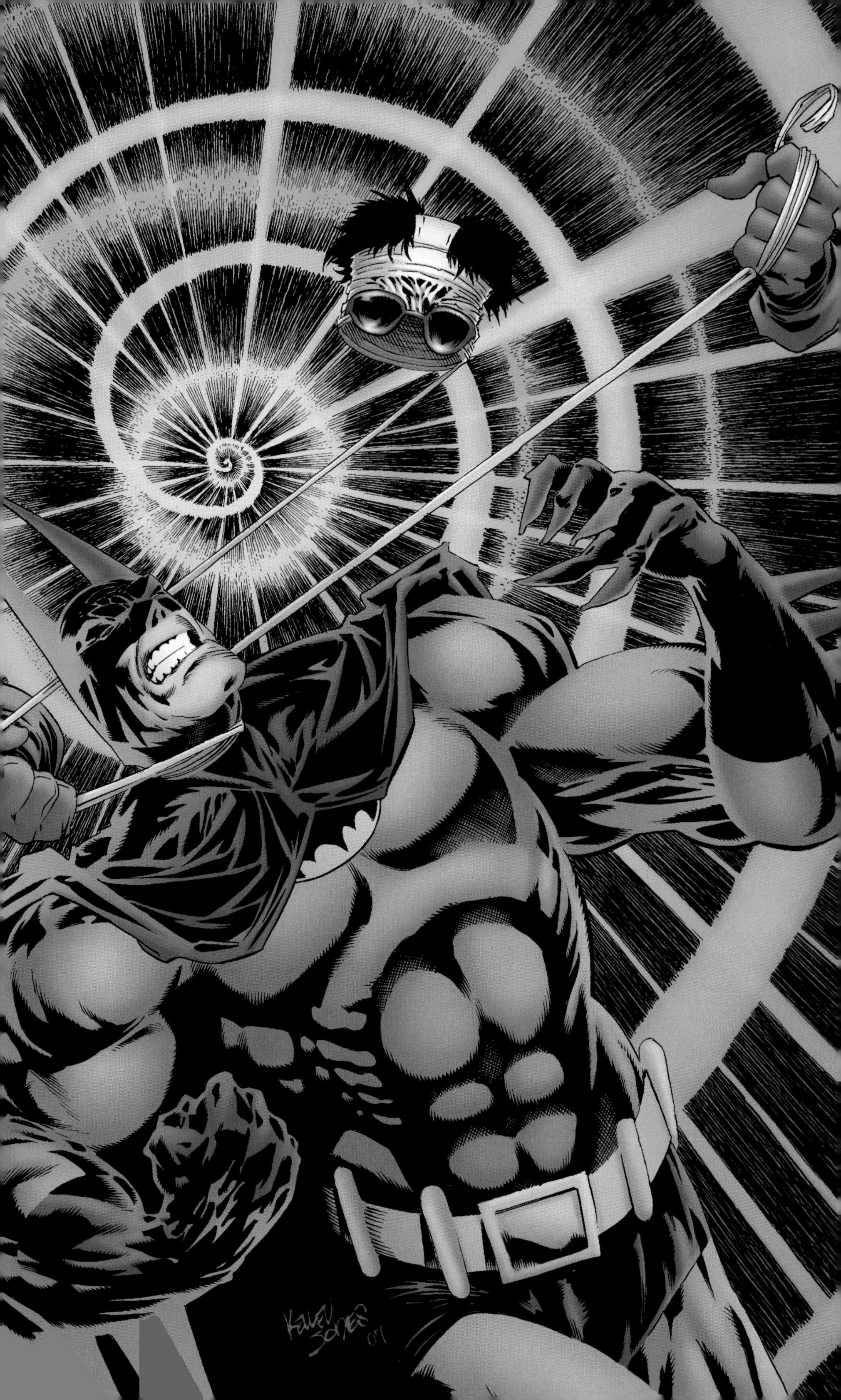
KELLEY JONES 07

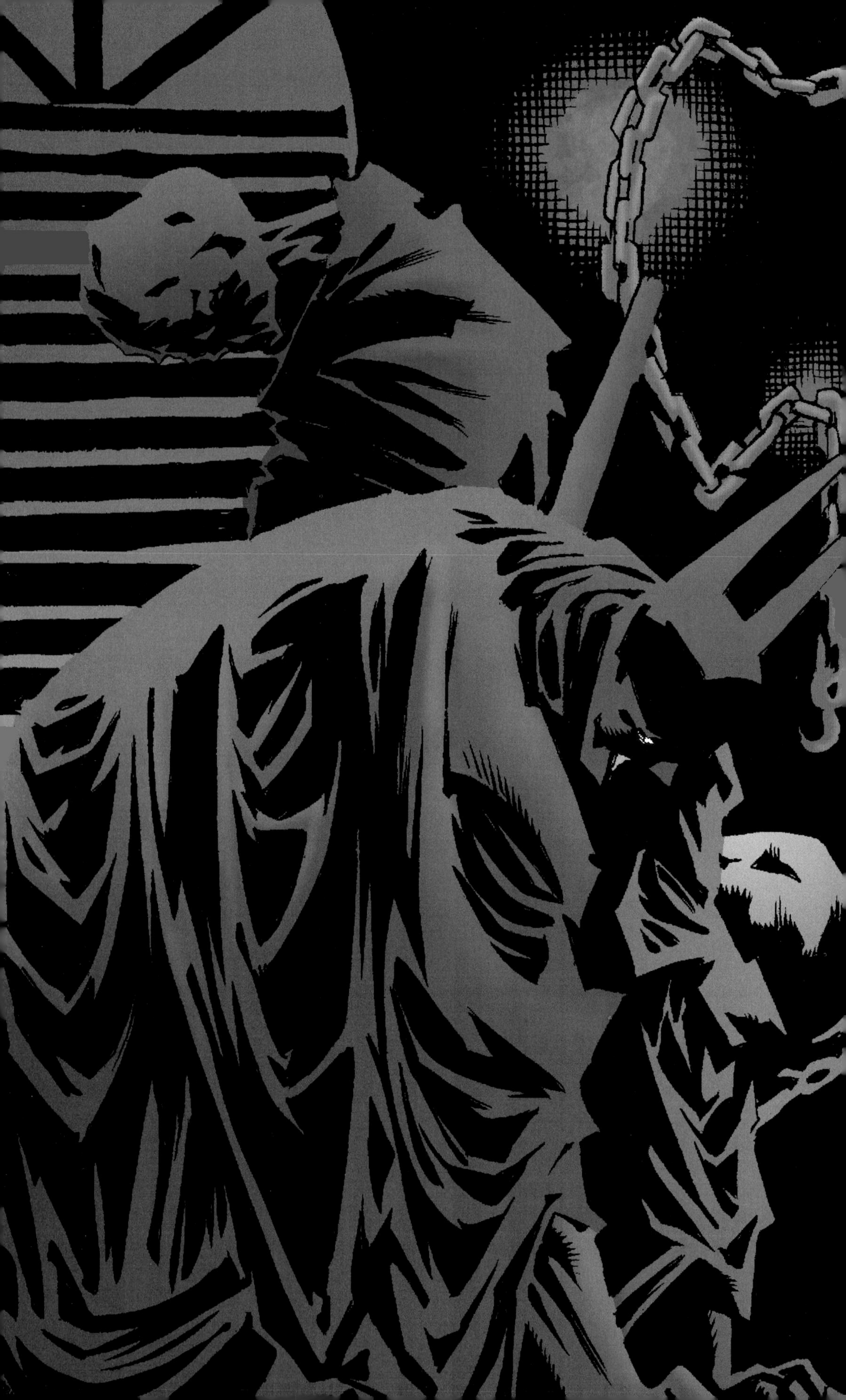

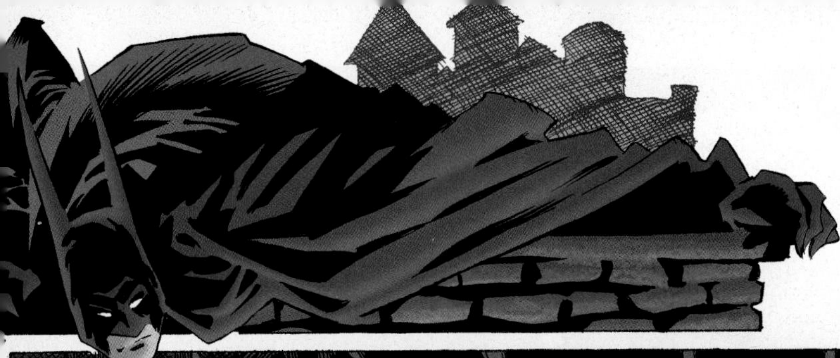

—PART 3—
GHOST-KILLER

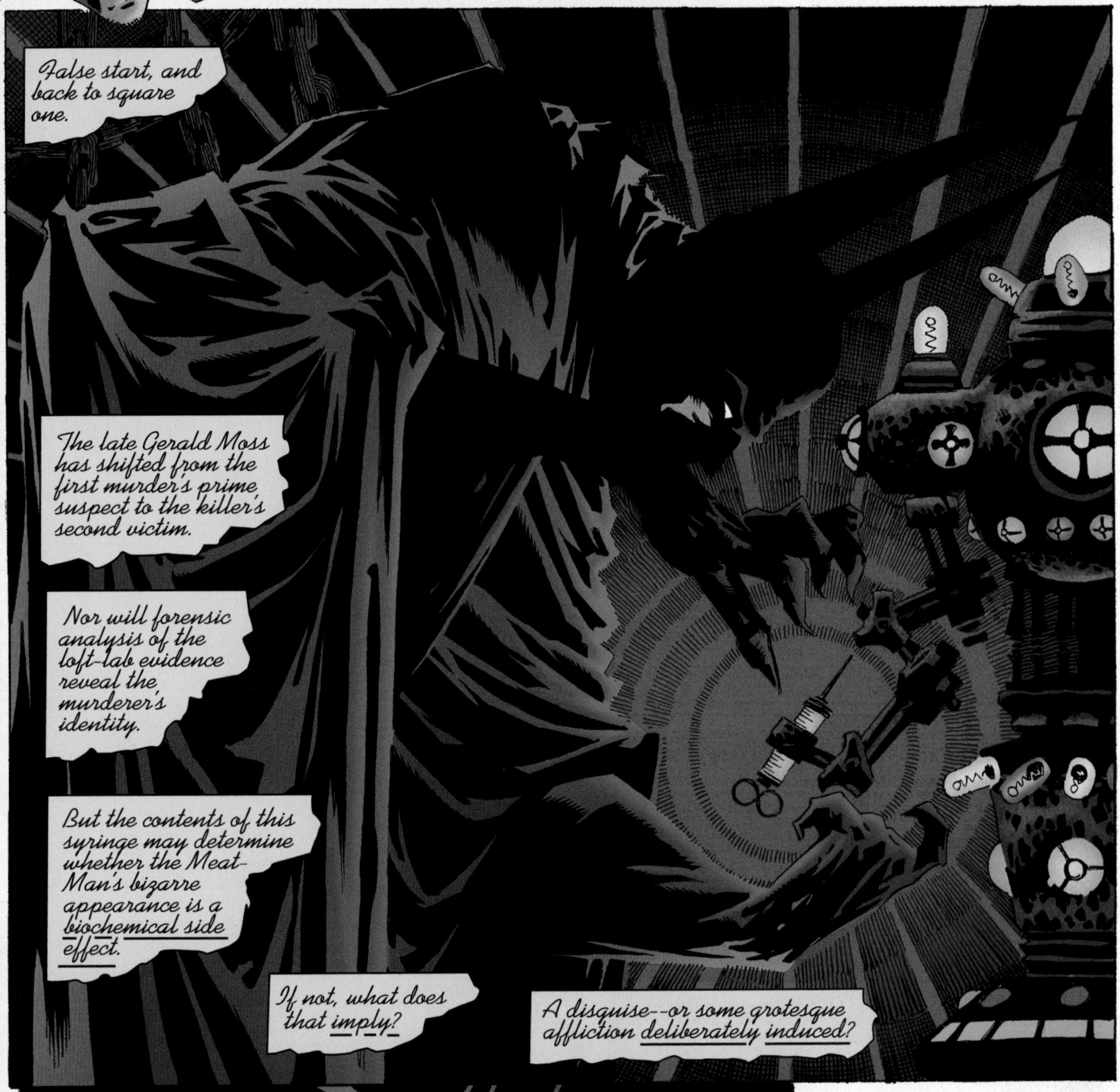
False start, and back to square one.
The late Gerald Moss has shifted from the first murder's prime suspect to the killer's second victim.
Nor will forensic analysis of the loft-lab evidence reveal the murderer's identity.
But the contents of this syringe may determine whether the Meat-Man's bizarre appearance is a biochemical side effect.
If not, what does that imply?
A disguise--or some grotesque affliction deliberately induced?

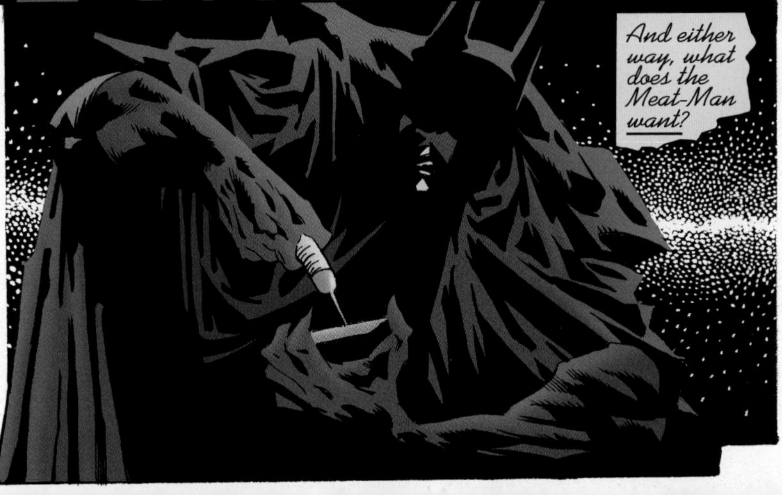
And either way, what does the Meat-Man want?

Chapter 1
Vengeance

MY DEAR INVISIBLE NIGEL, SURELY YOU DON'T INTEND TO *SHOOT* ME?

CROSS YOUR UGLY EYES AND *WATCH*.

BUT YOU DON'T *WANT* TO SHOOT ME.

SAYS YOU...

KLEKT

...FACING A *BULLET* BETWEEN YOUR UGLY CROSSED EYES.

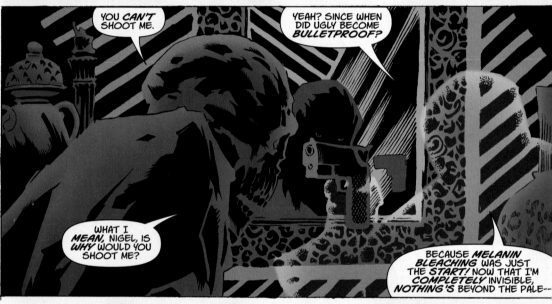

YOU *CAN'T* SHOOT ME.

YEAH? SINCE WHEN DID UGLY BECOME *BULLETPROOF*?

WHAT I *MEAN*, NIGEL, IS *WHY* WOULD YOU SHOOT ME?

BECAUSE *MELANIN BLEACHING* WAS JUST THE *START!* NOW THAT I'M *COMPLETELY* INVISIBLE, *NOTHING'S* BEYOND THE PALE--

--NOT EVEN BRIGHT RED REVENGE ON *EVERYONE* WHO EVER USED OR *ABUSED* ME!

YOU *SEE*? WE BOTH WANT THE *SAME THING*.

WHAT ARE YOU *BABBLING* ABOUT?

FACES AND *MASKS*, NIGEL--MY OWN *LOST* FACE AND THE DARK MASK THAT *STOLE* IT.

IF I MAY CONTINUE...?

ONLY IF THAT LIPLESS MOUTH RUNS *BULLET-FAST!*

FLITCH

ALL RIGHT...

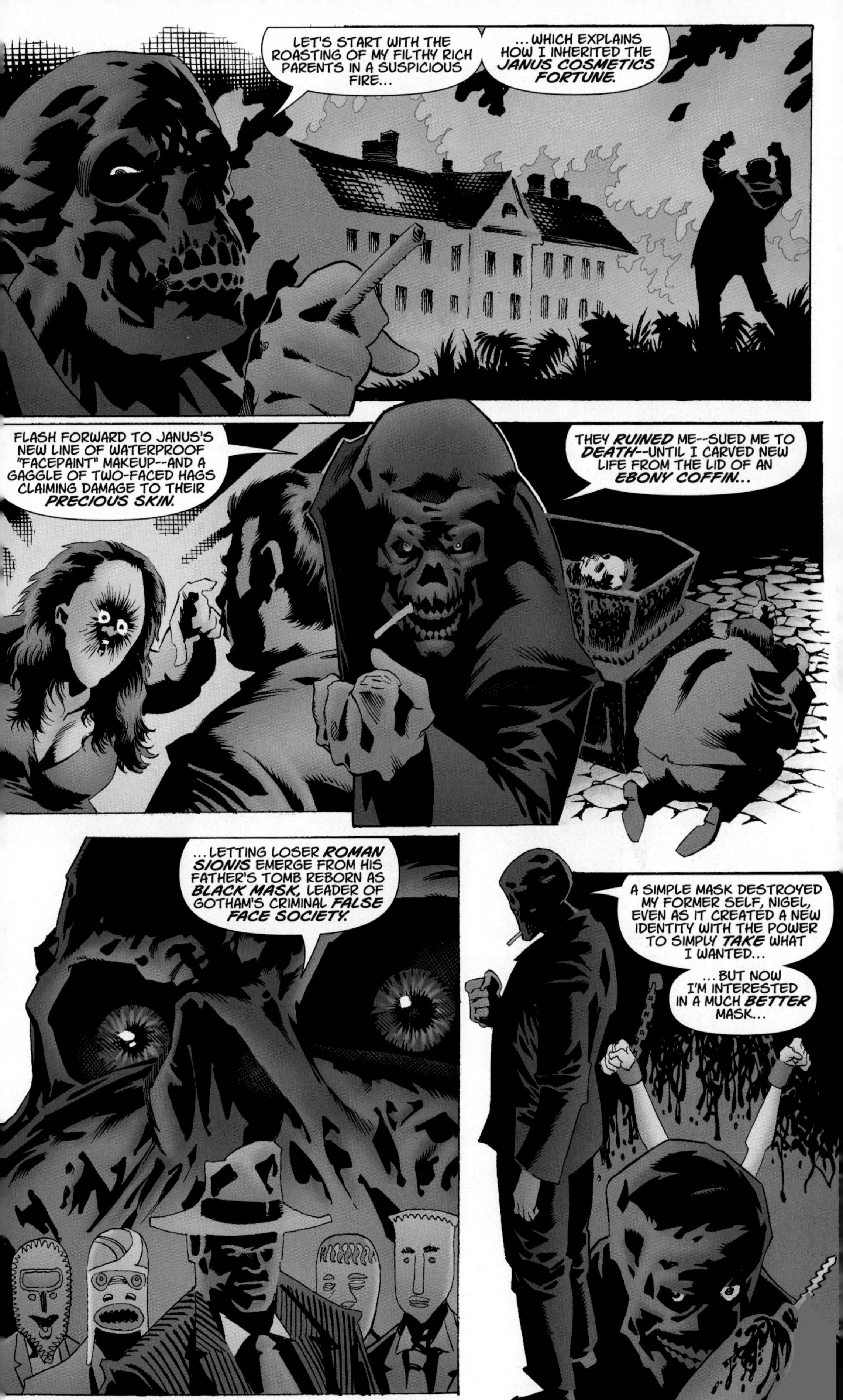
LET'S START WITH THE ROASTING OF MY FILTHY RICH PARENTS IN A SUSPICIOUS FIRE...
...WHICH EXPLAINS HOW I INHERITED THE JANUS COSMETICS FORTUNE.
FLASH FORWARD TO JANUS'S NEW LINE OF WATERPROOF "FACEPAINT" MAKEUP--AND A GAGGLE OF TWO-FACED HAGS CLAIMING DAMAGE TO THEIR PRECIOUS SKIN.
THEY RUINED ME--SUED ME TO DEATH--UNTIL I CARVED NEW LIFE FROM THE LID OF AN EBONY COFFIN...
...LETTING LOSER ROMAN SIONIS EMERGE FROM HIS FATHER'S TOMB REBORN AS BLACK MASK, LEADER OF GOTHAM'S CRIMINAL FALSE FACE SOCIETY.
A SIMPLE MASK DESTROYED MY FORMER SELF, NIGEL, EVEN AS IT CREATED A NEW IDENTITY WITH THE POWER TO SIMPLY TAKE WHAT I WANTED...
...BUT NOW I'M INTERESTED IN A MUCH BETTER MASK...

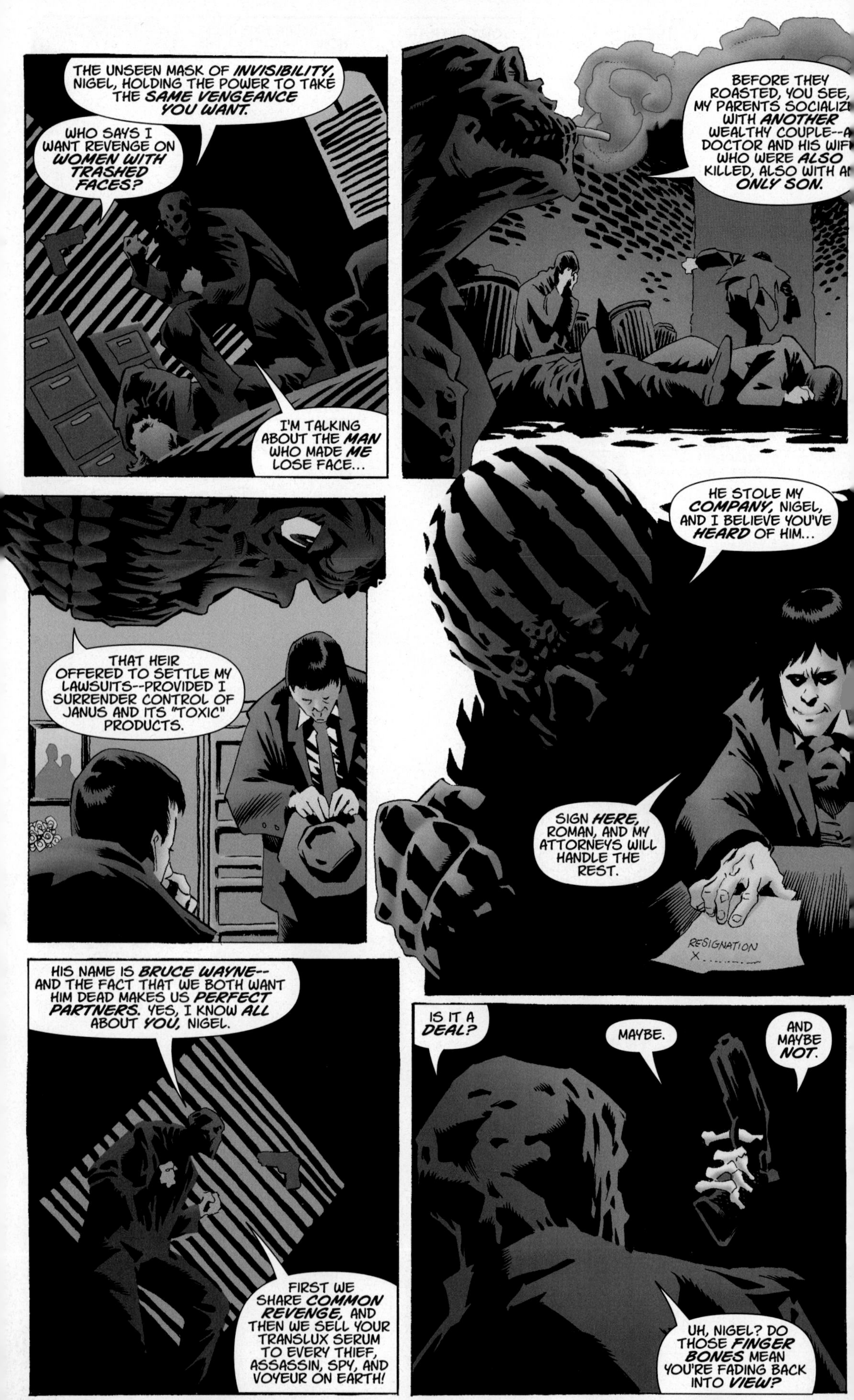

THE UNSEEN MASK OF *INVISIBILITY,* NIGEL, HOLDING THE POWER TO TAKE THE *SAME VENGEANCE YOU WANT.*
WHO SAYS I WANT REVENGE ON *WOMEN WITH TRASHED FACES?*
I'M TALKING ABOUT THE *MAN* WHO MADE *ME* LOSE FACE...
BEFORE THEY ROASTED, YOU SEE, MY PARENTS SOCIALIZ WITH *ANOTHER* WEALTHY COUPLE--A DOCTOR AND HIS WIF WHO WERE *ALSO* KILLED, ALSO WITH A *ONLY SON.*
THAT HEIR OFFERED TO SETTLE MY LAWSUITS--PROVIDED I SURRENDER CONTROL OF JANUS AND ITS "TOXIC" PRODUCTS.
HE STOLE MY *COMPANY,* NIGEL, AND I BELIEVE YOU'VE *HEARD* OF HIM...
SIGN *HERE,* ROMAN, AND MY ATTORNEYS WILL HANDLE THE REST.
RESIGNATION
X..........
HIS NAME IS *BRUCE WAYNE*-- AND THE FACT THAT WE BOTH WANT HIM DEAD MAKES US *PERFECT PARTNERS.* YES, I KNOW *ALL* ABOUT *YOU,* NIGEL.
FIRST WE SHARE *COMMON REVENGE,* AND THEN WE SELL YOUR TRANSLUX SERUM TO EVERY THIEF, ASSASSIN, SPY, AND VOYEUR ON EARTH!
IS IT A *DEAL?*
MAYBE.
AND MAYBE *NOT.*
UH, NIGEL? DO THOSE *FINGER BONES* MEAN YOU'RE FADING BACK INTO *VIEW?*

**Chapter 2
Betrayal**

SWUKT

GUH-H!

BUT *RIGHT NOW,* FOOL...

...I NEED MORE TRANSLUX FOR *MYSELF*-- MORE AND MORE *ALL THE TIME.*

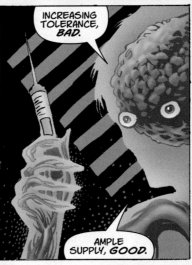

INCREASING TOLERANCE, *BAD.*

AMPLE SUPPLY, *GOOD.*

AND I'LL INJECT *GALLONS* OF THE STUFF...

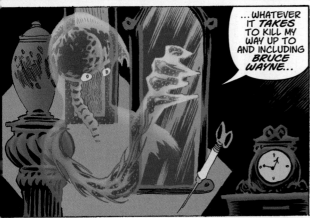

...WHATEVER IT *TAKES* TO KILL MY WAY UP TO AND INCLUDING *BRUCE WAYNE*...

...IN A CAMPAIGN OF *MIRACULOUS VENGEANCE* STARTING *NOW.*

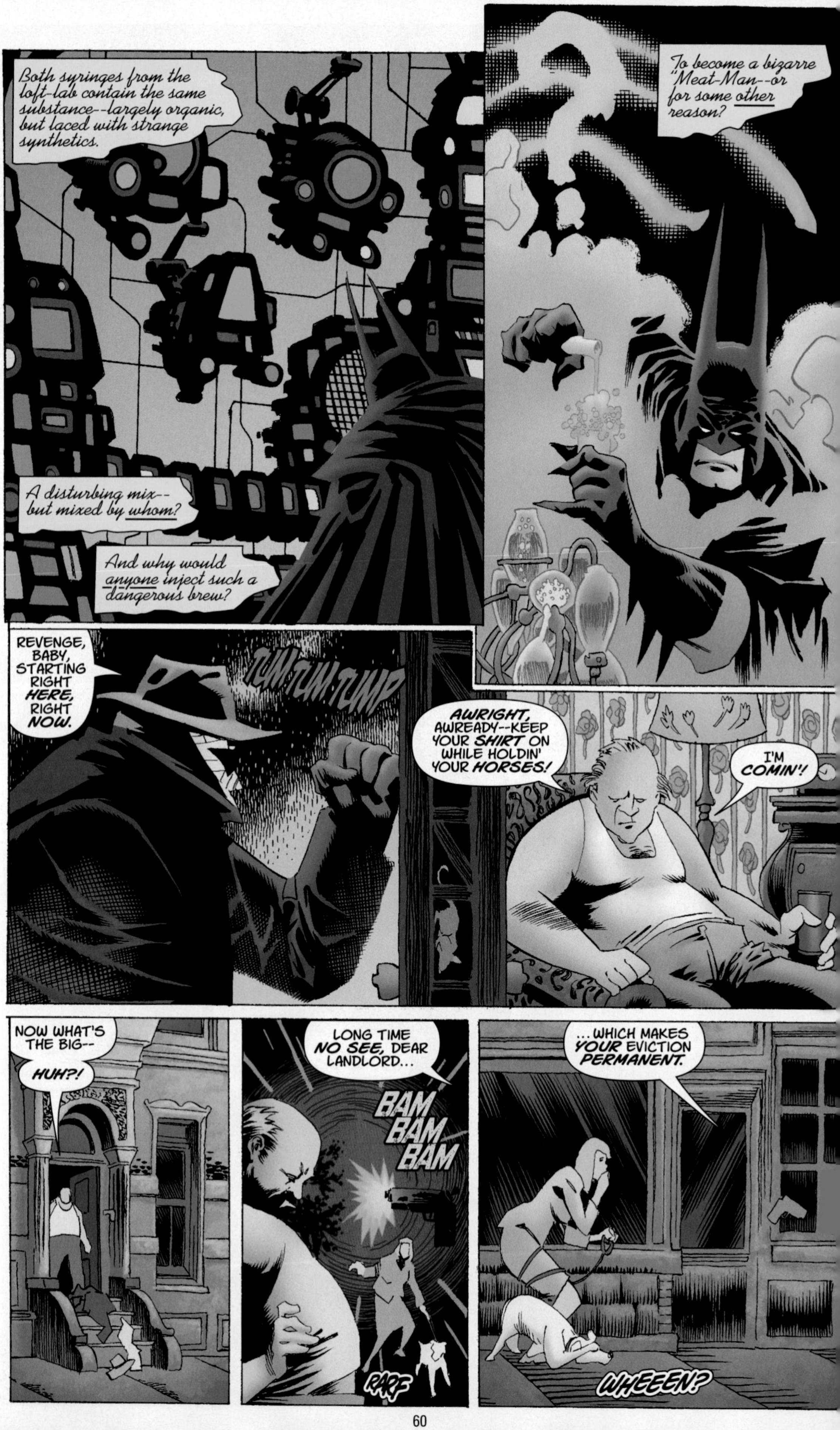

Both syringes from the loft-lab contain the same substance--largely organic, but laced with strange synthetics.
A disturbing mix--but mixed by whom?
And why would anyone inject such a dangerous brew?
To become a bizarre "Meat-Man--or for some other reason?
REVENGE, BABY, STARTING RIGHT HERE, RIGHT NOW.
TUMP TUMP TUMP
AWRIGHT, AWREADY--KEEP YOUR SHIRT ON WHILE HOLDIN' YOUR HORSES!
I'M COMIN'!
NOW WHAT'S THE BIG--
HUH?!
LONG TIME NO SEE, DEAR LANDLORD...
BAM BAM BAM
RARF
...WHICH MAKES YOUR EVICTION PERMANENT.
WHEEEN?

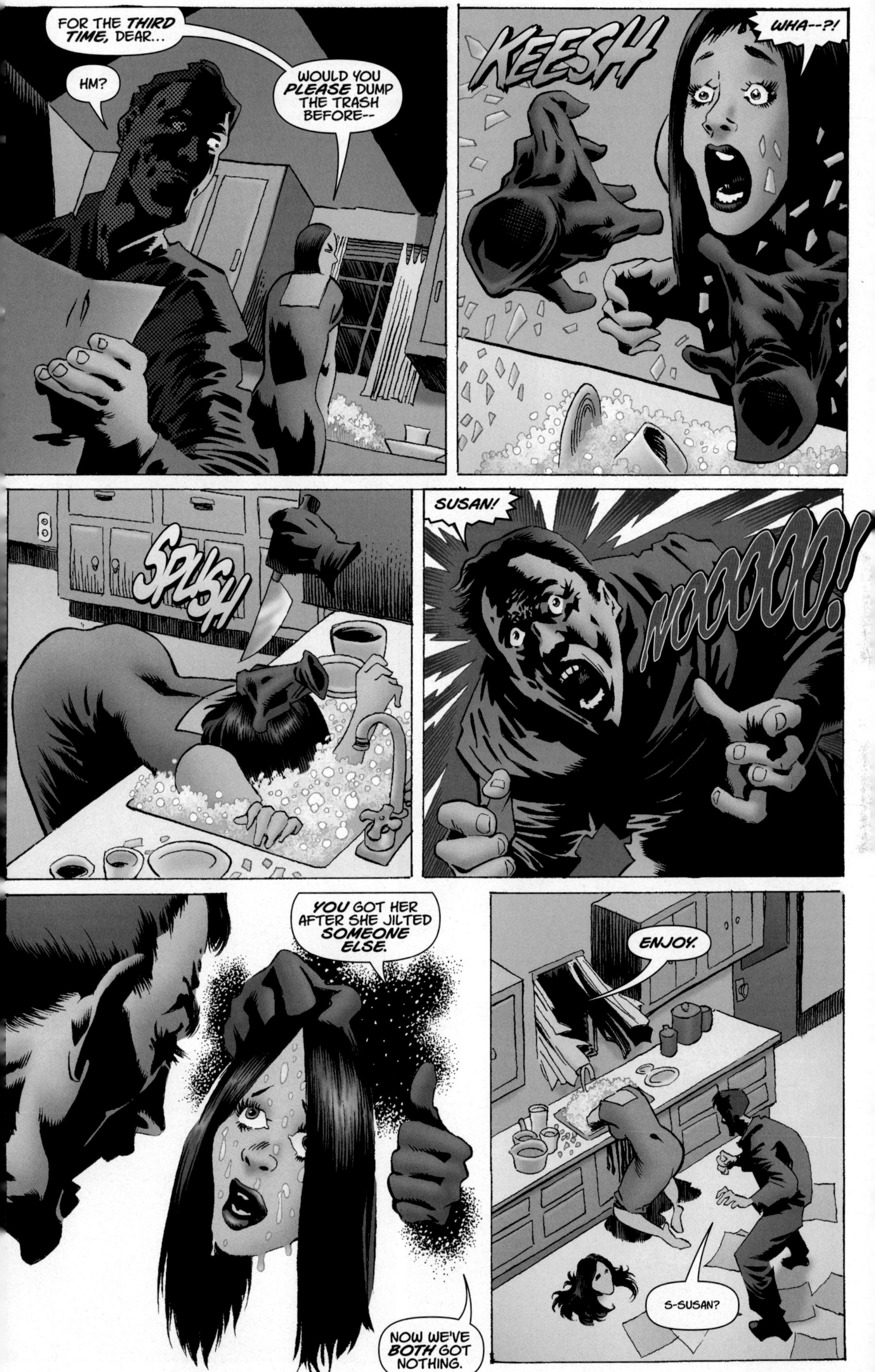
FOR THE THIRD TIME, DEAR...
HM?
WOULD YOU PLEASE DUMP THE TRASH BEFORE--
KEESH
WHA--?!
SPLISH
SUSAN!
NOOOOO!
YOU GOT HER AFTER SHE JILTED SOMEONE ELSE.
NOW WE'VE BOTH GOT NOTHING.
ENJOY.
S-SUSAN?

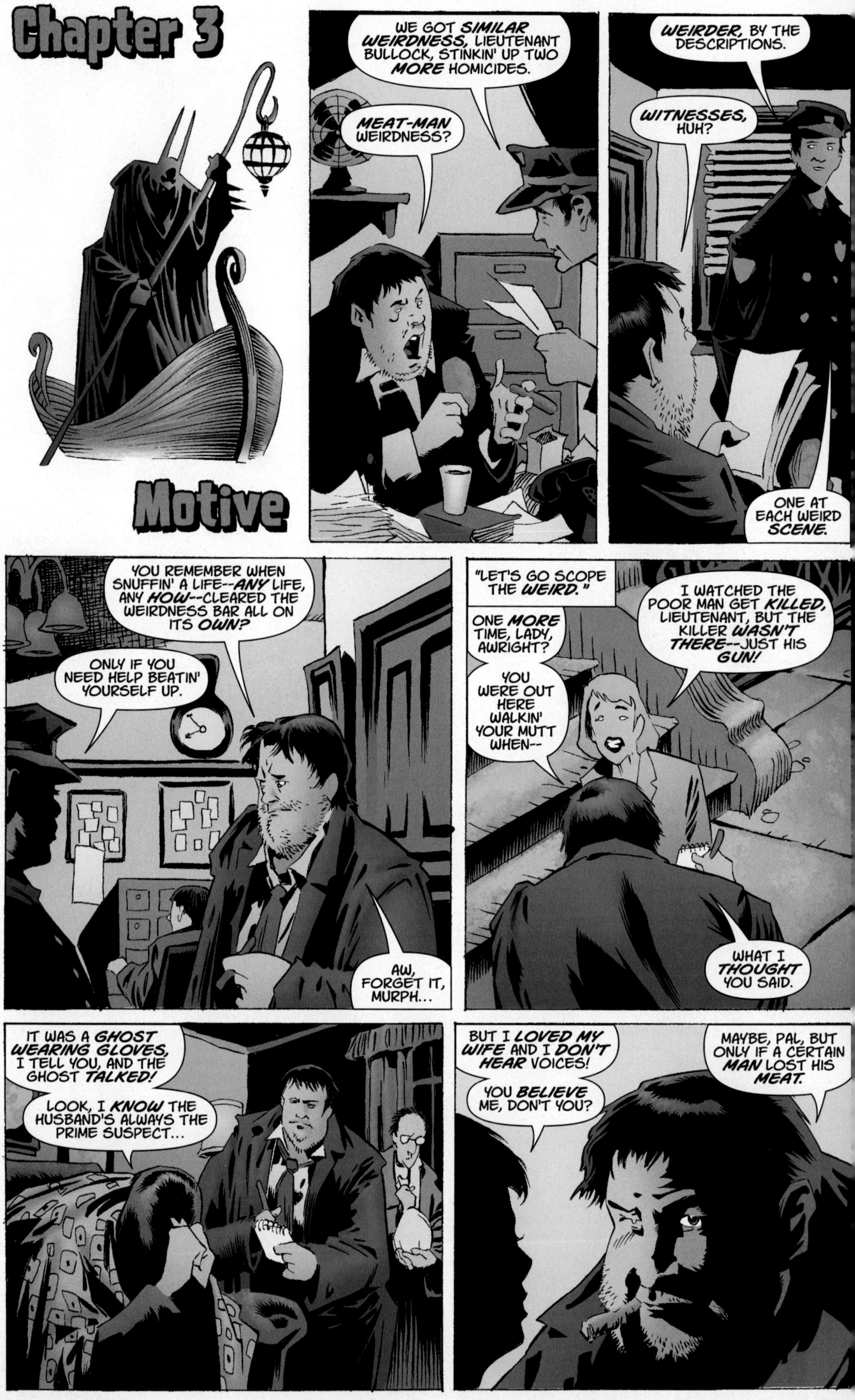
Chapter 3
Motive
WE GOT SIMILAR WEIRDNESS, LIEUTENANT BULLOCK, STINKIN' UP TWO MORE HOMICIDES.
MEAT-MAN WEIRDNESS?
WEIRDER, BY THE DESCRIPTIONS.
WITNESSES, HUH?
ONE AT EACH WEIRD SCENE.
YOU REMEMBER WHEN SNUFFIN' A LIFE--ANY LIFE, ANY HOW--CLEARED THE WEIRDNESS BAR ALL ON ITS OWN?
ONLY IF YOU NEED HELP BEATIN' YOURSELF UP.
AW, FORGET IT, MURPH...
"LET'S GO SCOPE THE WEIRD."
ONE MORE TIME, LADY, AWRIGHT?
YOU WERE OUT HERE WALKIN' YOUR MUTT WHEN--
I WATCHED THE POOR MAN GET KILLED, LIEUTENANT, BUT THE KILLER WASN'T THERE--JUST HIS GUN!
WHAT I THOUGHT YOU SAID.
IT WAS A GHOST WEARING GLOVES, I TELL YOU, AND THE GHOST TALKED!
LOOK, I KNOW THE HUSBAND'S ALWAYS THE PRIME SUSPECT...
BUT I LOVED MY WIFE AND I DON'T HEAR VOICES!
YOU BELIEVE ME, DON'T YOU?
MAYBE, PAL, BUT ONLY IF A CERTAIN MAN LOST HIS MEAT.

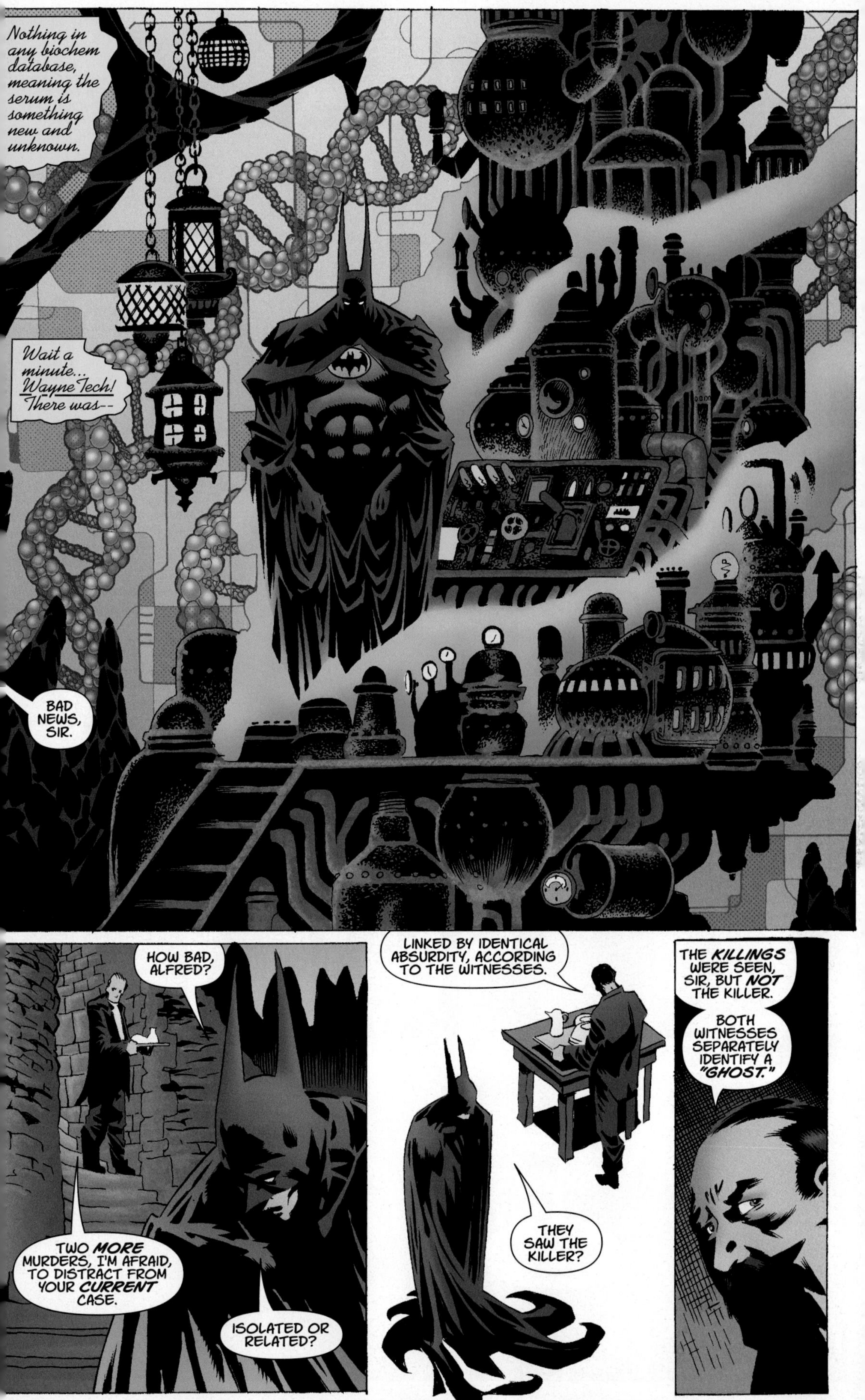
Nothing in any biochem database, meaning the serum is something new and unknown.
Wait a minute... WayneTech! There was--
BAD NEWS, SIR.
HOW BAD, ALFRED?
TWO MORE MURDERS, I'M AFRAID, TO DISTRACT FROM YOUR CURRENT CASE.
ISOLATED OR RELATED?
LINKED BY IDENTICAL ABSURDITY, ACCORDING TO THE WITNESSES.
THEY SAW THE KILLER?
THE KILLINGS WERE SEEN, SIR, BUT NOT THE KILLER.
BOTH WITNESSES SEPARATELY IDENTIFY A "GHOST."

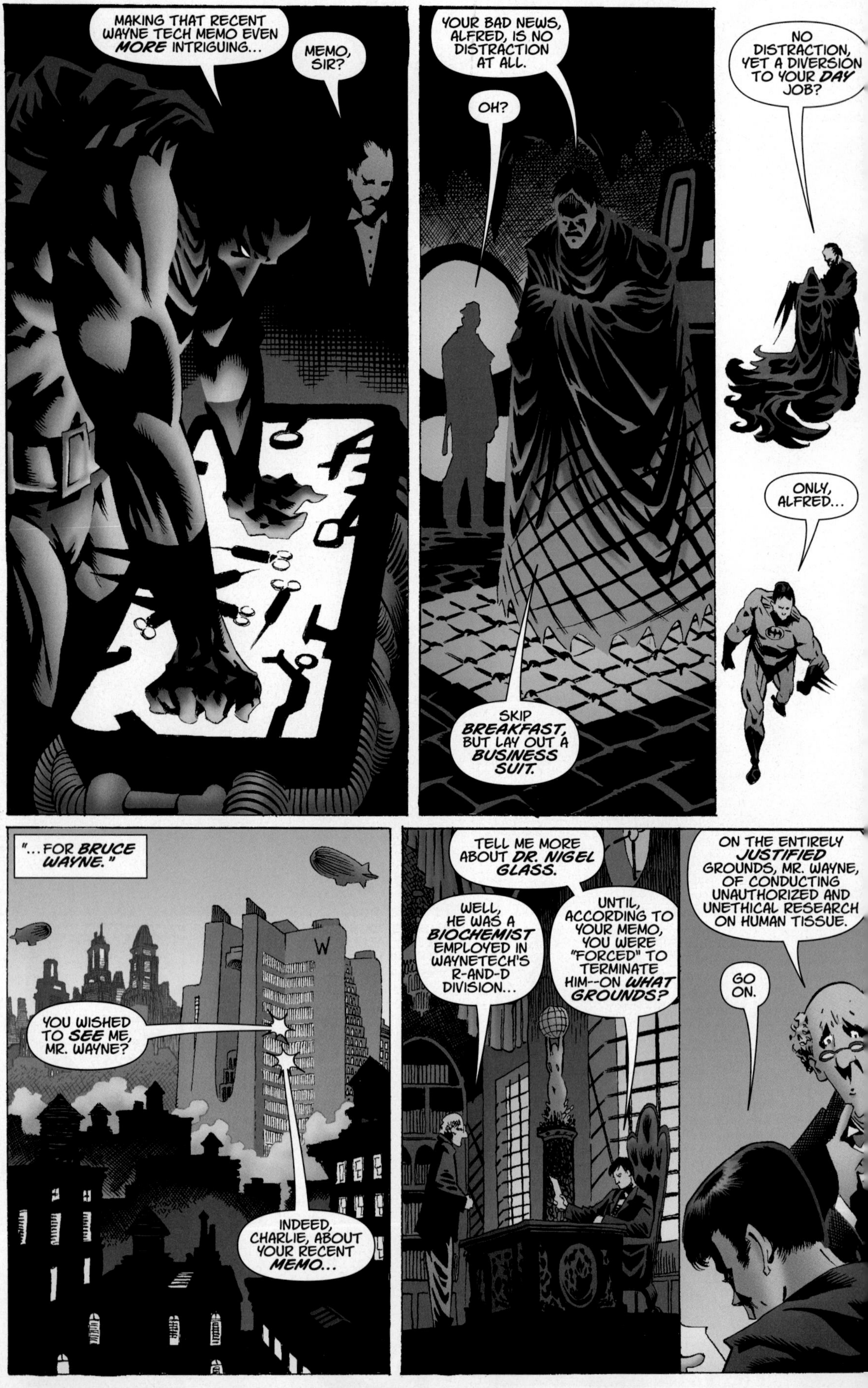

MAKING THAT RECENT WAYNE TECH MEMO EVEN *MORE* INTRIGUING...
MEMO, SIR?
YOUR BAD NEWS, ALFRED, IS NO DISTRACTION AT ALL.
OH?
SKIP *BREAKFAST*, BUT LAY OUT A *BUSINESS SUIT.*
NO DISTRACTION, YET A DIVERSION TO YOUR *DAY* JOB?
ONLY, ALFRED...
"...FOR *BRUCE WAYNE.*"
YOU WISHED TO *SEE* ME, MR. WAYNE?
INDEED, CHARLIE, ABOUT YOUR RECENT *MEMO...*
TELL ME MORE ABOUT *DR. NIGEL GLASS.*
WELL, HE WAS A *BIOCHEMIST* EMPLOYED IN WAYNETECH'S R-AND-D DIVISION...
UNTIL, ACCORDING TO YOUR MEMO, YOU WERE "FORCED" TO TERMINATE HIM--ON *WHAT GROUNDS?*
ON THE ENTIRELY *JUSTIFIED* GROUNDS, MR. WAYNE, OF CONDUCTING UNAUTHORIZED AND UNETHICAL RESEARCH ON HUMAN TISSUE.
GO ON.

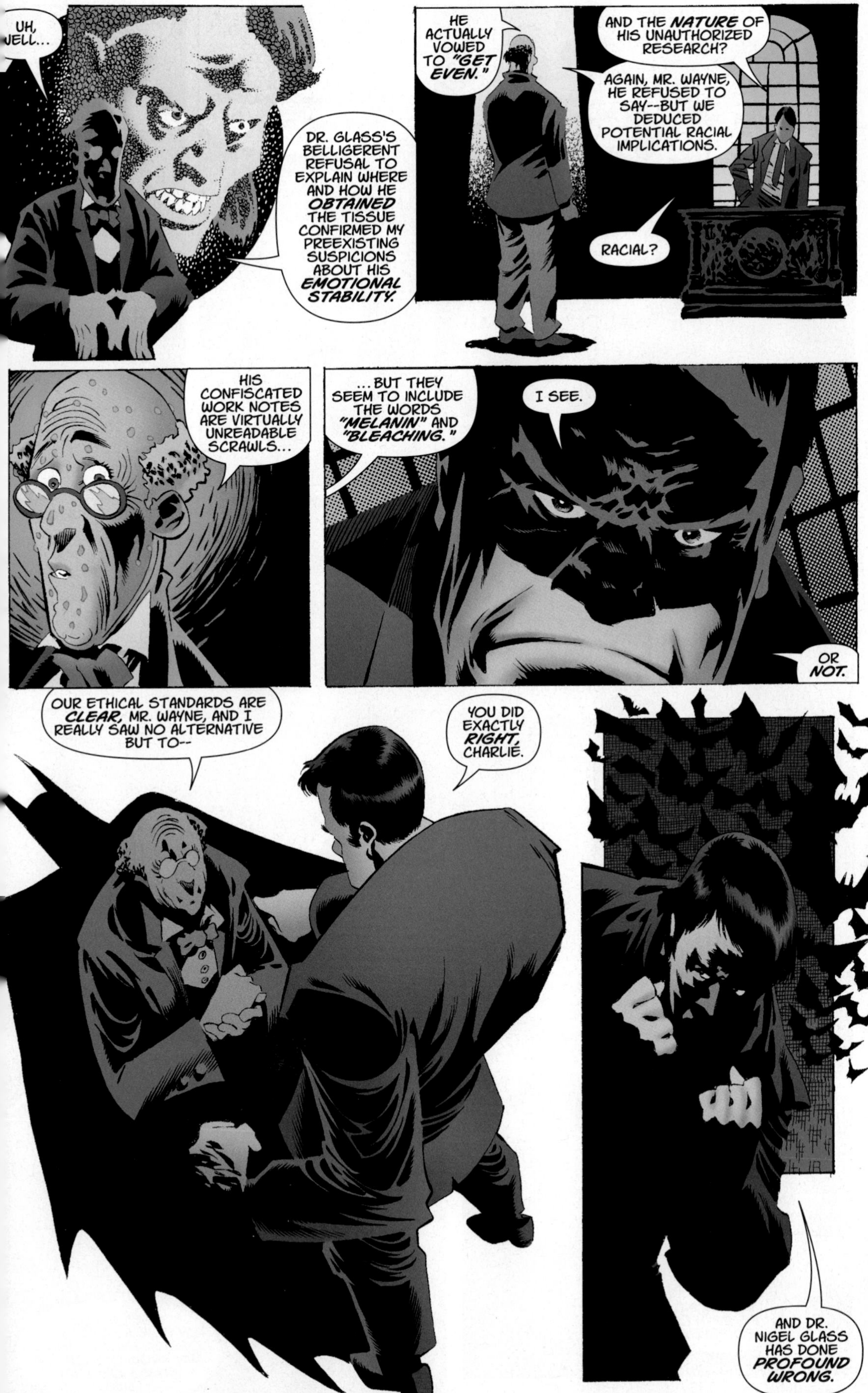

UH, WELL...
DR. GLASS'S BELLIGERENT REFUSAL TO EXPLAIN WHERE AND HOW HE *OBTAINED* THE TISSUE CONFIRMED MY PREEXISTING SUSPICIONS ABOUT HIS *EMOTIONAL STABILITY.*
HE ACTUALLY VOWED TO *"GET EVEN."*
AND THE *NATURE* OF HIS UNAUTHORIZED RESEARCH?
AGAIN, MR. WAYNE, HE REFUSED TO SAY--BUT WE DEDUCED POTENTIAL RACIAL IMPLICATIONS.
RACIAL?
HIS CONFISCATED WORK NOTES ARE VIRTUALLY UNREADABLE SCRAWLS...
...BUT THEY SEEM TO INCLUDE THE WORDS *"MELANIN"* AND *"BLEACHING."*
I SEE.
OR *NOT.*
OUR ETHICAL STANDARDS ARE *CLEAR,* MR. WAYNE, AND I REALLY SAW NO ALTERNATIVE BUT TO--
YOU DID EXACTLY *RIGHT,* CHARLIE.
AND DR. NIGEL GLASS HAS DONE *PROFOUND WRONG.*

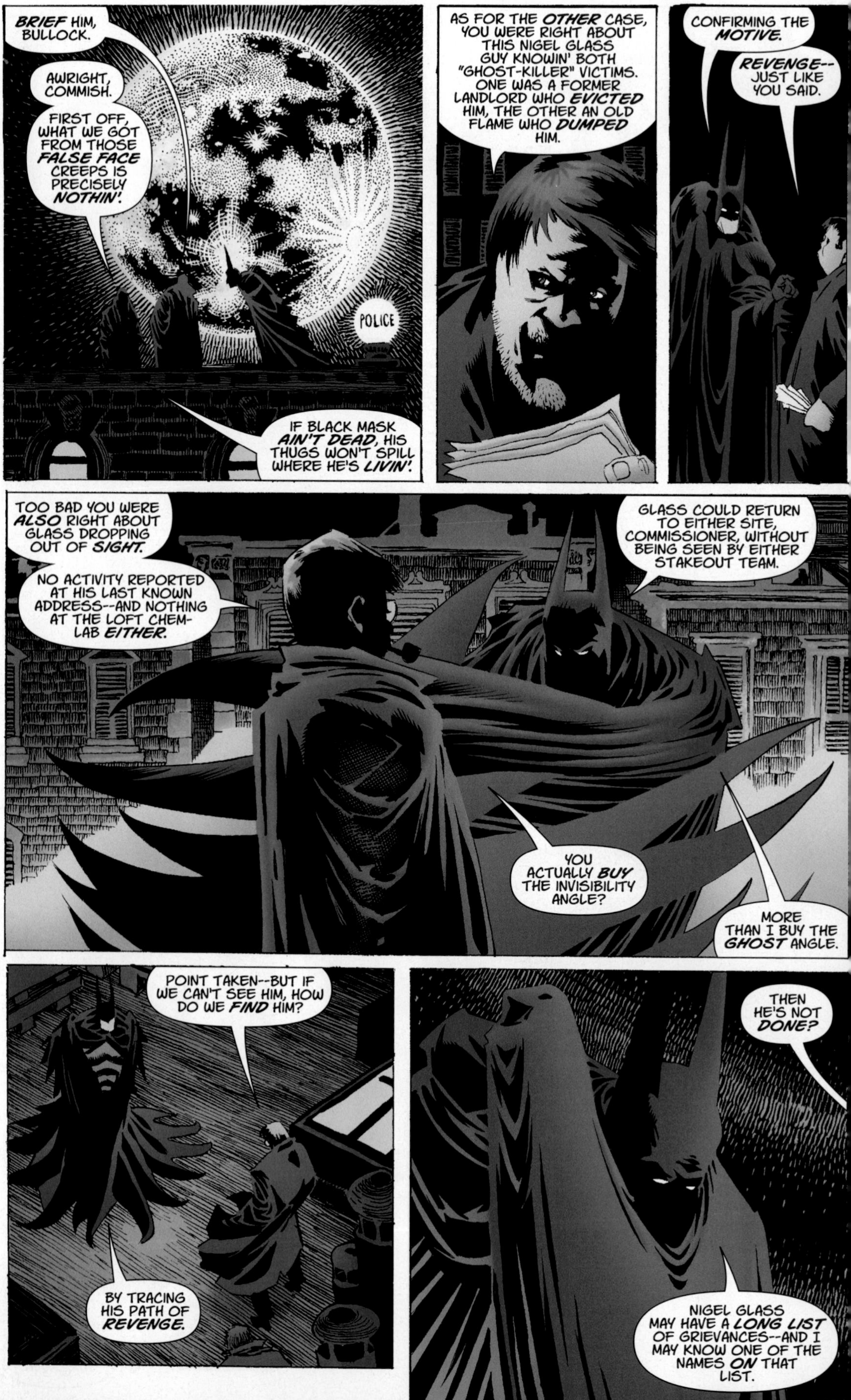
BRIEF HIM, BULLOCK.
AWRIGHT, COMMISH.
FIRST OFF, WHAT WE GOT FROM THOSE FALSE FACE CREEPS IS PRECISELY NOTHIN'.
POLICE
IF BLACK MASK AIN'T DEAD, HIS THUGS WON'T SPILL WHERE HE'S LIVIN'.
AS FOR THE OTHER CASE, YOU WERE RIGHT ABOUT THIS NIGEL GLASS GUY KNOWIN' BOTH "GHOST-KILLER" VICTIMS. ONE WAS A FORMER LANDLORD WHO EVICTED HIM, THE OTHER AN OLD FLAME WHO DUMPED HIM.
CONFIRMING THE MOTIVE.
REVENGE-- JUST LIKE YOU SAID.
TOO BAD YOU WERE ALSO RIGHT ABOUT GLASS DROPPING OUT OF SIGHT.
NO ACTIVITY REPORTED AT HIS LAST KNOWN ADDRESS--AND NOTHING AT THE LOFT CHEM-LAB EITHER.
GLASS COULD RETURN TO EITHER SITE, COMMISSIONER, WITHOUT BEING SEEN BY EITHER STAKEOUT TEAM.
YOU ACTUALLY BUY THE INVISIBILITY ANGLE?
MORE THAN I BUY THE GHOST ANGLE.
POINT TAKEN--BUT IF WE CAN'T SEE HIM, HOW DO WE FIND HIM?
BY TRACING HIS PATH OF REVENGE.
THEN HE'S NOT DONE?
NIGEL GLASS MAY HAVE A LONG LIST OF GRIEVANCES--AND I MAY KNOW ONE OF THE NAMES ON THAT LIST.

Chapter 4
Assault

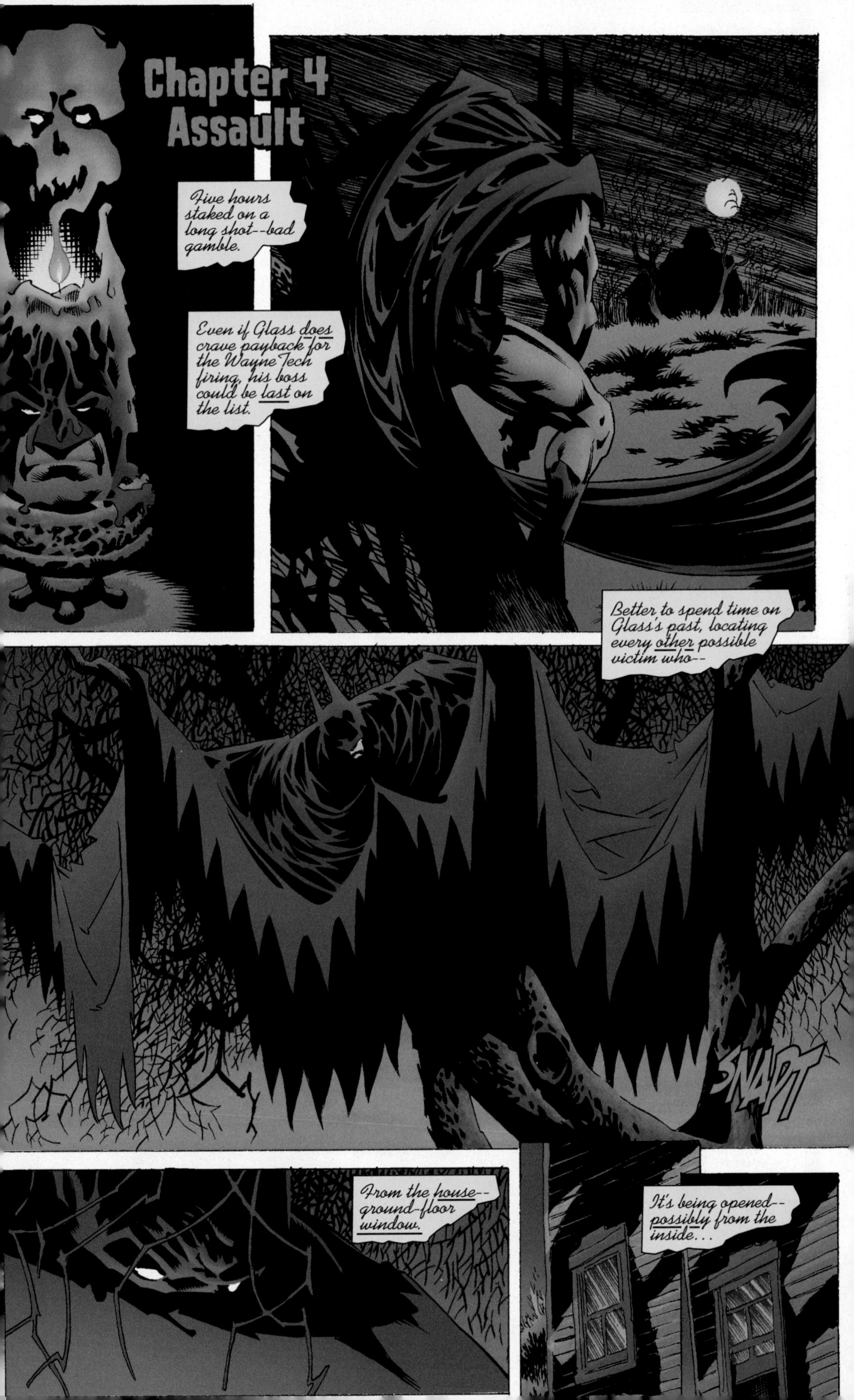

Five hours staked on a long shot--bad gamble.
Even if Glass does crave payback for the Wayne Tech firing, his boss could be last on the list.
Better to spend time on Glass's past, locating every other possible victim who--
SNAPT
From the house--ground-floor window.
It's being opened--possibly from the inside...

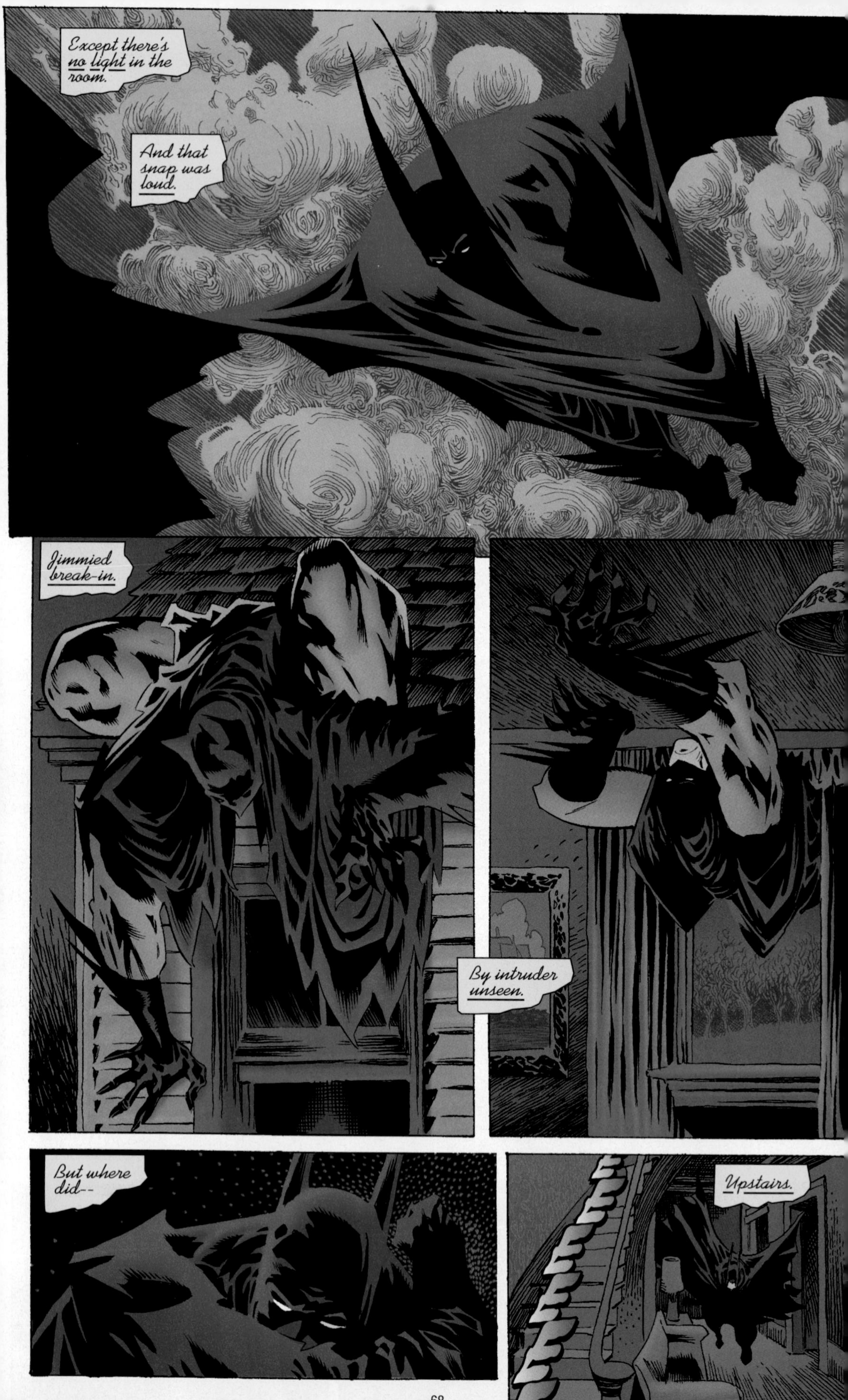
Except there's no light in the room.
And that snap was loud.
Jimmied break-in.
By intruder unseen.
But where did--
Upstairs.

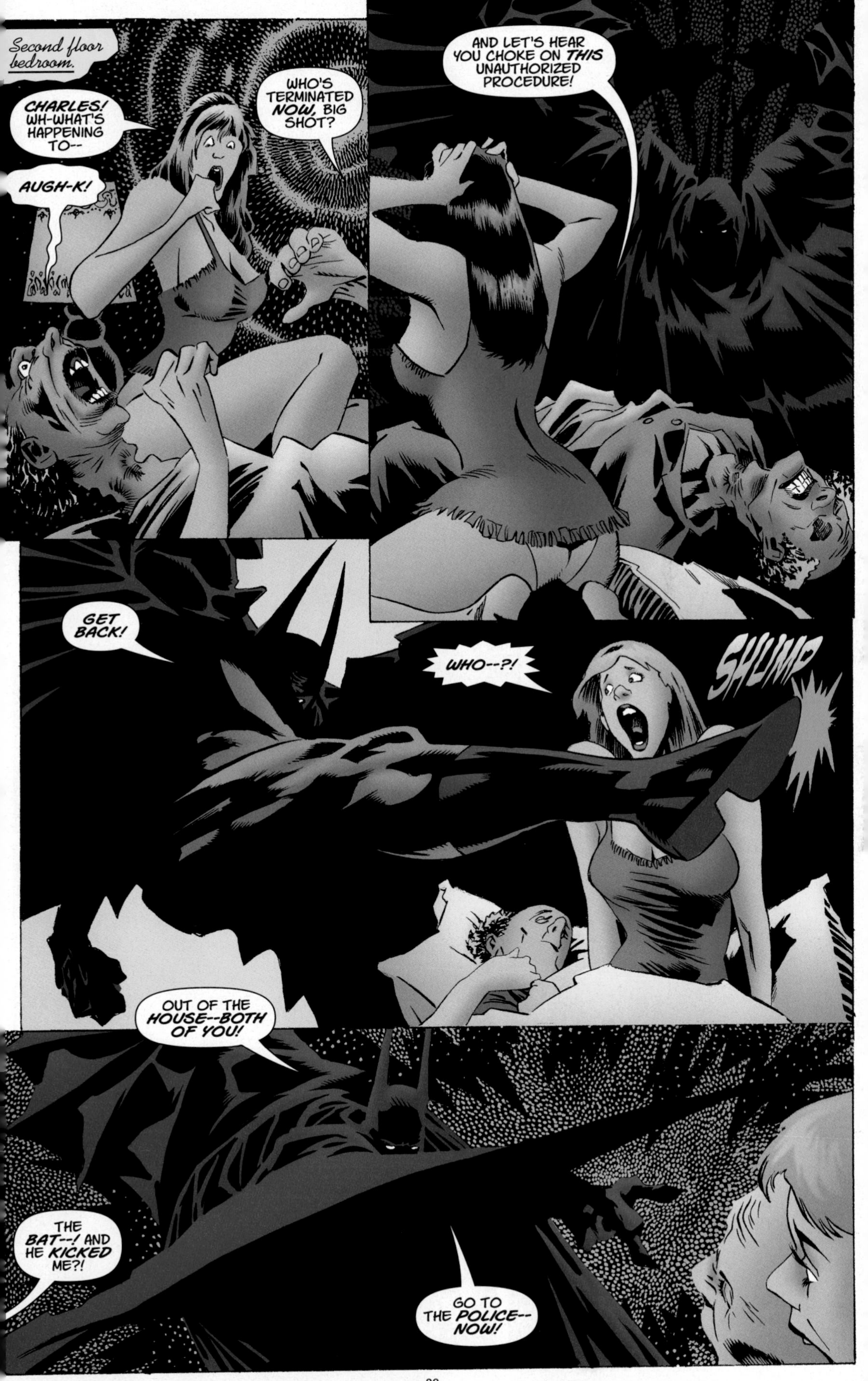
Second floor bedroom.
CHARLES! WH-WHAT'S HAPPENING TO--
AUGH-K!
WHO'S TERMINATED NOW, BIG SHOT?
AND LET'S HEAR YOU CHOKE ON THIS UNAUTHORIZED PROCEDURE!
GET BACK!
WHO--?!
SHUMP
OUT OF THE HOUSE--BOTH OF YOU!
THE BAT--! AND HE KICKED ME?!
GO TO THE POLICE-- NOW!

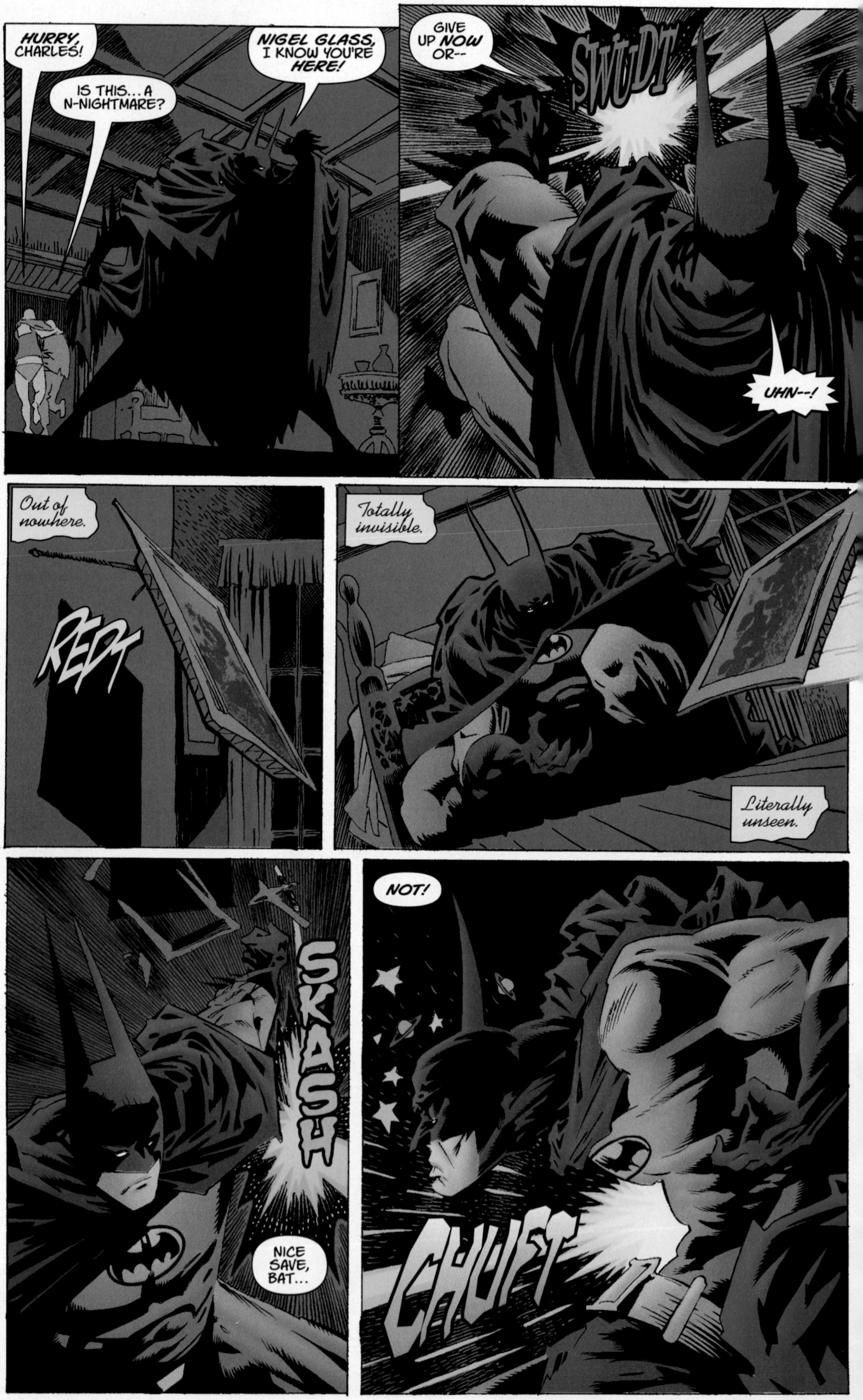
HURRY, CHARLES!
IS THIS... A N-NIGHTMARE?
NIGEL GLASS, I KNOW YOU'RE HERE!
GIVE UP NOW OR--
SWUDT
UHN--!
Out of nowhere.
REDT
Totally invisible.
Literally unseen.
SKASH
NICE SAVE, BAT...
NOT!
CHUFT

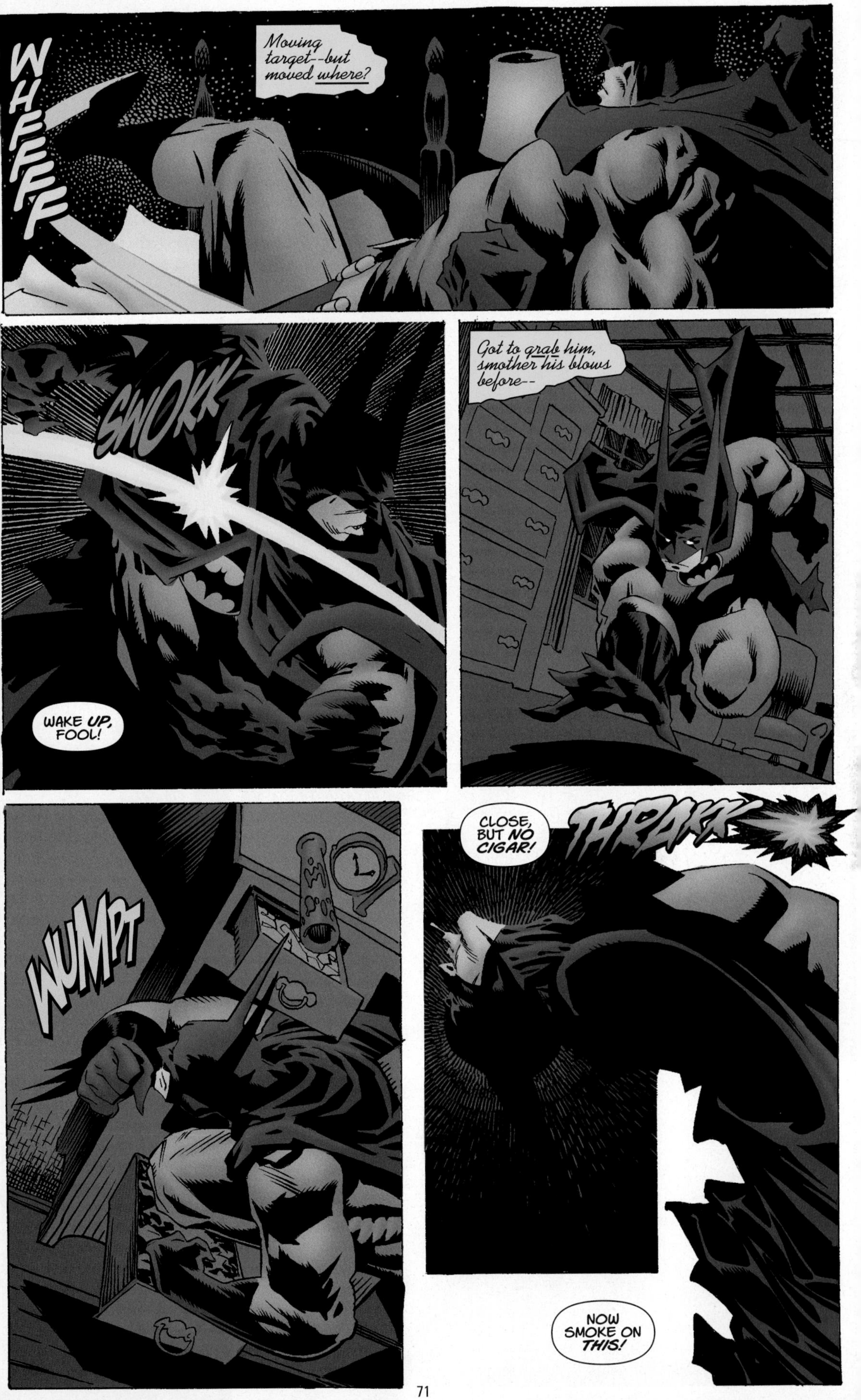
WHFFFF
Moving target--but moved where?
SWORKK
WAKE UP, FOOL!
Got to grab him, smother his blows before--
WUMPT
CLOSE, BUT NO CIGAR!
THPAKK
NOW SMOKE ON THIS!

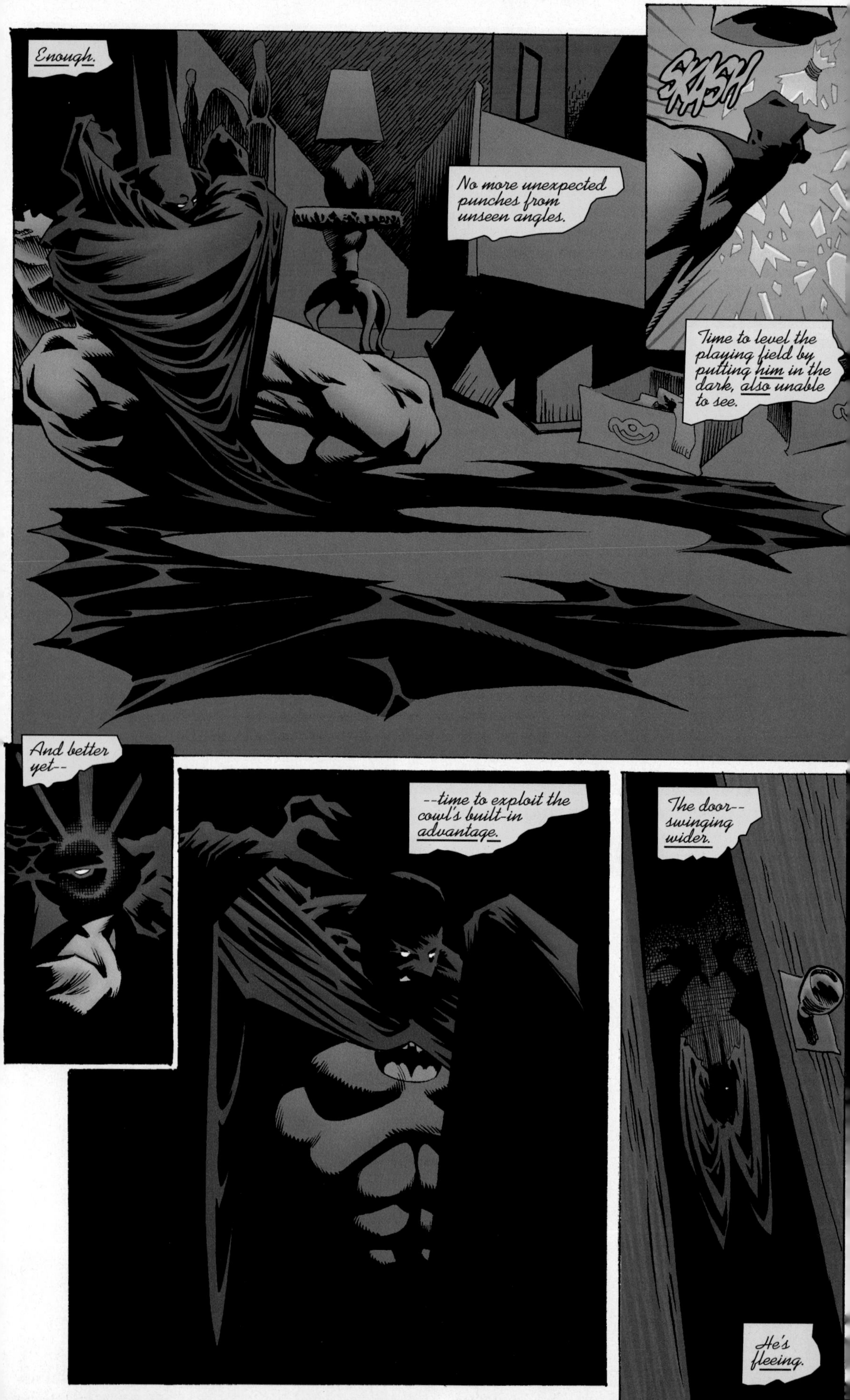
Enough.
No more unexpected punches from unseen angles.
SKASH
Time to level the playing field by putting him in the dark, also unable to see.
And better yet--
--time to exploit the cowl's built-in advantage.
The door-- swinging wider.
He's fleeing.

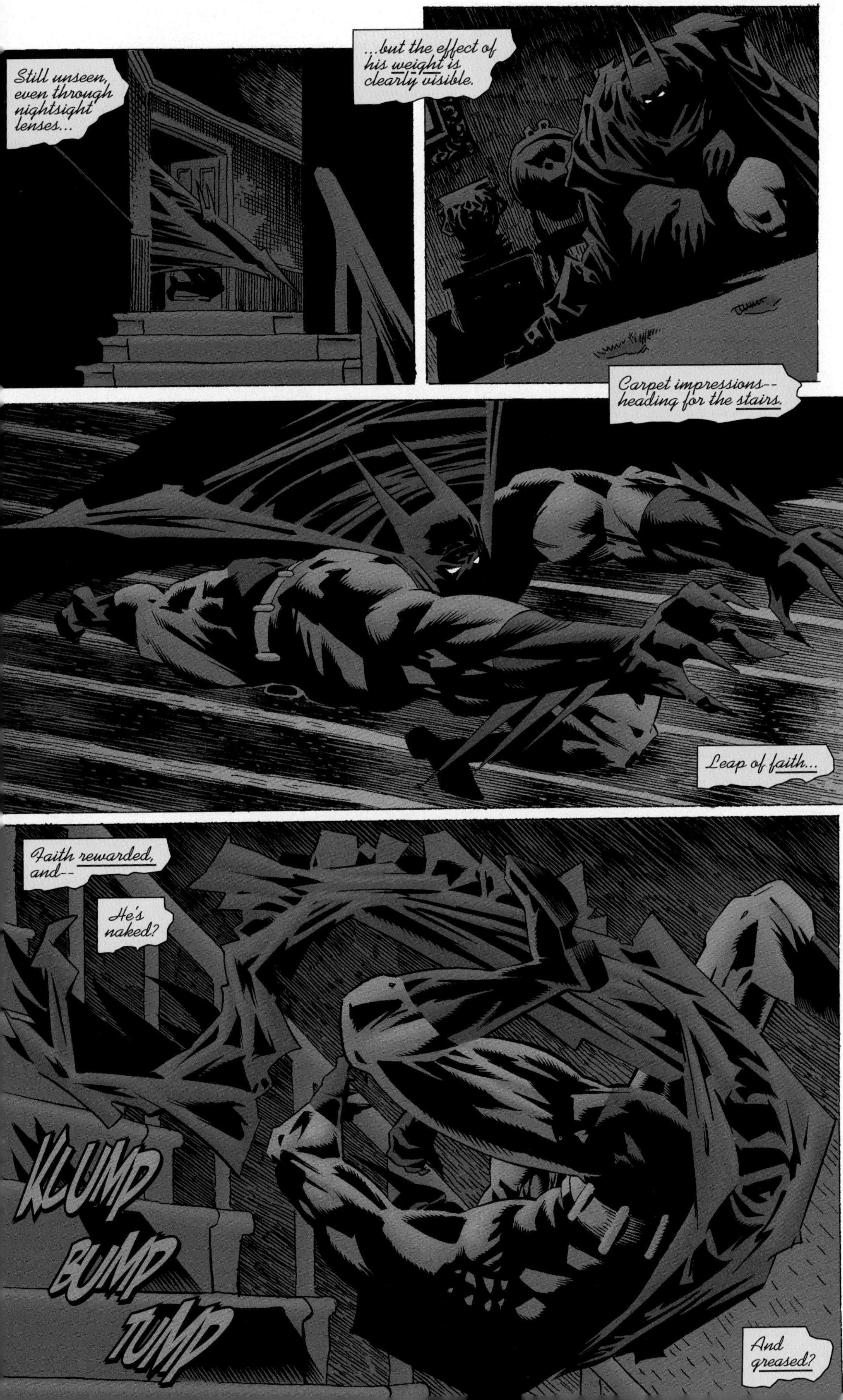
Still unseen, even through nightsight lenses...
...but the effect of his weight is clearly visible.
Carpet impressions--heading for the stairs.
Leap of faith...
Faith rewarded, and--
He's naked?
KLUMP
BUMP
TUMP
And greased?

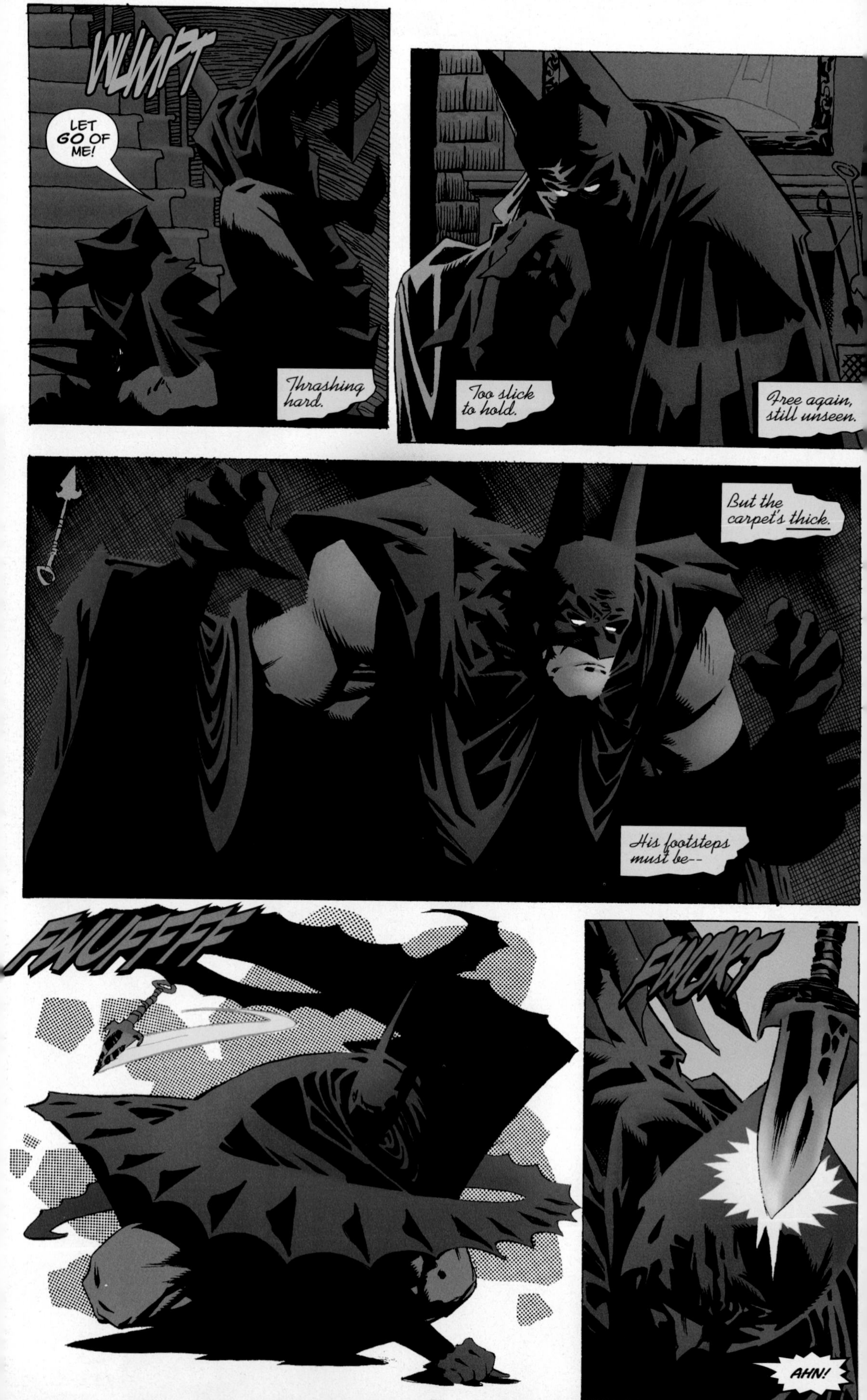
WUMPT
LET GO OF ME!
Thrashing hard.
Too slick to hold.
Free again, still unseen.
But the carpet's thick.
His footsteps must be--
FWUFFF
FWORT
AHN!

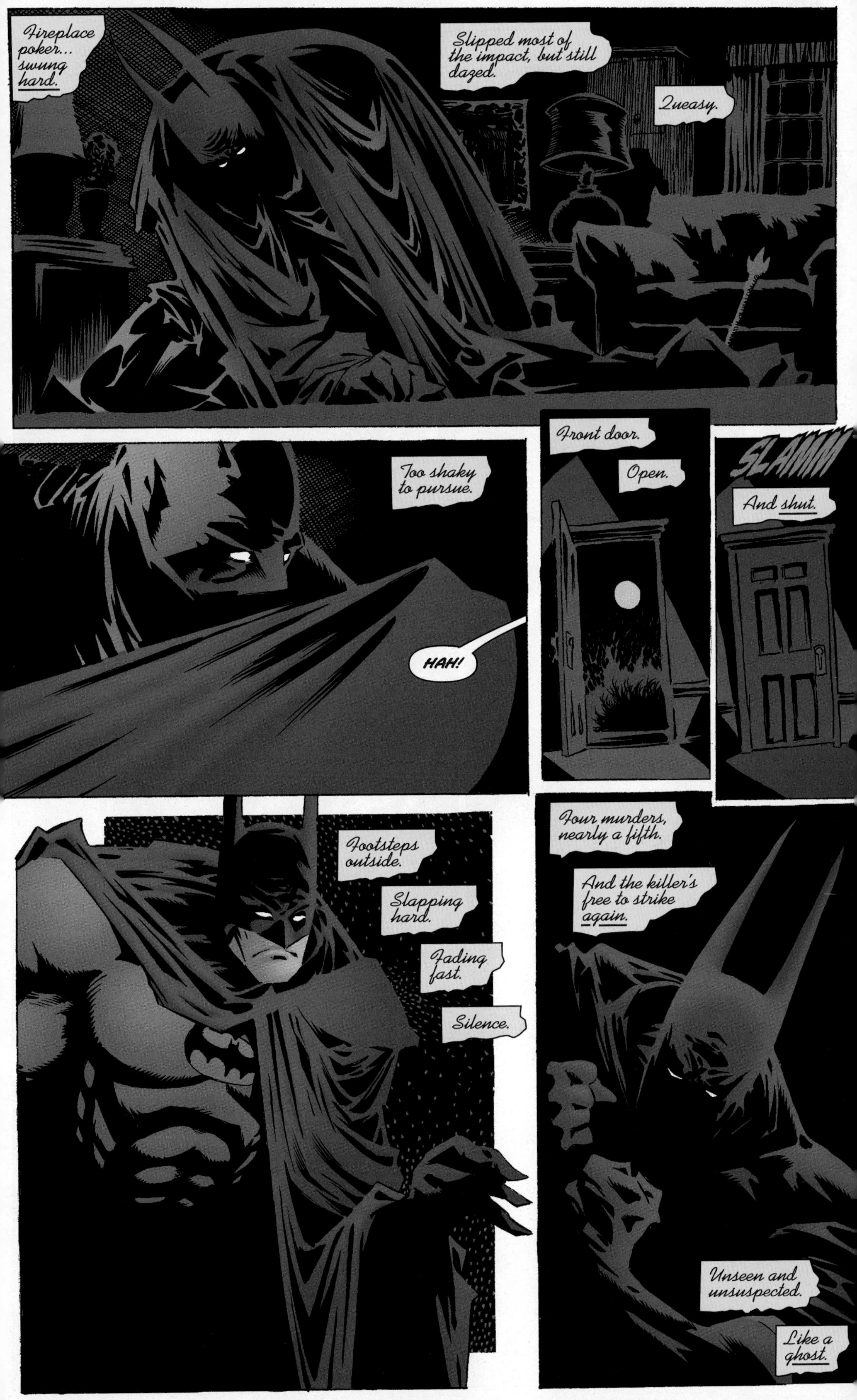
Fireplace poker... swung hard.
Slipped most of the impact, but still dazed.
Queasy.
Too shaky to pursue.
HAH!
Front door.
Open.
SLAMM
And shut.
Footsteps outside.
Slapping hard.
Fading fast.
Silence.
Four murders, nearly a fifth.
And the killer's free to strike again.
Unseen and unsuspected.
Like a ghost.

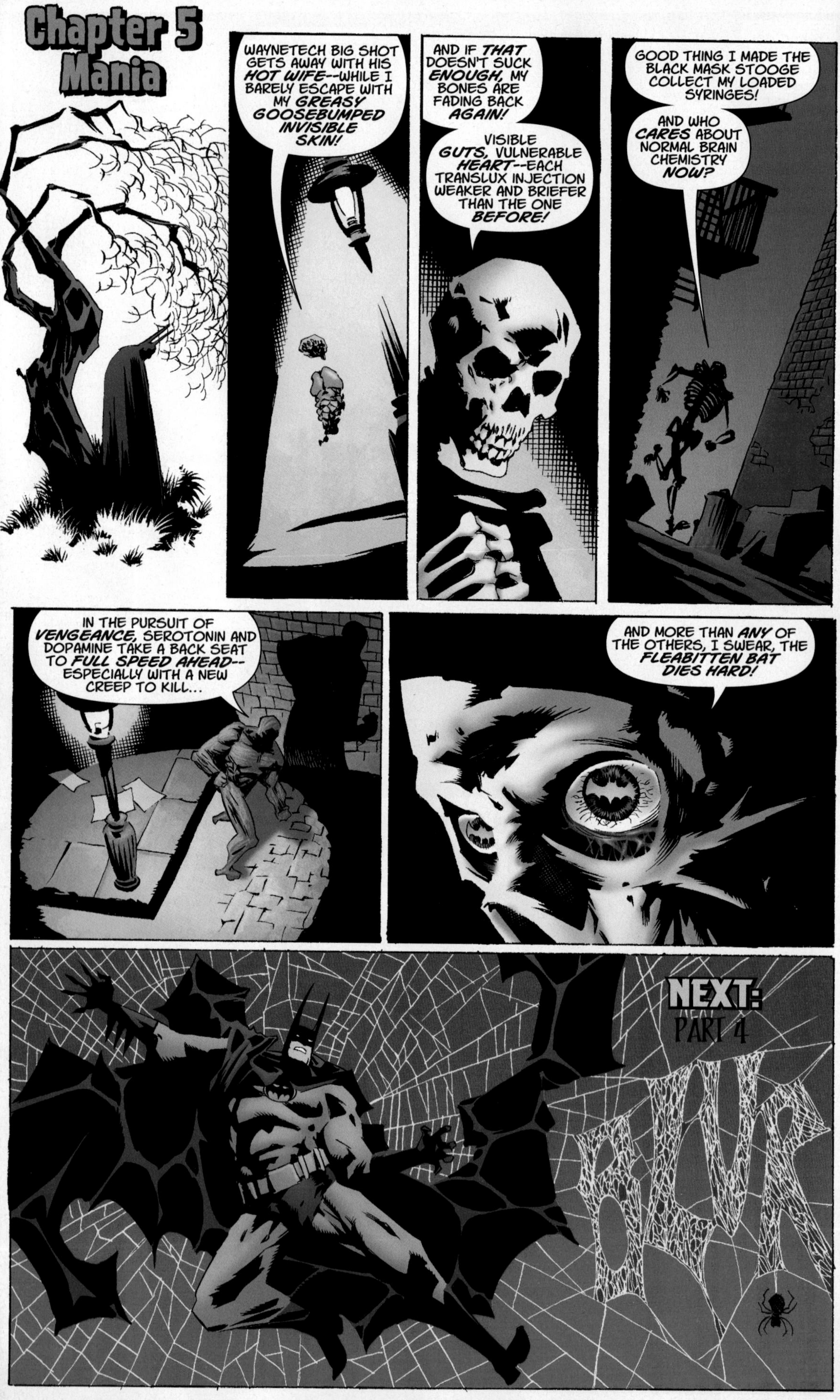
Chapter 5 Mania
WAYNETECH BIG SHOT GETS AWAY WITH HIS HOT WIFE--WHILE I BARELY ESCAPE WITH MY GREASY GOOSEBUMPED INVISIBLE SKIN!
AND IF THAT DOESN'T SUCK ENOUGH, MY BONES ARE FADING BACK AGAIN!
VISIBLE GUTS, VULNERABLE HEART--EACH TRANSLUX INJECTION WEAKER AND BRIEFER THAN THE ONE BEFORE!
GOOD THING I MADE THE BLACK MASK STOOGE COLLECT MY LOADED SYRINGES!
AND WHO CARES ABOUT NORMAL BRAIN CHEMISTRY NOW?
IN THE PURSUIT OF VENGEANCE, SEROTONIN AND DOPAMINE TAKE A BACK SEAT TO FULL SPEED AHEAD--ESPECIALLY WITH A NEW CREEP TO KILL...
AND MORE THAN ANY OF THE OTHERS, I SWEAR, THE FLEABITTEN BAT DIES HARD!
NEXT:
PART 4
BLUR

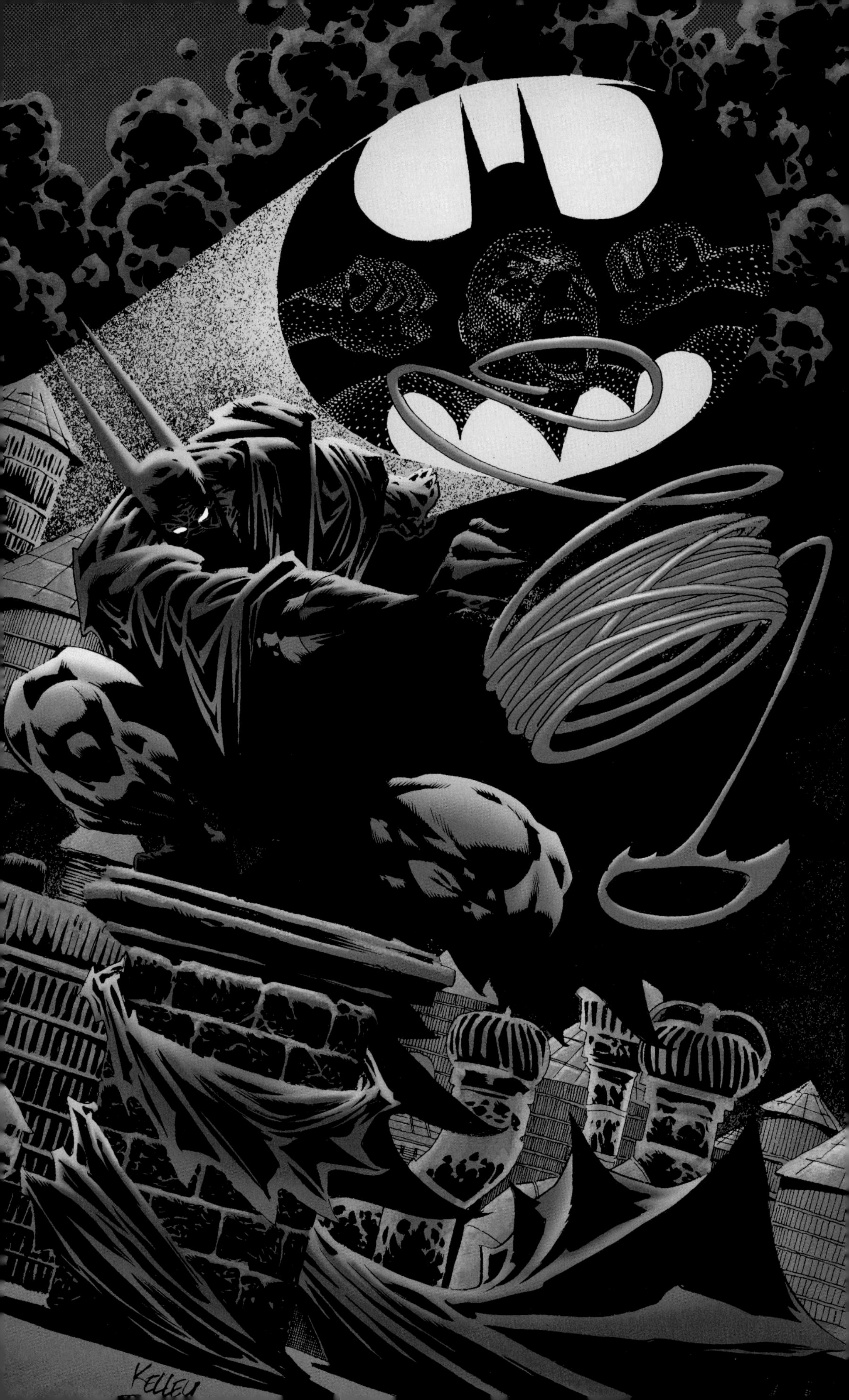
KELLEY

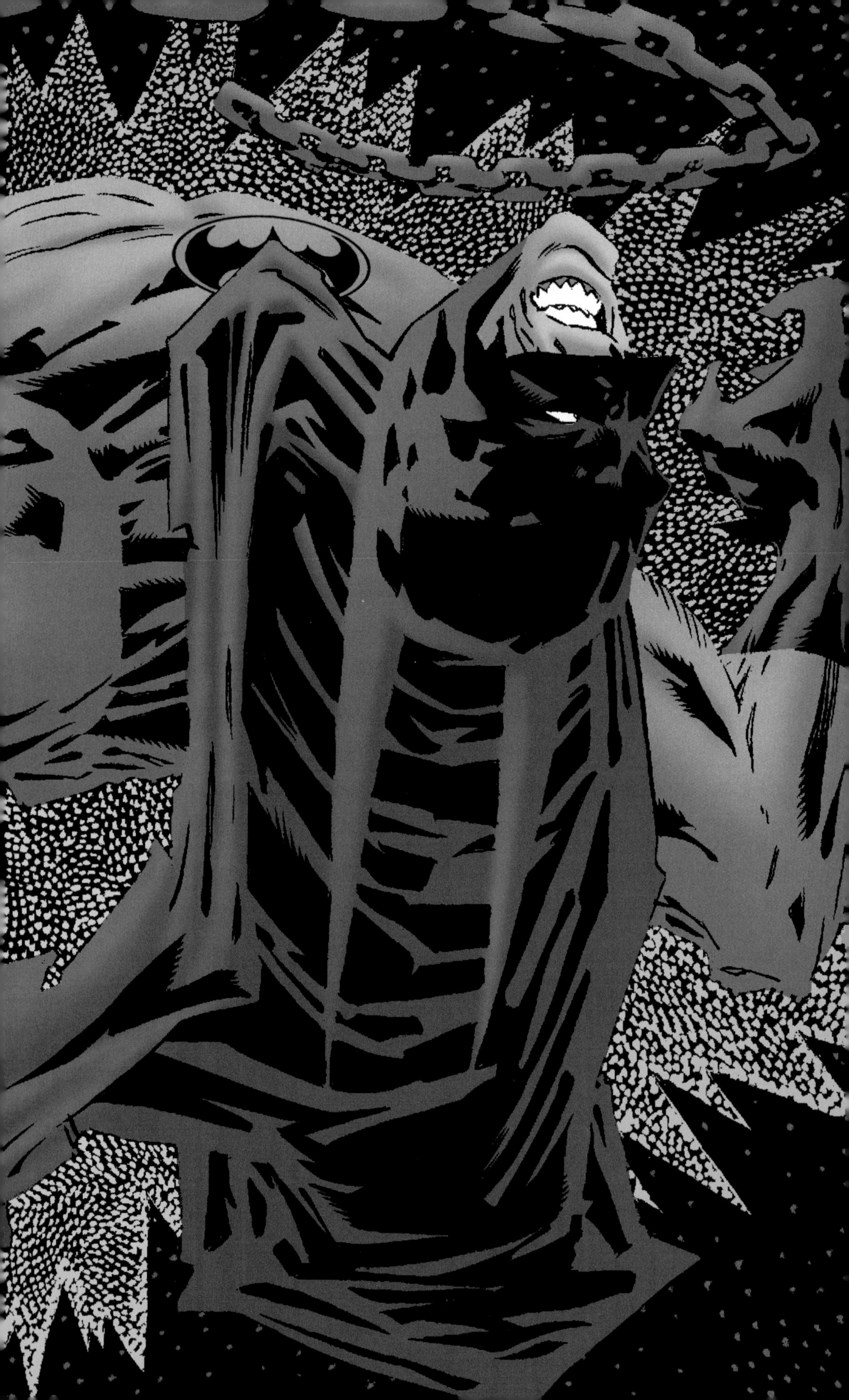

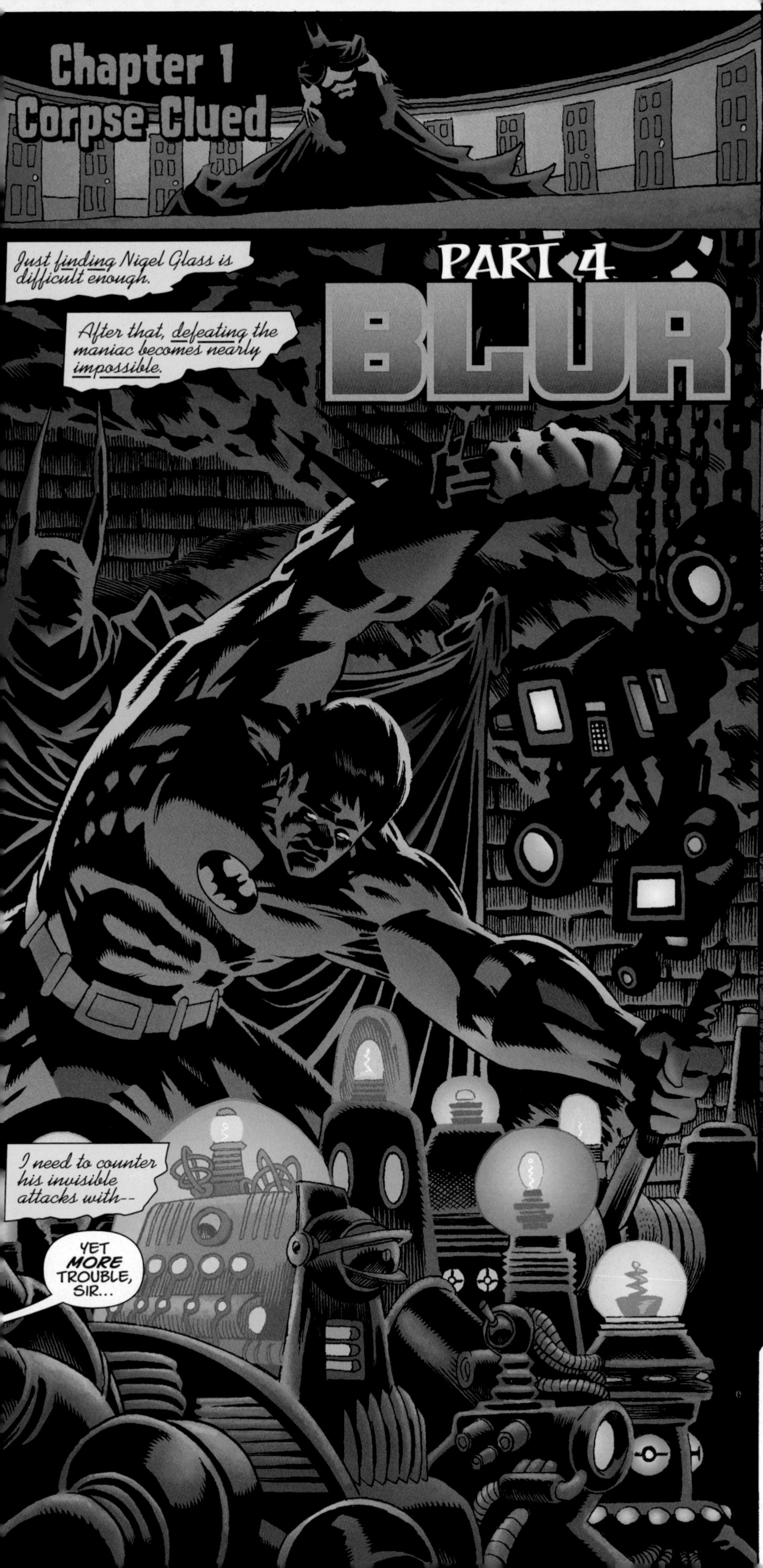
Chapter 1
Corpse-Clued
Just finding Nigel Glass is difficult enough.
PART 4
BLUR
After that, defeating the maniac becomes nearly impossible.
I need to counter his invisible attacks with--
YET MORE TROUBLE, SIR...
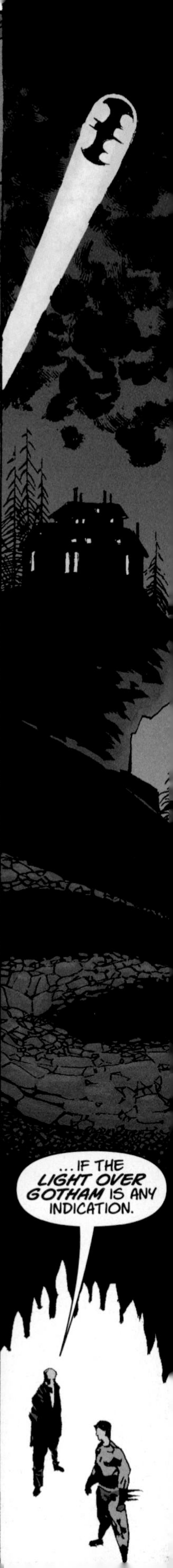
...IF THE LIGHT OVER GOTHAM IS ANY INDICATION.

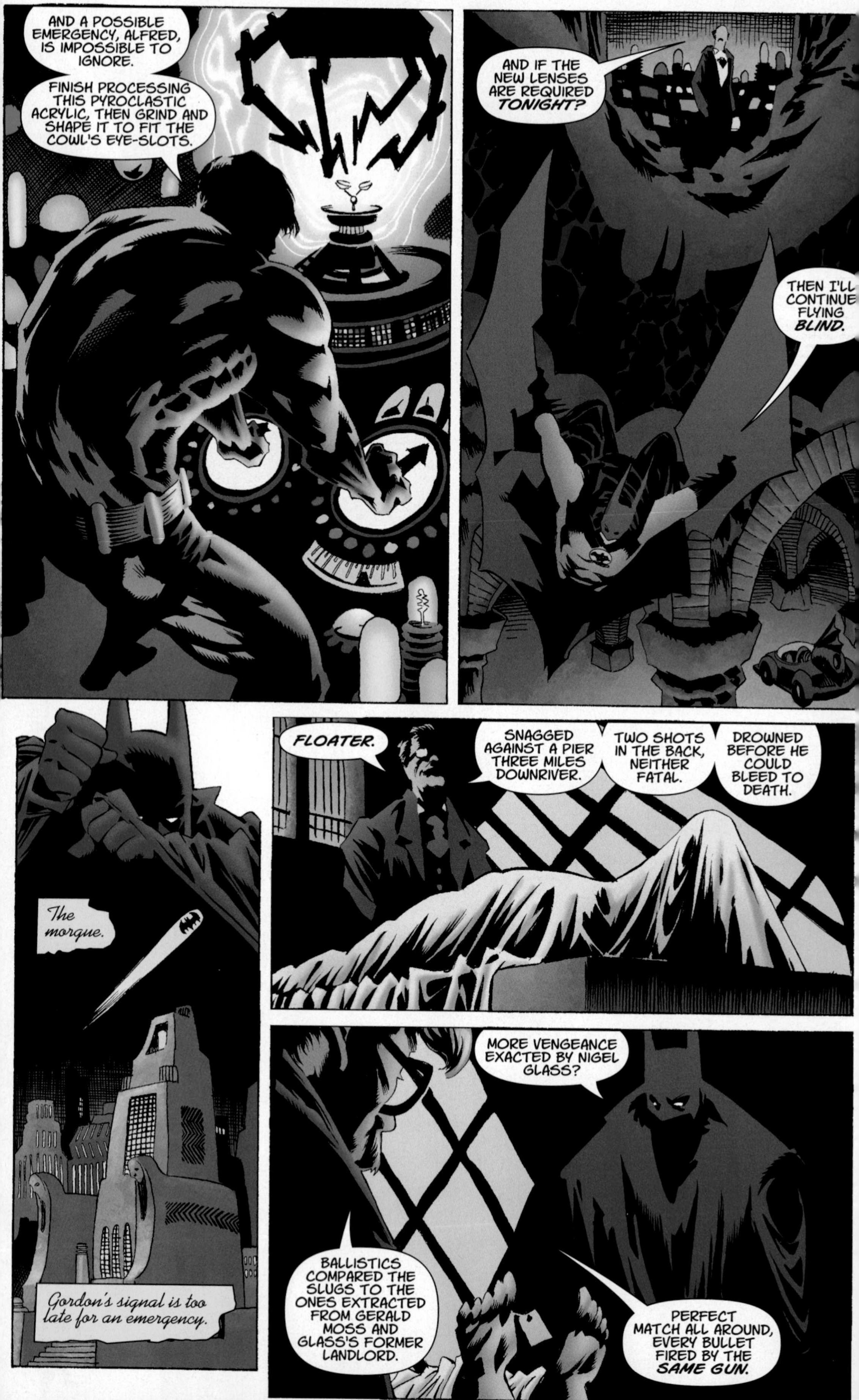
AND A POSSIBLE EMERGENCY, ALFRED, IS IMPOSSIBLE TO IGNORE.
FINISH PROCESSING THIS PYROCLASTIC ACRYLIC, THEN GRIND AND SHAPE IT TO FIT THE COWL'S EYE-SLOTS.
AND IF THE NEW LENSES ARE REQUIRED *TONIGHT?*
THEN I'LL CONTINUE FLYING *BLIND.*
The morgue.
Gordon's signal is too late for an emergency.
FLOATER.
SNAGGED AGAINST A PIER THREE MILES DOWNRIVER.
TWO SHOTS IN THE BACK, NEITHER FATAL.
DROWNED BEFORE HE COULD BLEED TO DEATH.
MORE VENGEANCE EXACTED BY NIGEL GLASS?
BALLISTICS COMPARED THE SLUGS TO THE ONES EXTRACTED FROM GERALD MOSS AND GLASS'S FORMER LANDLORD.
PERFECT MATCH ALL AROUND, EVERY BULLET FIRED BY THE *SAME GUN.*

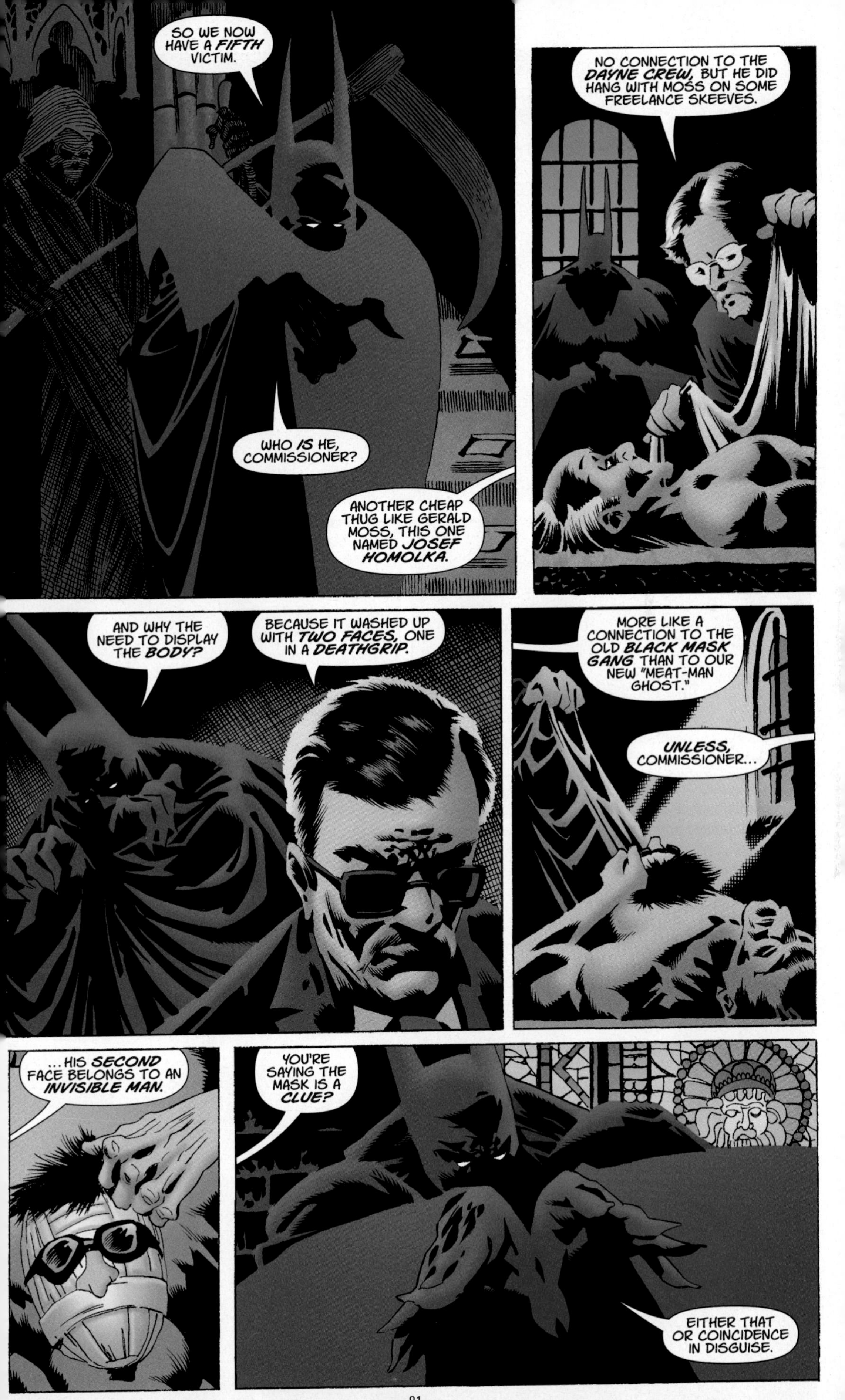
SO WE NOW HAVE A *FIFTH* VICTIM.
WHO *IS* HE, COMMISSIONER?
ANOTHER CHEAP THUG LIKE GERALD MOSS, THIS ONE NAMED *JOSEF HOMOLKA*.
NO CONNECTION TO THE *DAYNE CREW,* BUT HE DID HANG WITH MOSS ON SOME FREELANCE SKEEVES.
AND WHY THE NEED TO DISPLAY THE *BODY?*
BECAUSE IT WASHED UP WITH *TWO FACES,* ONE IN A *DEATHGRIP*.
MORE LIKE A CONNECTION TO THE OLD *BLACK MASK GANG* THAN TO OUR NEW "MEAT-MAN GHOST."
UNLESS, COMMISSIONER...
...HIS *SECOND* FACE BELONGS TO AN *INVISIBLE MAN*.
YOU'RE SAYING THE MASK IS A *CLUE?*
EITHER THAT OR COINCIDENCE IN DISGUISE.

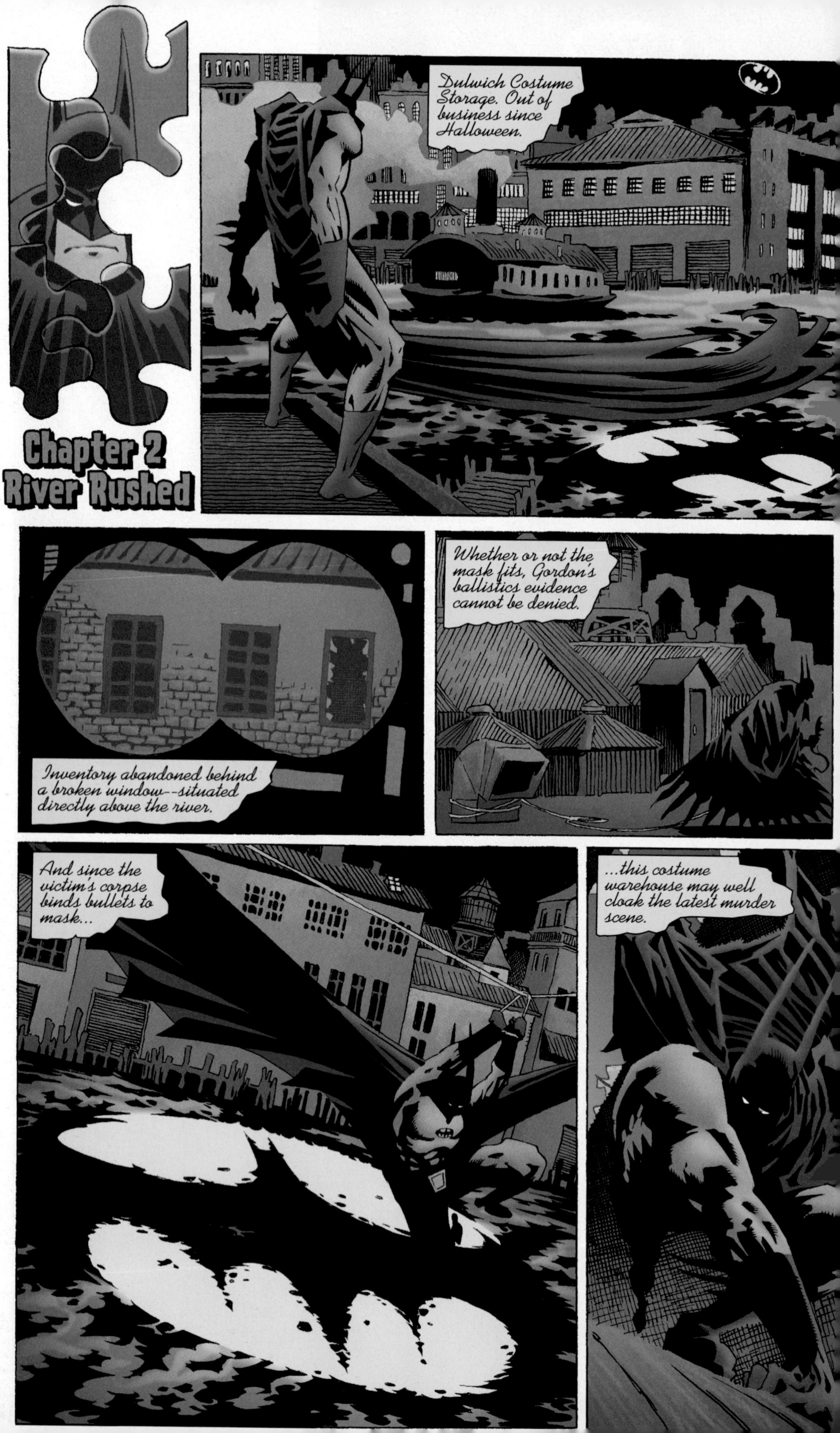
Chapter 2
River Rushed
Dulwich Costume Storage. Out of business since Halloween.
Inventory abandoned behind a broken window--situated directly above the river.
Whether or not the mask fits, Gordon's ballistics evidence cannot be denied.
And since the victim's corpse binds bullets to mask...
...this costume warehouse may well cloak the latest murder scene.

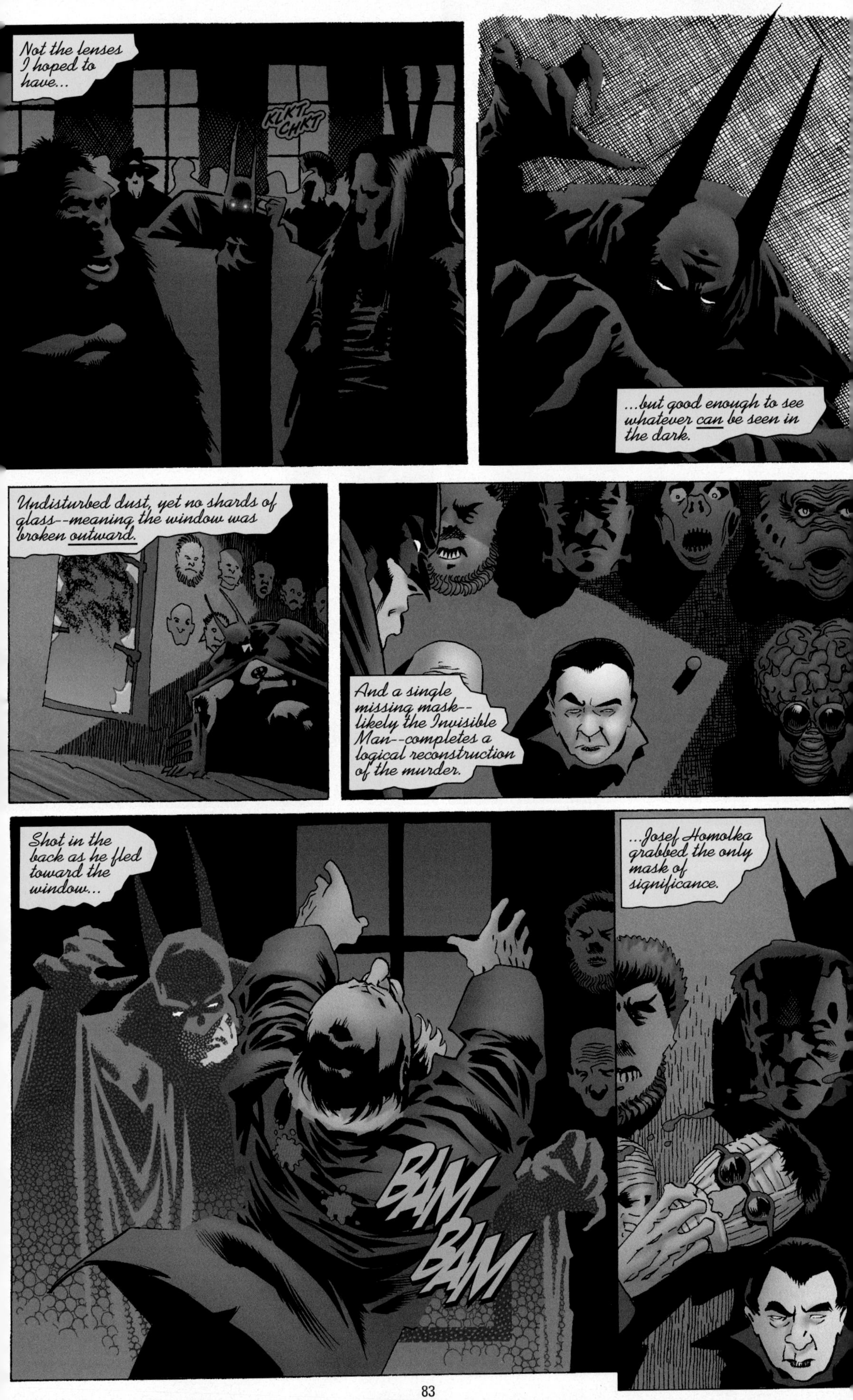
Not the lenses I hoped to have...
KLKT CHKT
...but good enough to see whatever can be seen in the dark.
Undisturbed dust, yet no shards of glass--meaning the window was broken outward.
And a single missing mask--likely the Invisible Man--completes a logical reconstruction of the murder.
Shot in the back as he fled toward the window...
BAM BAM
...Josef Homolka grabbed the only mask of significance.

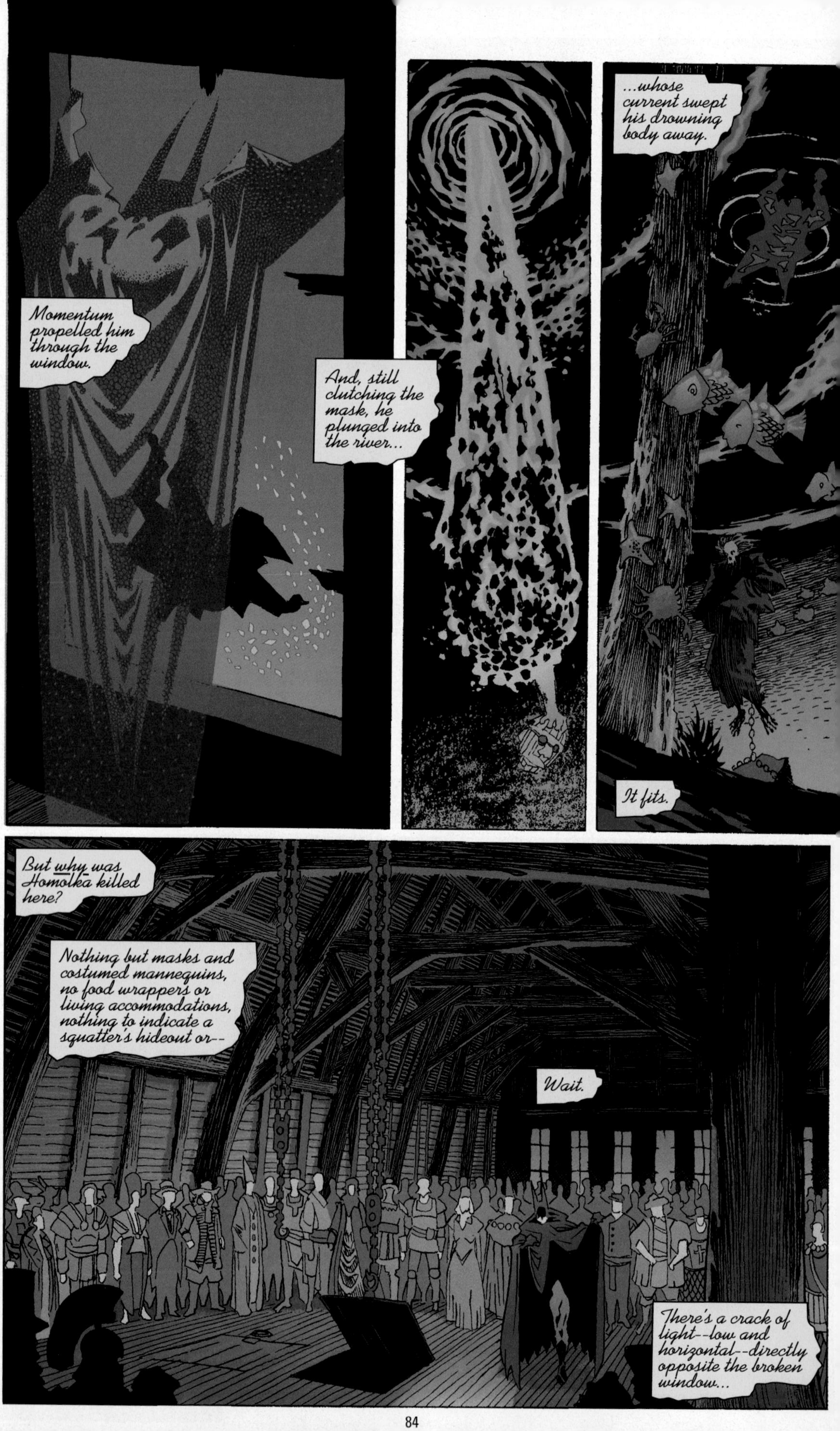
Momentum propelled him through the window.
And, still clutching the mask, he plunged into the river...
...whose current swept his drowning body away.
It fits.
But why was Homolka killed here?
Nothing but masks and costumed mannequins, no food wrappers or living accommodations, nothing to indicate a squatter's hideout or--
Wait.
There's a crack of light--low and horizontal--directly opposite the broken window...

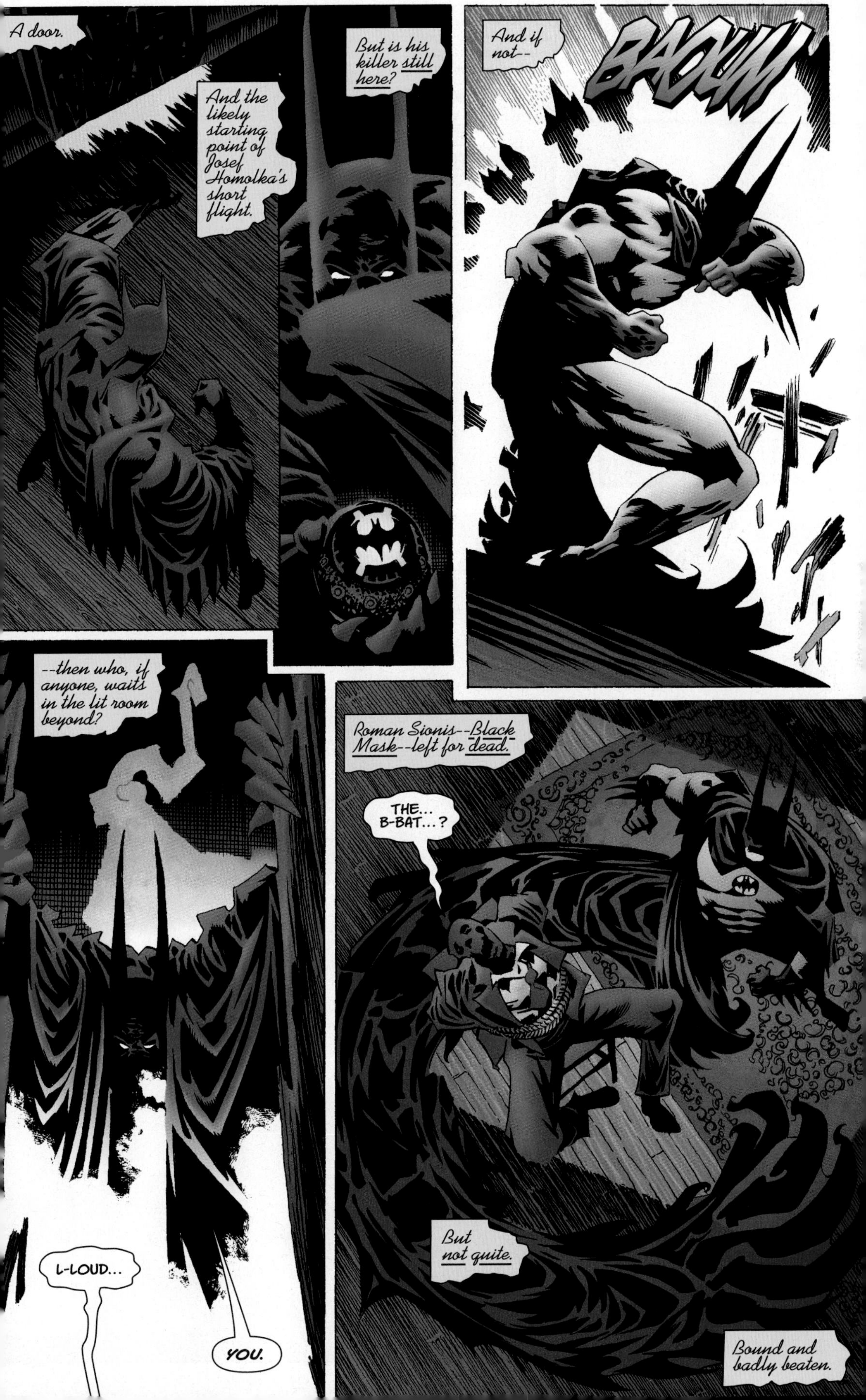
A door.
And the likely starting point of Josef Homolka's short flight.
But is his killer still here?
And if not--
BAOUM
--then who, if anyone, waits in the lit room beyond?
L-LOUD...
YOU.
Roman Sionis--Black Mask--left for dead.
THE... B-BAT...?
But not quite.
Bound and badly beaten.

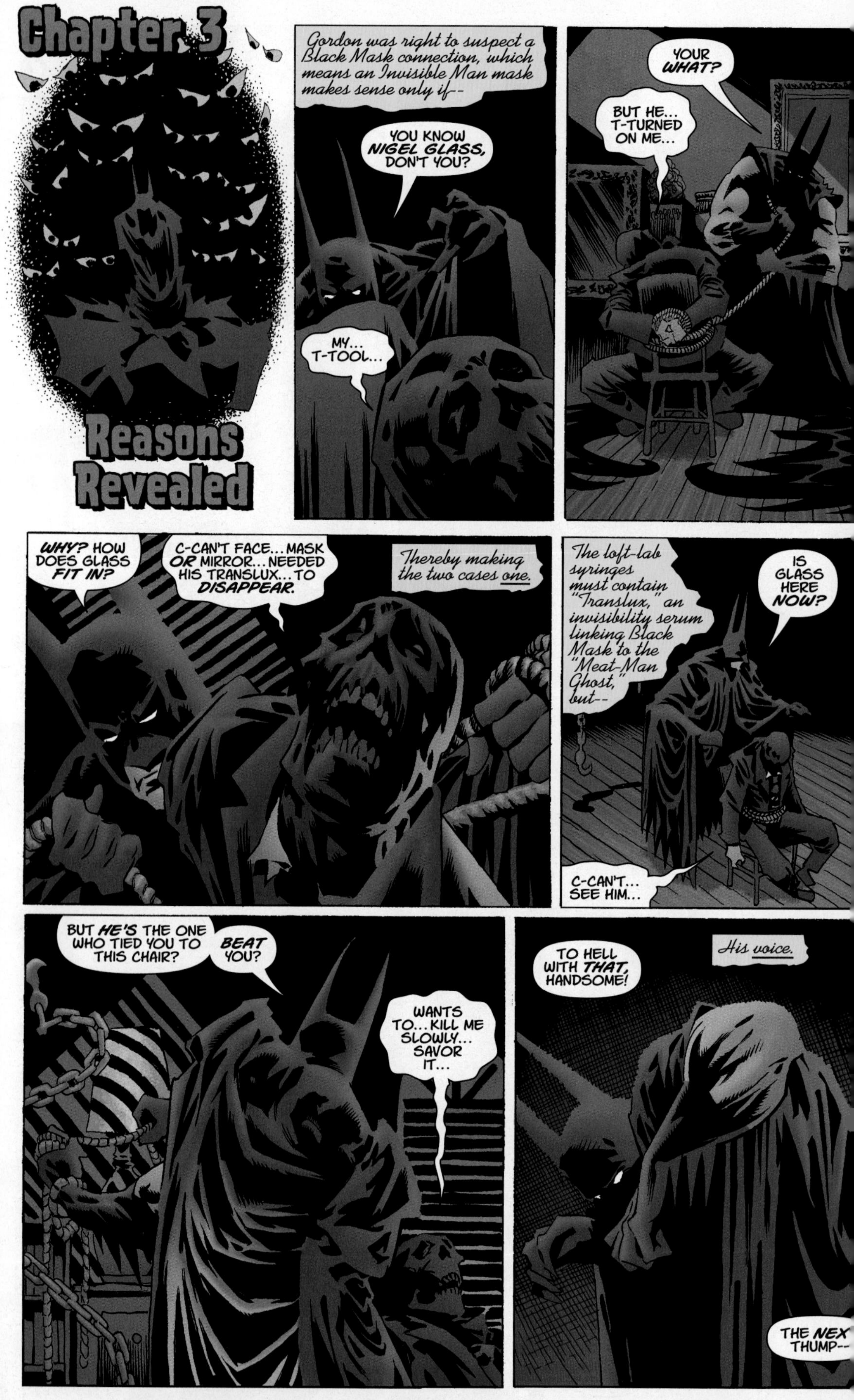
Chapter 3
Reasons Revealed
Gordon was right to suspect a Black Mask connection, which means an Invisible Man mask makes sense only if--
YOU KNOW NIGEL GLASS, DON'T YOU?
MY... T-TOOL...
YOUR WHAT?
BUT HE... T-TURNED ON ME...
WHY? HOW DOES GLASS FIT IN?
C-CAN'T FACE... MASK OR MIRROR... NEEDED HIS TRANSLUX... TO DISAPPEAR.
Thereby making the two cases one.
The loft-lab syringes must contain "Translux," an invisibility serum linking Black Mask to the "Meat-Man Ghost," but--
IS GLASS HERE NOW?
C-CAN'T... SEE HIM...
BUT HE'S THE ONE WHO TIED YOU TO THIS CHAIR?
BEAT YOU?
WANTS TO... KILL ME SLOWLY... SAVOR IT...
TO HELL WITH THAT, HANDSOME!
His voice.
THE NEX
THUMP--

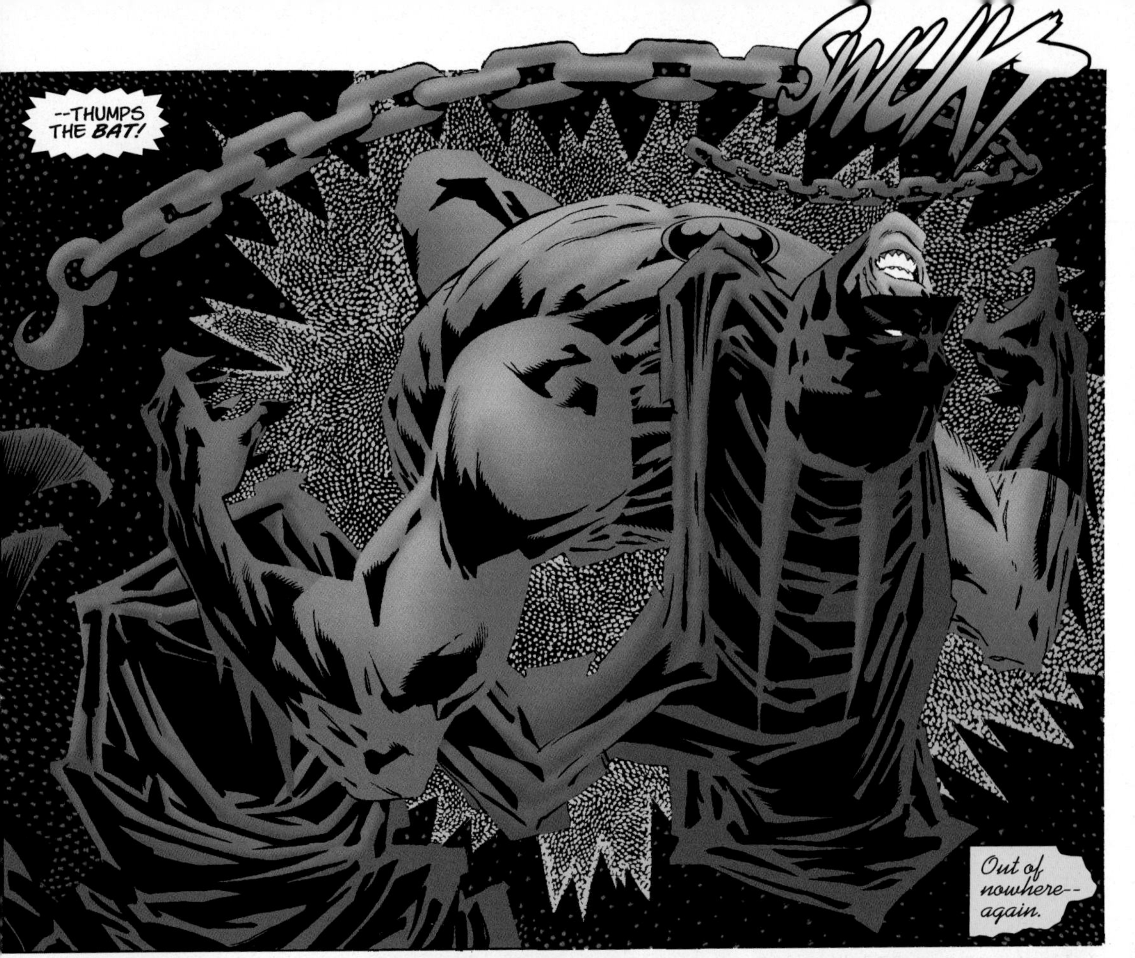
--THUMPS THE BAT!
Out of nowhere--again.

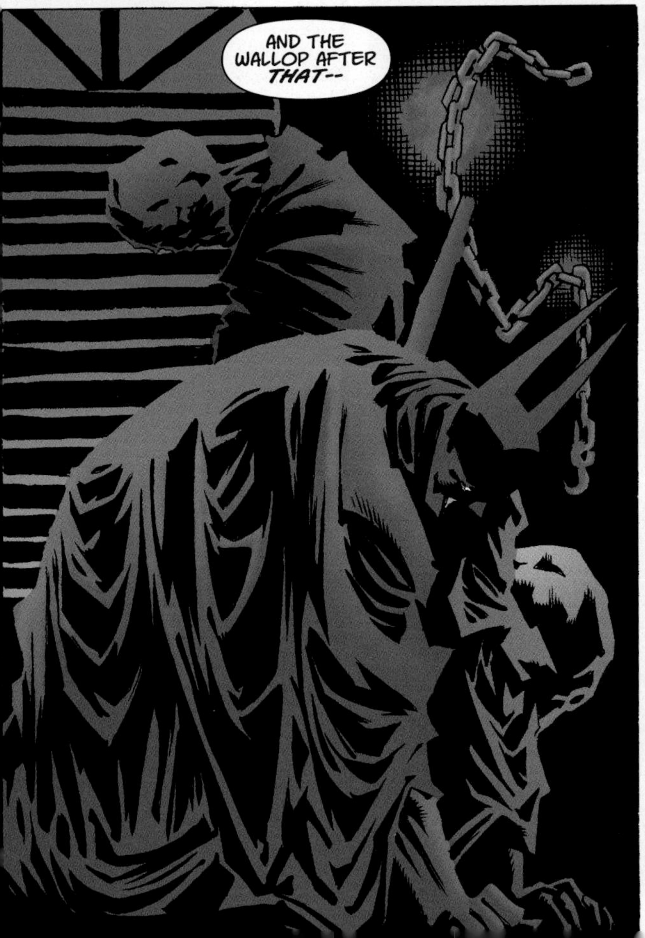
AND THE WALLOP AFTER THAT--

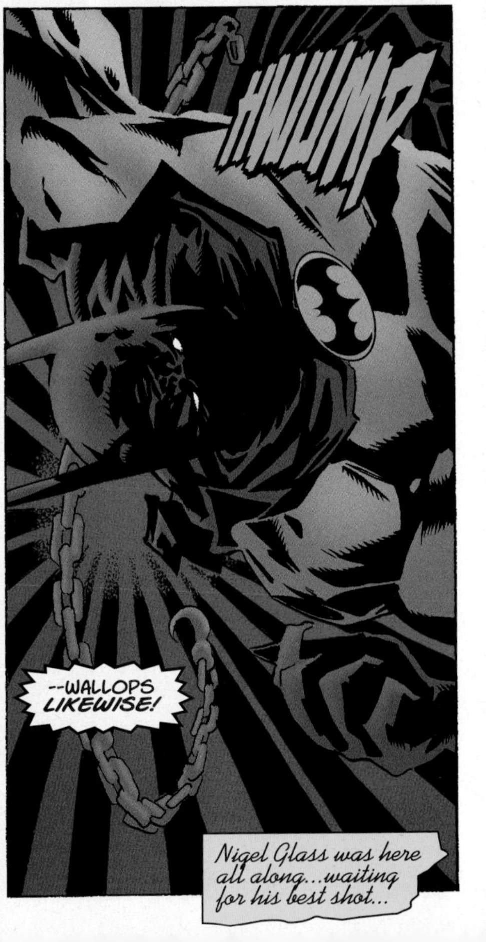
--WALLOPS LIKEWISE!
Nigel Glass was here all along...waiting for his best shot...

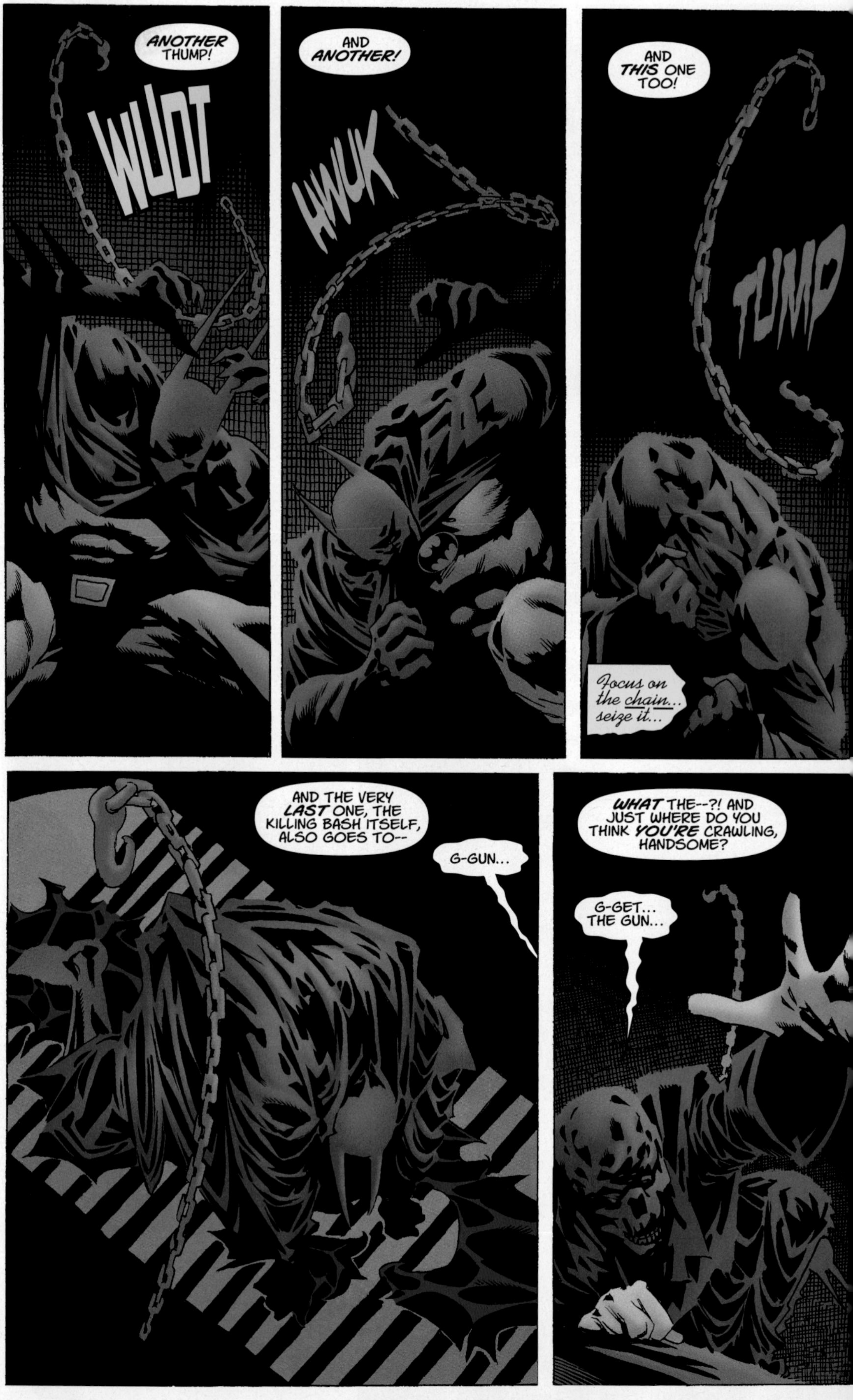
ANOTHER THUMP!
WUDT
AND ANOTHER!
HWUK
AND THIS ONE TOO!
TUMP
Focus on the chain... seize it...
AND THE VERY LAST ONE, THE KILLING BASH ITSELF, ALSO GOES TO--
G-GUN...
WHAT THE--?! AND JUST WHERE DO YOU THINK YOU'RE CRAWLING, HANDSOME?
G-GET... THE GUN...

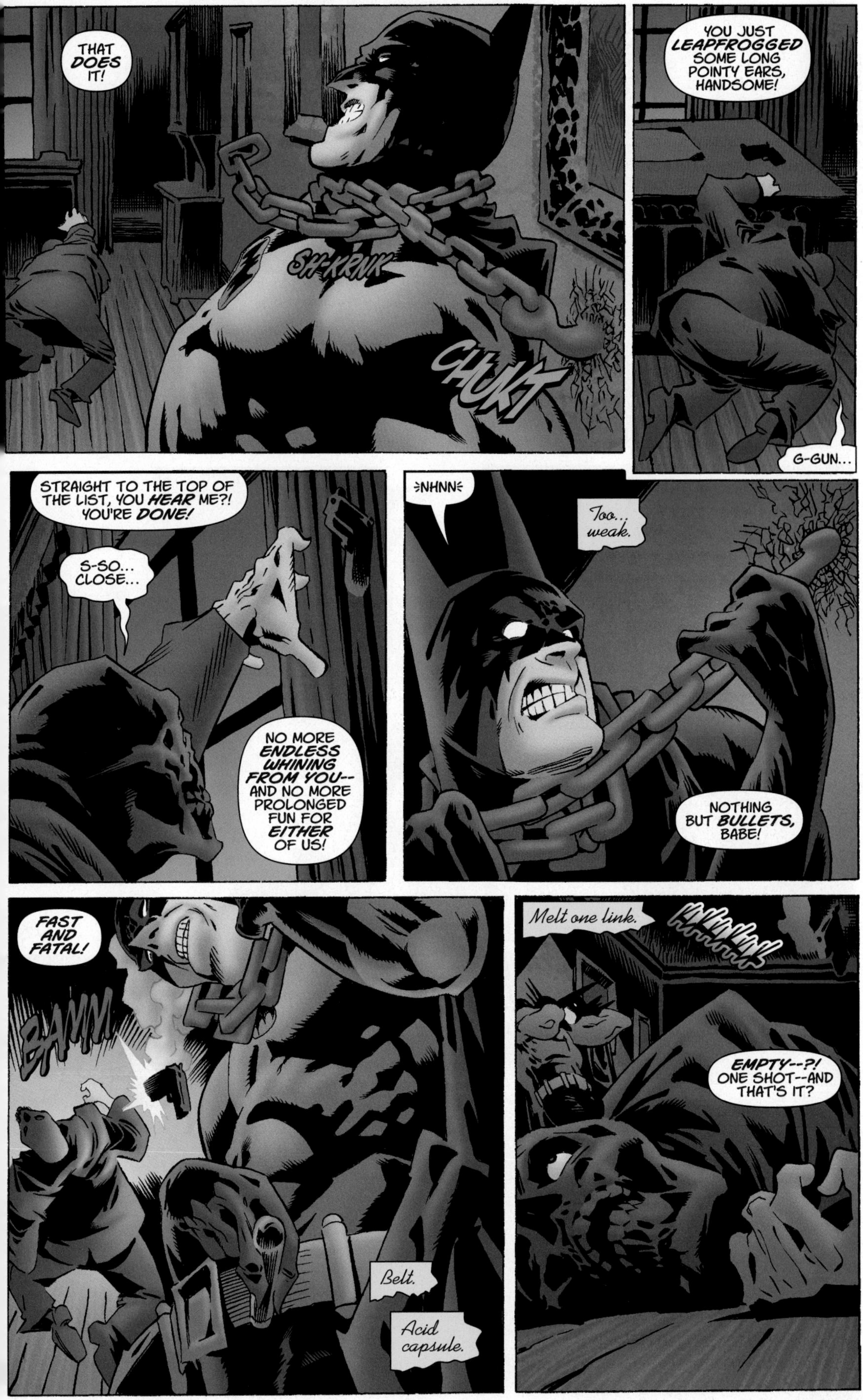
THAT DOES IT!
SH-KRNK
CHUKT
YOU JUST LEAPFROGGED SOME LONG POINTY EARS, HANDSOME!
G-GUN...
STRAIGHT TO THE TOP OF THE LIST, YOU HEAR ME?! YOU'RE DONE!
S-SO... CLOSE...
NO MORE ENDLESS WHINING FROM YOU-- AND NO MORE PROLONGED FUN FOR EITHER OF US!
NHNN
Too... weak.
NOTHING BUT BULLETS, BABE!
FAST AND FATAL!
BAMM
Belt.
Acid capsule.
Melt one link.
EMPTY--?! ONE SHOT--AND THAT'S IT?

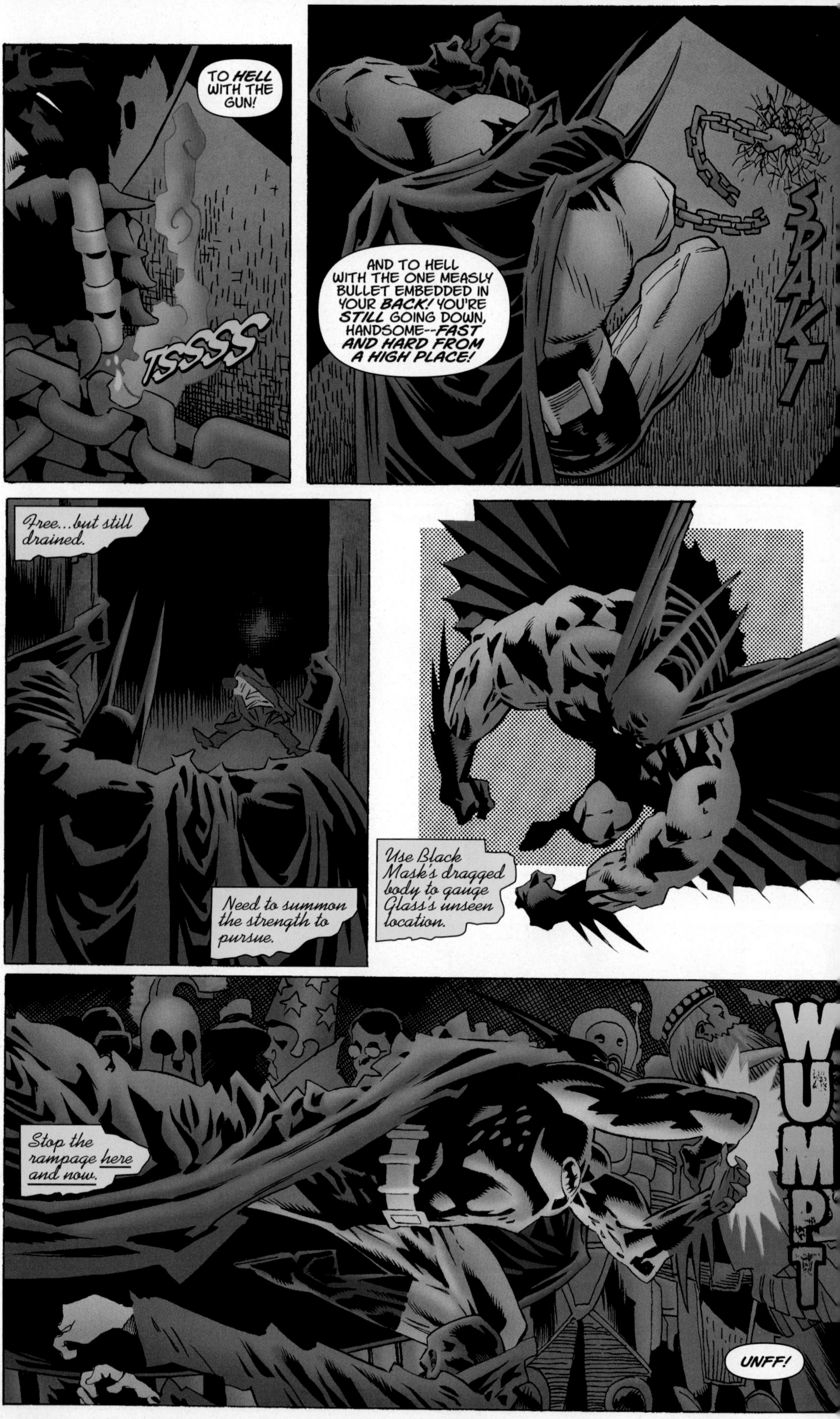
TO HELL WITH THE GUN!
TSSSS
AND TO HELL WITH THE ONE MEASLY BULLET EMBEDDED IN YOUR BACK! YOU'RE STILL GOING DOWN, HANDSOME--FAST AND HARD FROM A HIGH PLACE!
SPAKT
Free...but still drained.
Need to summon the strength to pursue.
Use Black Mask's dragged body to gauge Glass's unseen location.
Stop the rampage here and now.
WUMPT
UNFF!

ailed to secure him,
ut closed the gap.

CHUFT

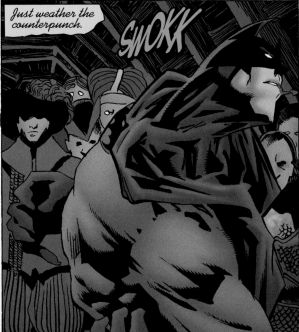

Just weather the
counterpunch.

SWOKK

WHA--?! I
CAN'T
SEE!

FWUFFF

Use the cloak.

LET GO
OF ME!

And give it
everything.

HWURK

Not
enough.

Still sapped
from the
beating...

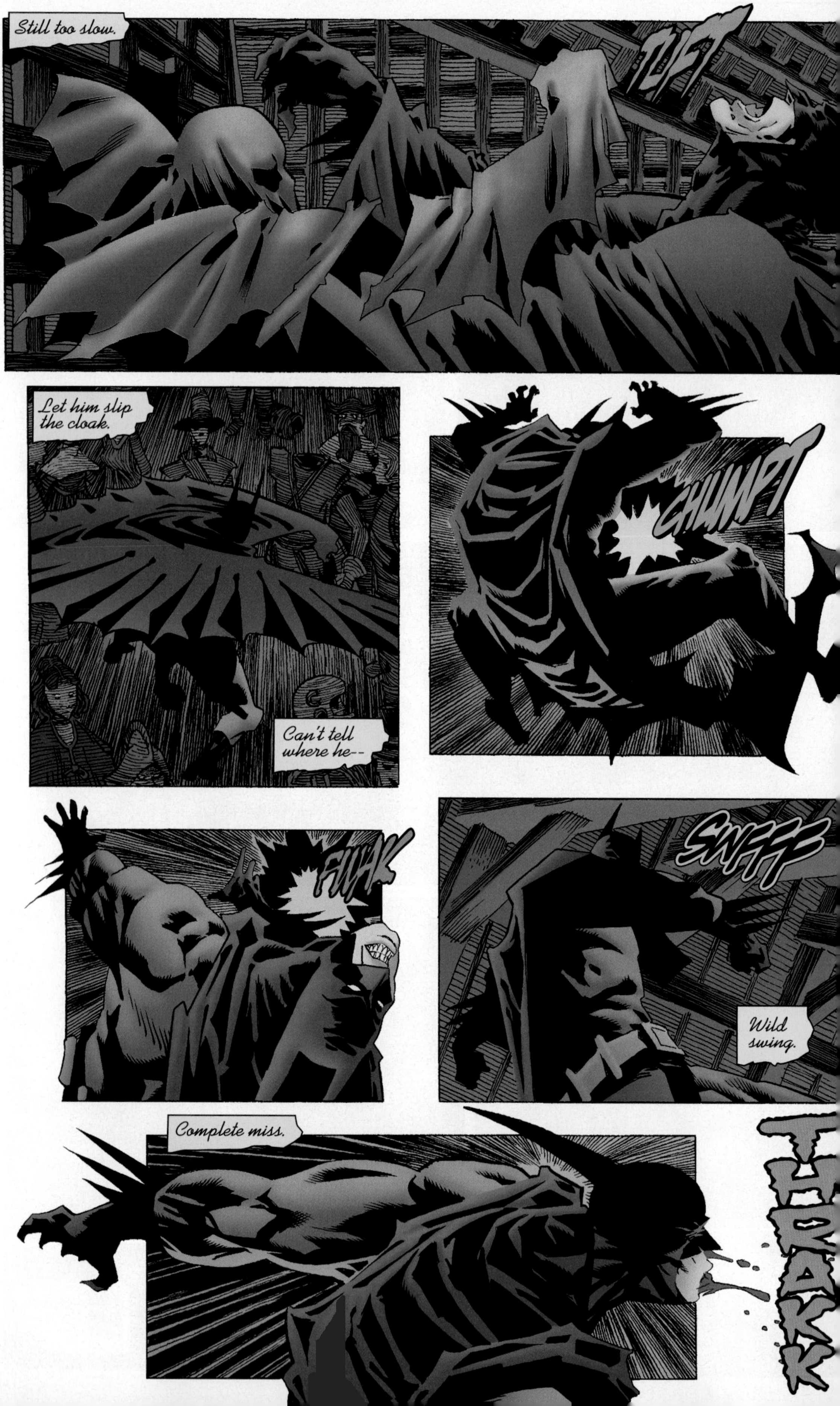

Still too slow.
Let him slip the cloak.
Can't tell where he--
CHUMPT
SNFFF
Wild swing.
Complete miss.
THRAKK

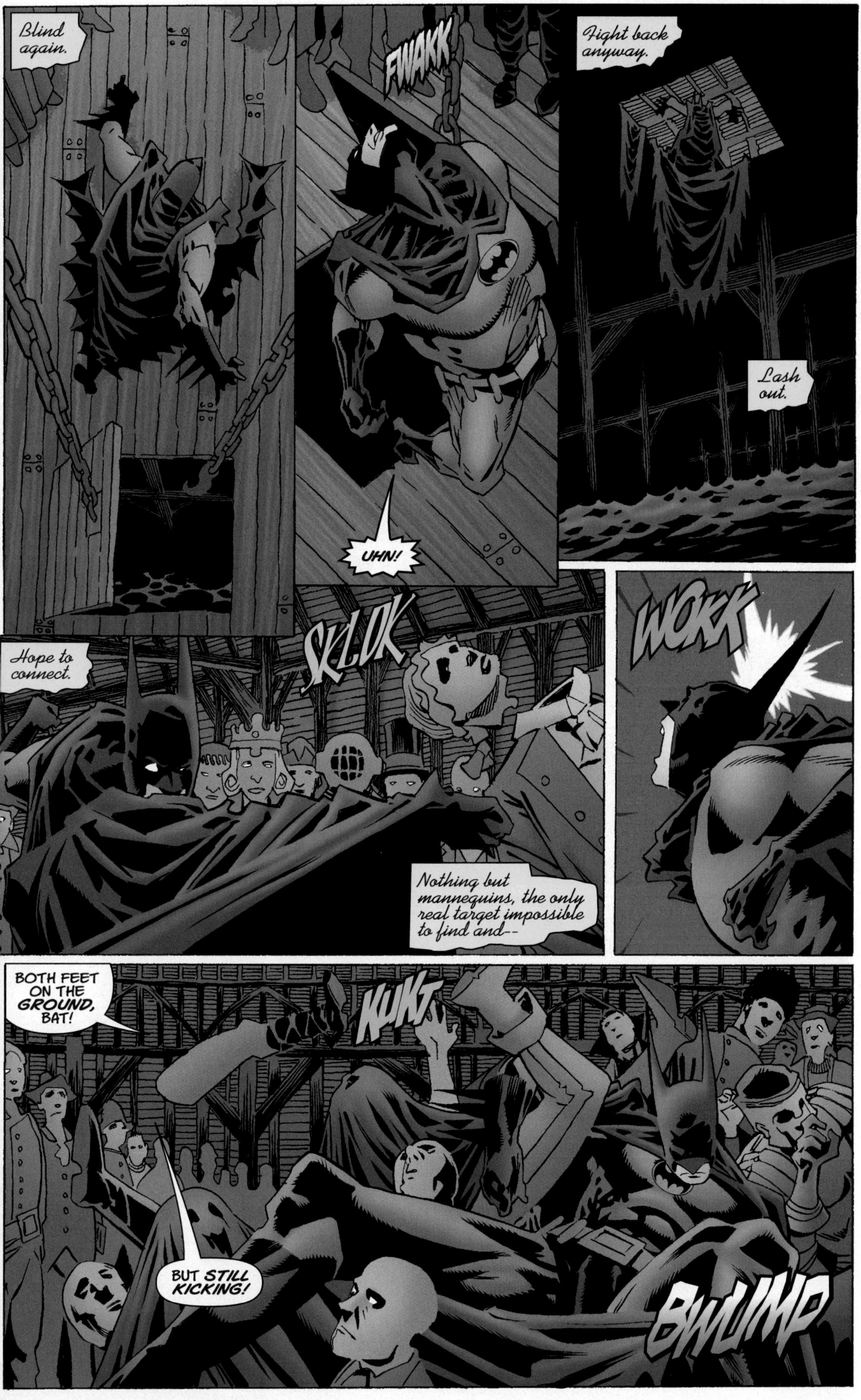
Blind again.
FWAKK
UHN!
Fight back anyway.
Lash out.
Hope to connect.
SKLOK
Nothing but mannequins, the only real target impossible to find and--
WOKK
BOTH FEET ON THE GROUND, BAT!
KUNT
BUT STILL KICKING!
BWUMP

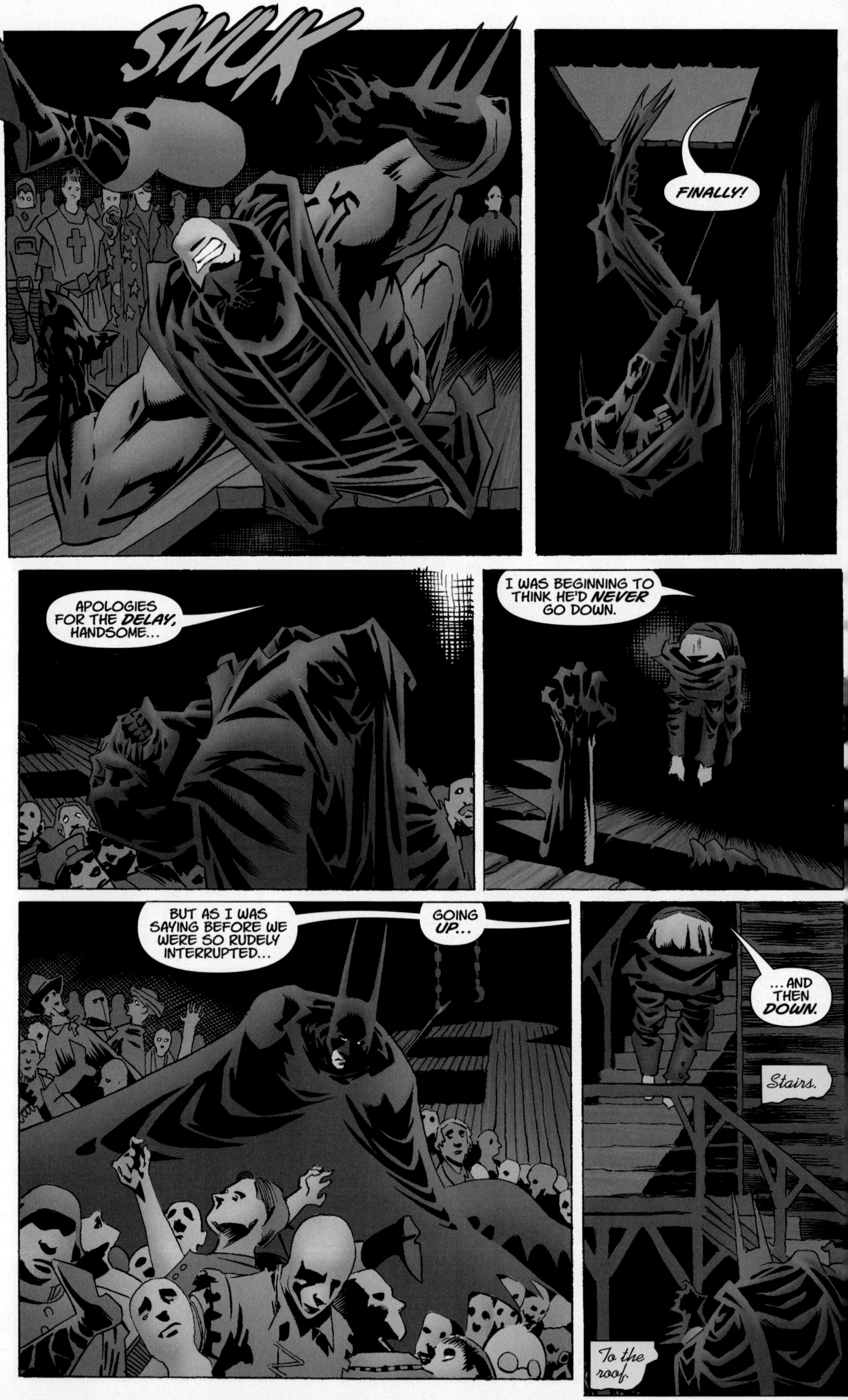
SWUK
FINALLY!
APOLOGIES FOR THE DELAY, HANDSOME...
I WAS BEGINNING TO THINK HE'D NEVER GO DOWN.
BUT AS I WAS SAYING BEFORE WE WERE SO RUDELY INTERRUPTED...
GOING UP...
...AND THEN DOWN.
Stairs.
To the roof.

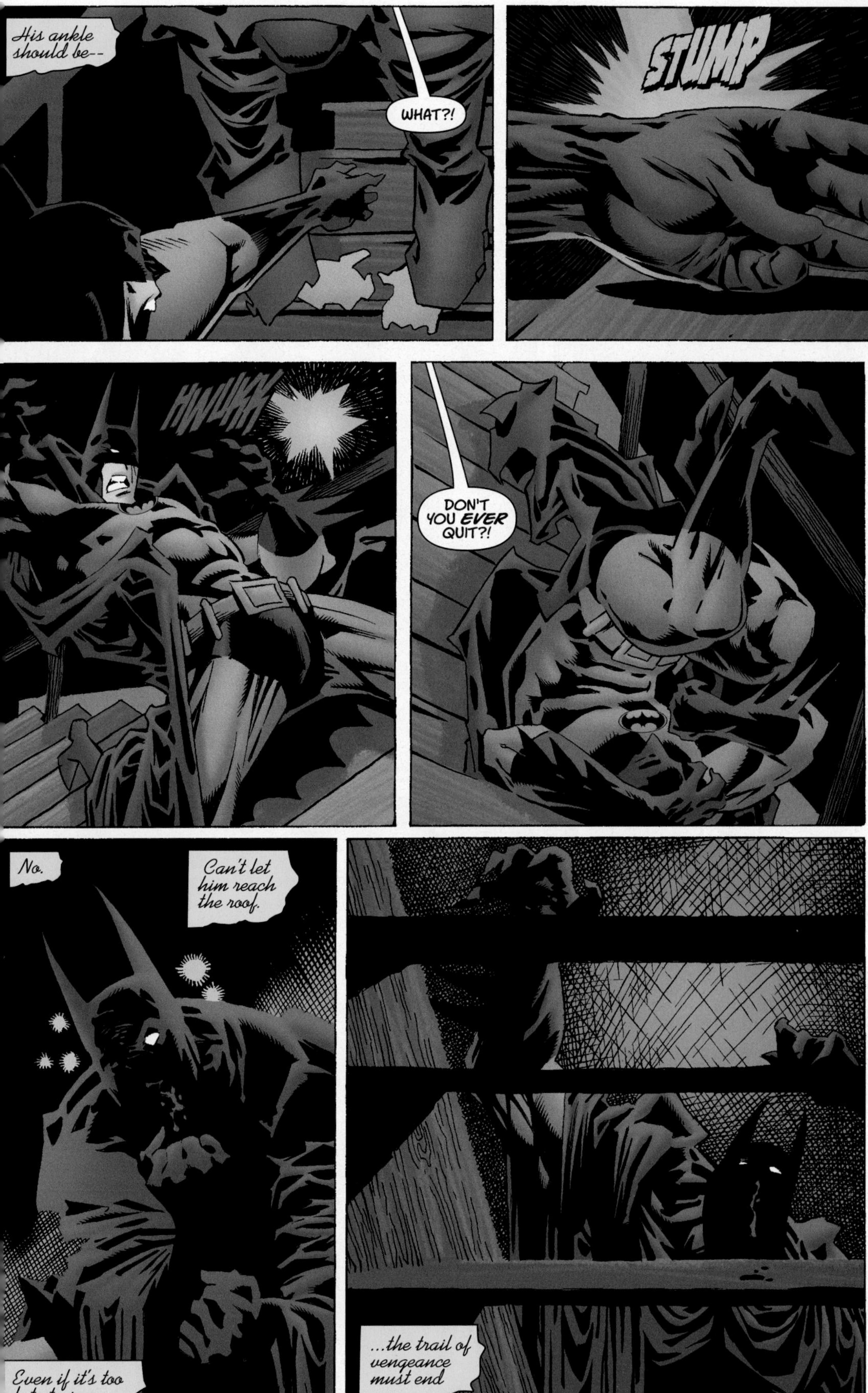

His ankle should be--
WHAT?!
STUMP
HWUHH
DON'T YOU EVER QUIT?!
No.
Can't let him reach the roof.
Even if it's too late to save Black Mask...
...the trail of vengeance must end now.

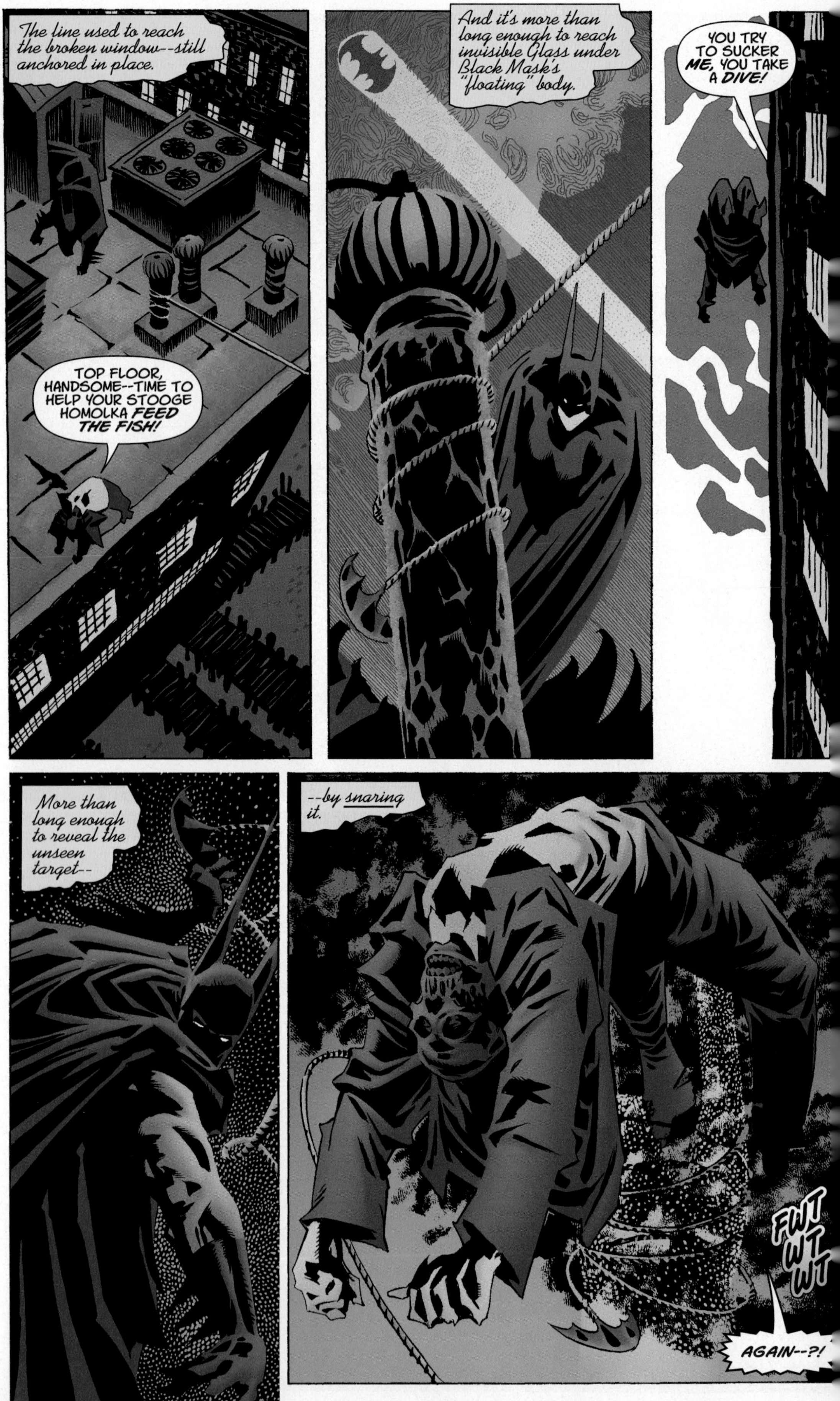
The line used to reach the broken window--still anchored in place.
TOP FLOOR, HANDSOME--TIME TO HELP YOUR STOOGE HOMOLKA FEED THE FISH!
And it's more than long enough to reach invisible Glass under Black Mask's "floating" body.
YOU TRY TO SUCKER ME, YOU TAKE A DIVE!
More than long enough to reveal the unseen target--
--by snaring it.
FWT WT WT
AGAIN--?!

Now--pull him back from the edge.

HEY!

Hold fast.

YOU MADE ME THROW SHORT!

I MISSED THE RIVER COMPLETELY-- DIDN'T EVEN CLEAR THE ROOF!

And reel him in before--

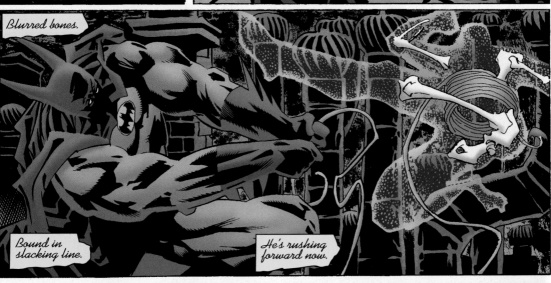

Blurred bones.

Bound in slacking line.

He's rushing forward now.

TUP

Attacking.

But he's also turning visible.

SCHUNK

Finally making a mistake.

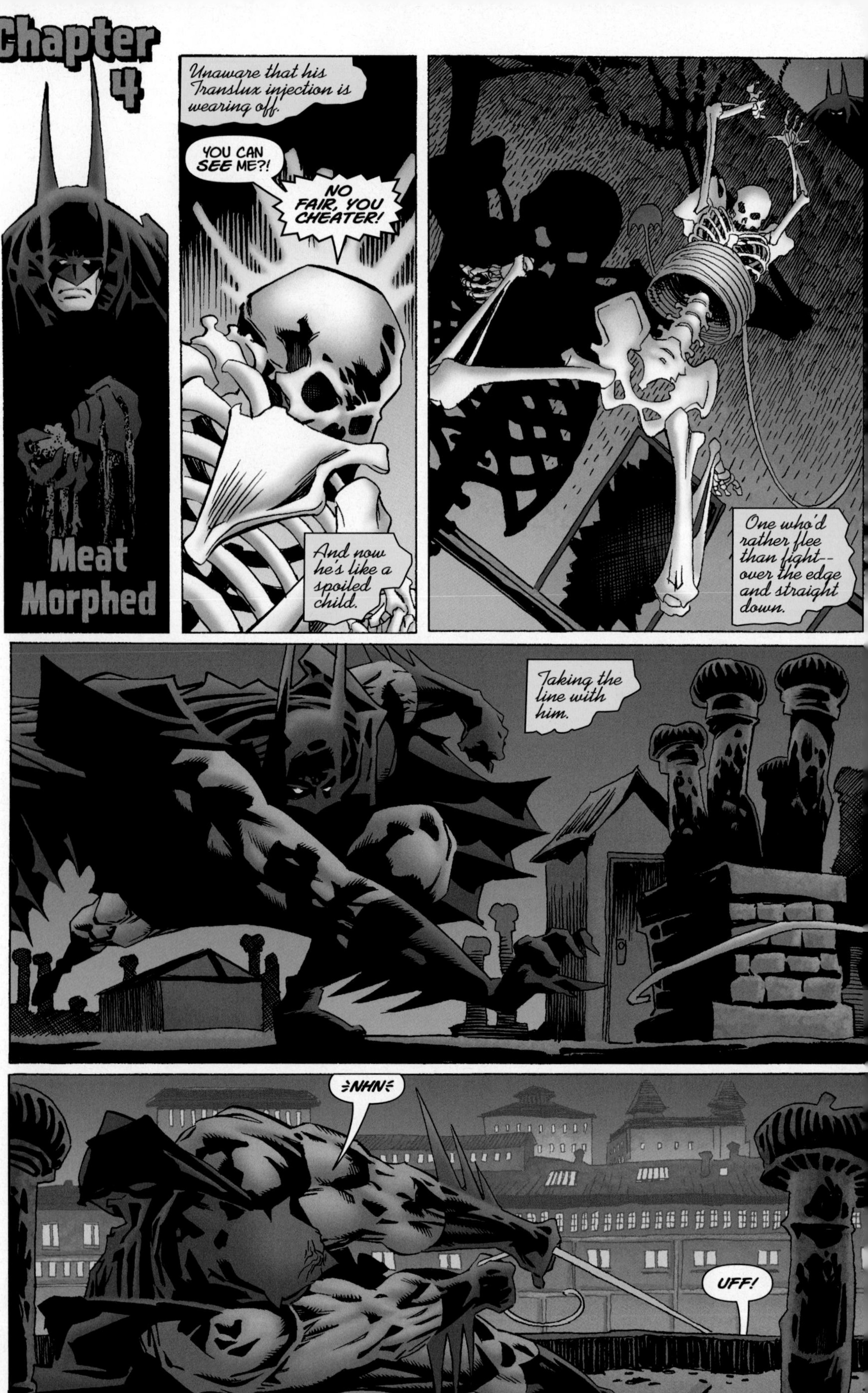
Chapter 4
Meat Morphed
Unaware that his Translux injection is wearing off.
YOU CAN SEE ME?!
NO FAIR, YOU CHEATER!
And now he's like a spoiled child.
One who'd rather flee than fight-- over the edge and straight down.
Taking the line with him.
NHN
UFF!

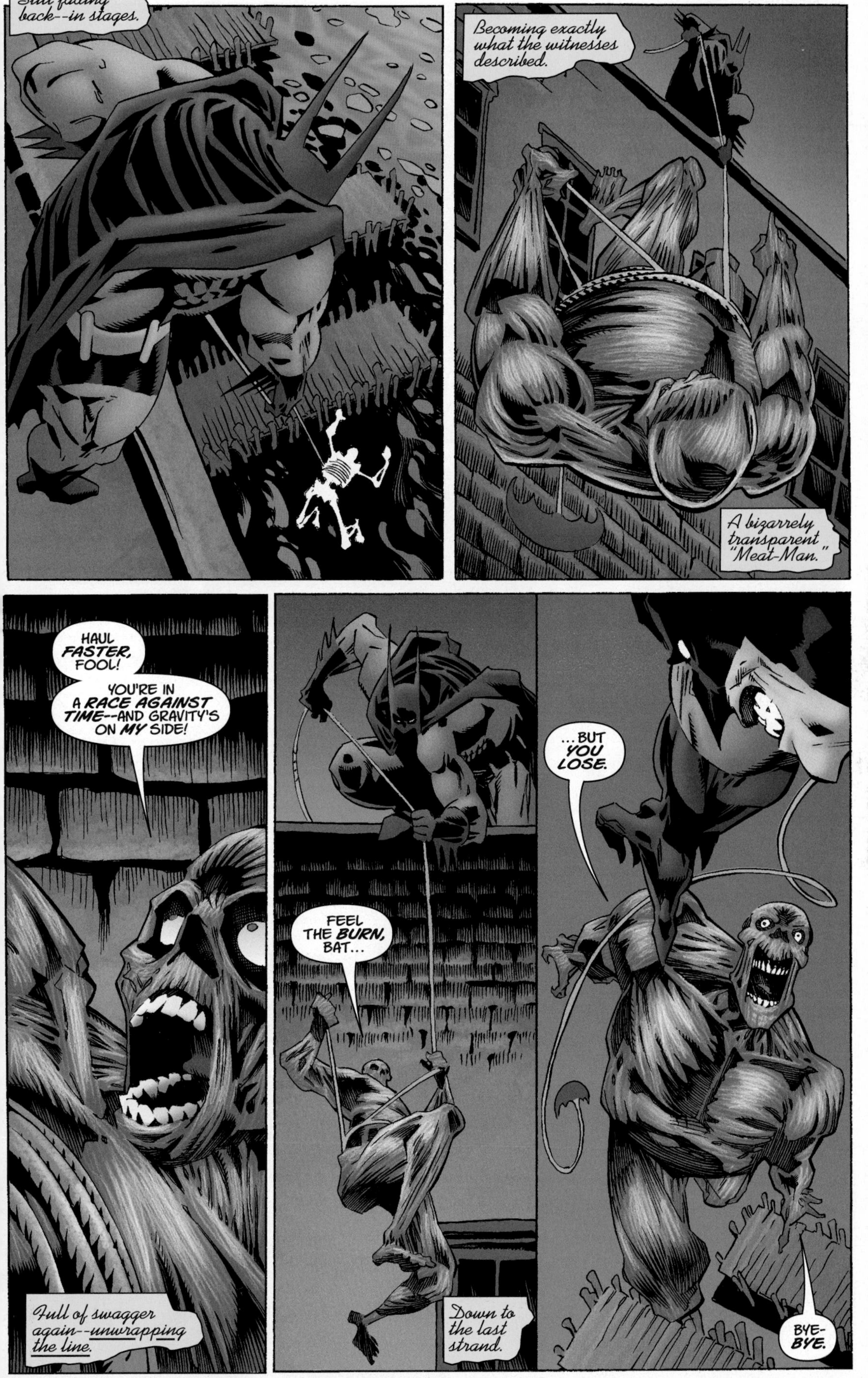

Still fading back--in stages.
Becoming exactly what the witnesses described.
A bizarrely transparent "Meat-Man."
HAUL FASTER, FOOL!
YOU'RE IN A RACE AGAINST TIME--AND GRAVITY'S ON MY SIDE!
Full of swagger again--unwrapping the line.
FEEL THE BURN, BAT...
Down to the last strand.
...BUT YOU LOSE.
BYE-BYE.

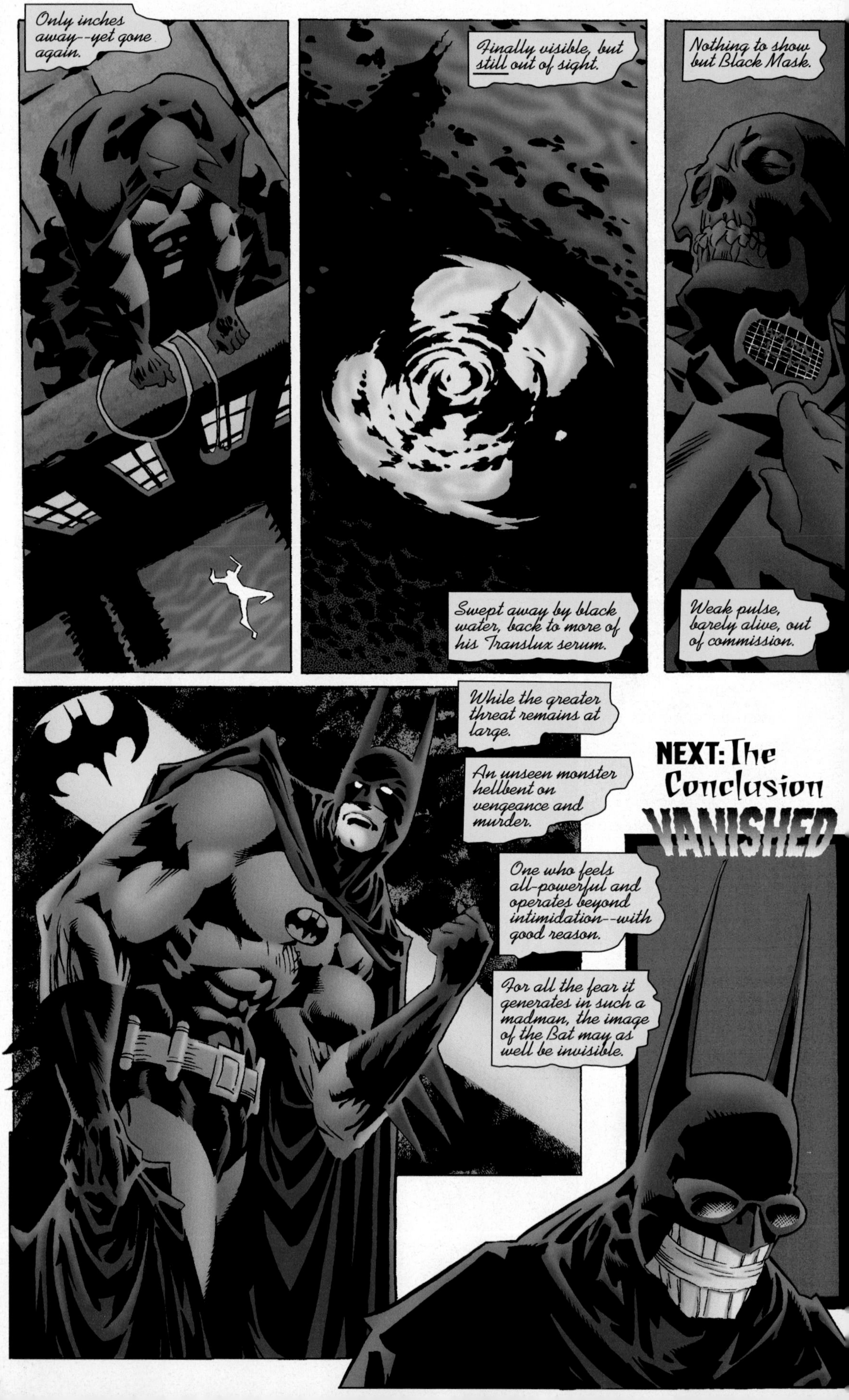
Only inches away--yet gone again.
Finally visible, but still out of sight.
Swept away by black water, back to more of his Translux serum.
Nothing to show but Black Mask.
Weak pulse, barely alive, out of commission.
While the greater threat remains at large.
An unseen monster hellbent on vengeance and murder.
One who feels all-powerful and operates beyond intimidation--with good reason.
For all the fear it generates in such a madman, the image of the Bat may as well be invisible.
NEXT: The Conclusion
VANISHED

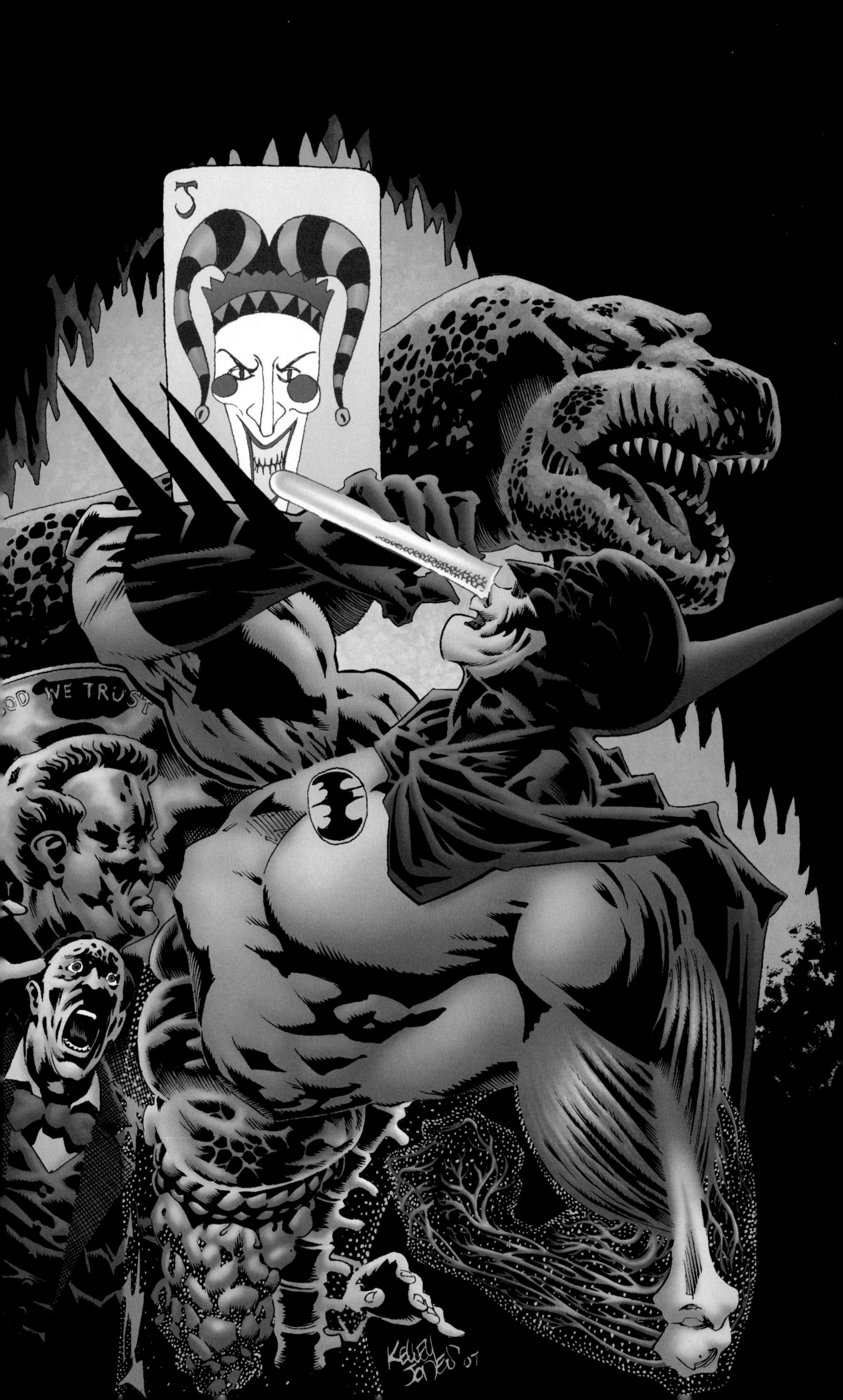
J
OD WE TRUST
KELLEY JONES '07

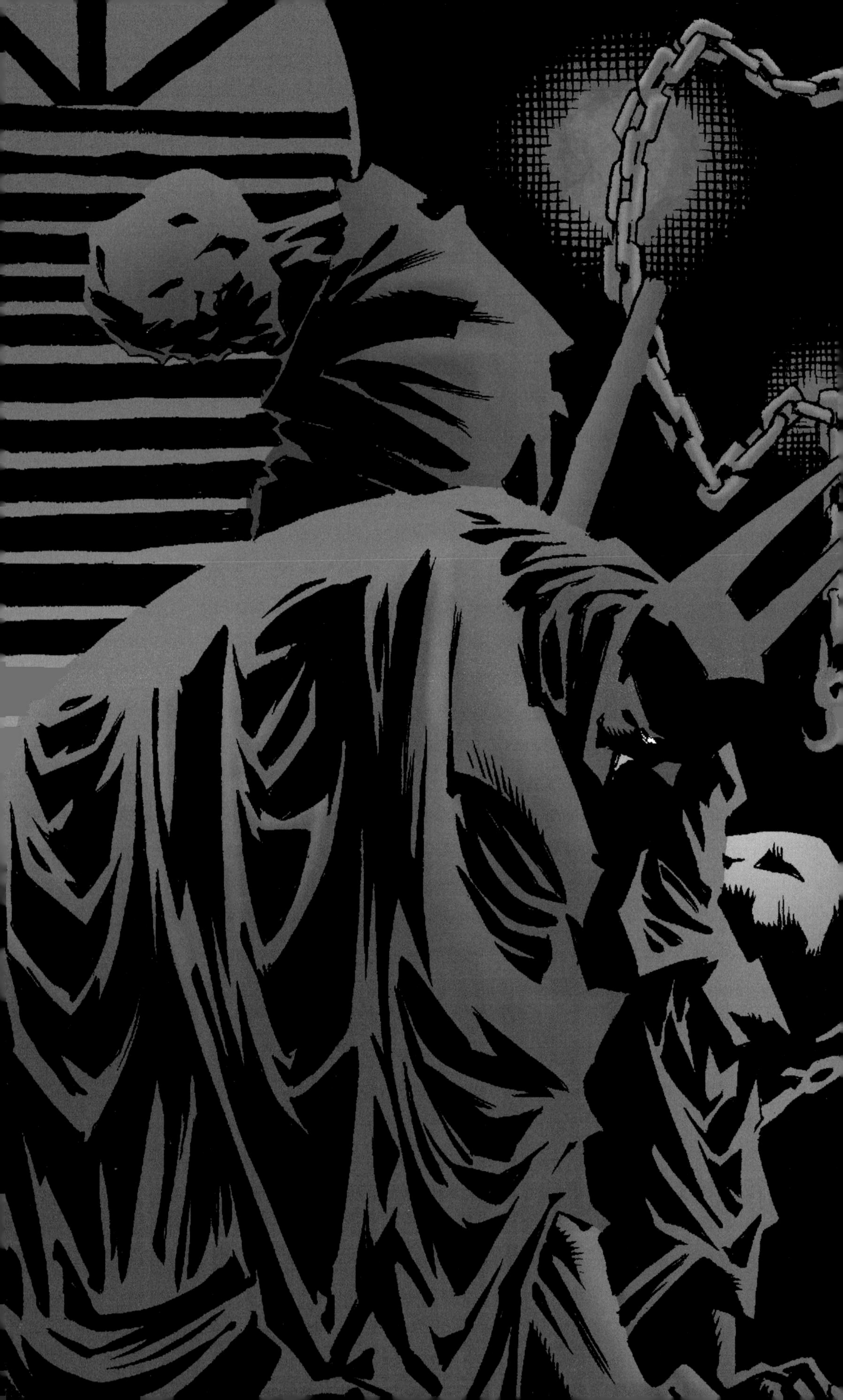

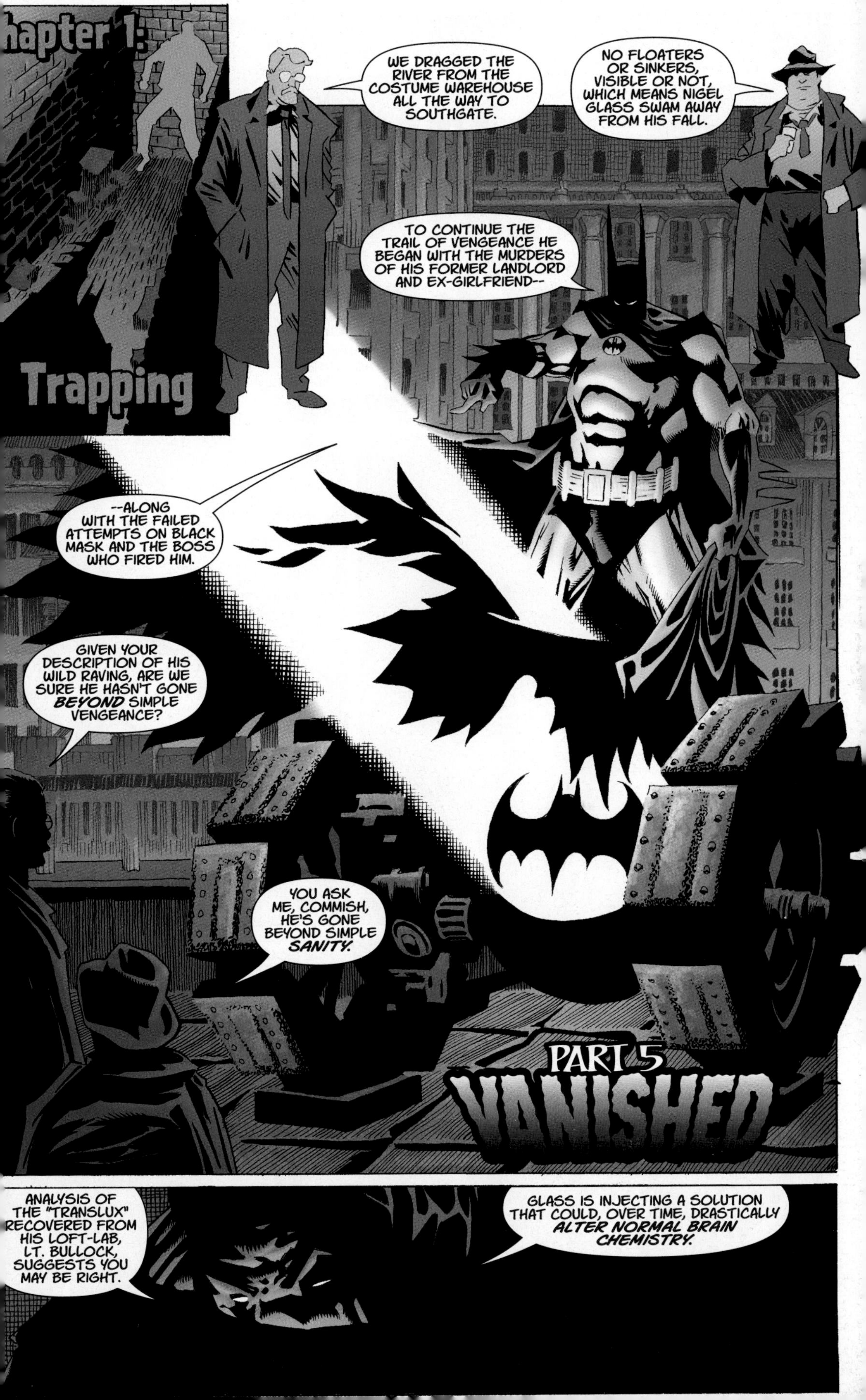
Chapter 1:
Trapping
WE DRAGGED THE RIVER FROM THE COSTUME WAREHOUSE ALL THE WAY TO SOUTHGATE.
NO FLOATERS OR SINKERS, VISIBLE OR NOT, WHICH MEANS NIGEL GLASS SWAM AWAY FROM HIS FALL.
TO CONTINUE THE TRAIL OF VENGEANCE HE BEGAN WITH THE MURDERS OF HIS FORMER LANDLORD AND EX-GIRLFRIEND--
--ALONG WITH THE FAILED ATTEMPTS ON BLACK MASK AND THE BOSS WHO FIRED HIM.
GIVEN YOUR DESCRIPTION OF HIS WILD RAVING, ARE WE SURE HE HASN'T GONE BEYOND SIMPLE VENGEANCE?
YOU ASK ME, COMMISH, HE'S GONE BEYOND SIMPLE SANITY.
PART 5
VANISHED
ANALYSIS OF THE "TRANSLUX" RECOVERED FROM HIS LOFT-LAB, LT. BULLOCK, SUGGESTS YOU MAY BE RIGHT.
GLASS IS INJECTING A SOLUTION THAT COULD, OVER TIME, DRASTICALLY ALTER NORMAL BRAIN CHEMISTRY.

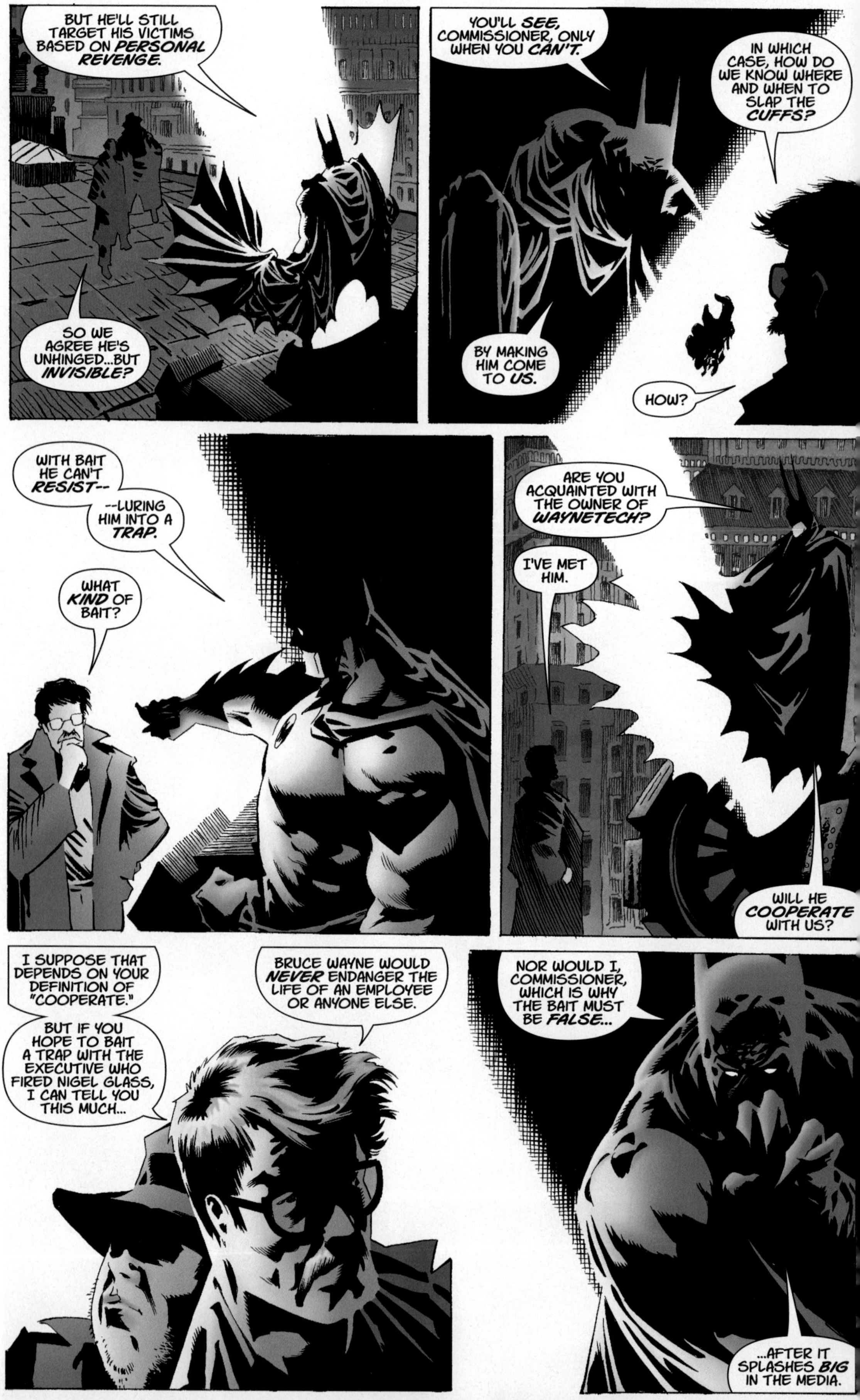
BUT HE'LL STILL TARGET HIS VICTIMS BASED ON PERSONAL REVENGE.
SO WE AGREE HE'S UNHINGED...BUT INVISIBLE?
YOU'LL SEE, COMMISSIONER, ONLY WHEN YOU CAN'T.
IN WHICH CASE, HOW DO WE KNOW WHERE AND WHEN TO SLAP THE CUFFS?
BY MAKING HIM COME TO US.
HOW?
WITH BAIT HE CAN'T RESIST--
--LURING HIM INTO A TRAP.
WHAT KIND OF BAIT?
ARE YOU ACQUAINTED WITH THE OWNER OF WAYNETECH?
I'VE MET HIM.
WILL HE COOPERATE WITH US?
I SUPPOSE THAT DEPENDS ON YOUR DEFINITION OF "COOPERATE."
BUT IF YOU HOPE TO BAIT A TRAP WITH THE EXECUTIVE WHO FIRED NIGEL GLASS, I CAN TELL YOU THIS MUCH...
BRUCE WAYNE WOULD NEVER ENDANGER THE LIFE OF AN EMPLOYEE OR ANYONE ELSE.
NOR WOULD I, COMMISSIONER, WHICH IS WHY THE BAIT MUST BE FALSE...
...AFTER IT SPLASHES BIG IN THE MEDIA.

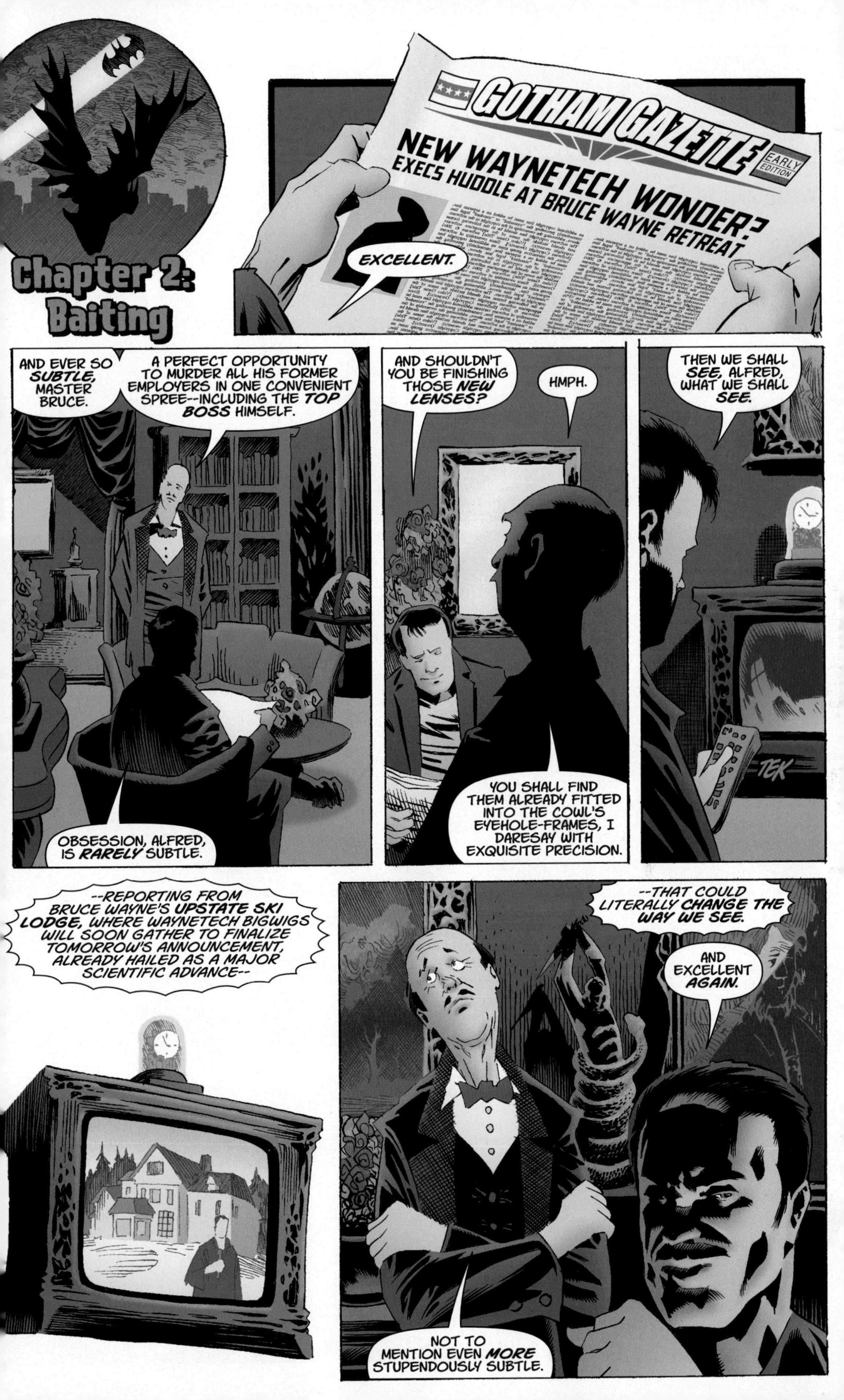
Chapter 2: Baiting
GOTHAM GAZETTE
EARLY EDITION
NEW WAYNETECH WONDER?
EXECS HUDDLE AT BRUCE WAYNE RETREAT
EXCELLENT.
AND EVER SO SUBTLE, MASTER BRUCE.
A PERFECT OPPORTUNITY TO MURDER ALL HIS FORMER EMPLOYERS IN ONE CONVENIENT SPREE--INCLUDING THE TOP BOSS HIMSELF.
OBSESSION, ALFRED, IS RARELY SUBTLE.
AND SHOULDN'T YOU BE FINISHING THOSE NEW LENSES?
HMPH.
YOU SHALL FIND THEM ALREADY FITTED INTO THE COWL'S EYEHOLE-FRAMES, I DARESAY WITH EXQUISITE PRECISION.
THEN WE SHALL SEE, ALFRED, WHAT WE SHALL SEE.
TEK
--REPORTING FROM BRUCE WAYNE'S UPSTATE SKI LODGE, WHERE WAYNETECH BIGWIGS WILL SOON GATHER TO FINALIZE TOMORROW'S ANNOUNCEMENT, ALREADY HAILED AS A MAJOR SCIENTIFIC ADVANCE--
--THAT COULD LITERALLY CHANGE THE WAY WE SEE.
AND EXCELLENT AGAIN.
NOT TO MENTION EVEN MORE STUPENDOUSLY SUBTLE.

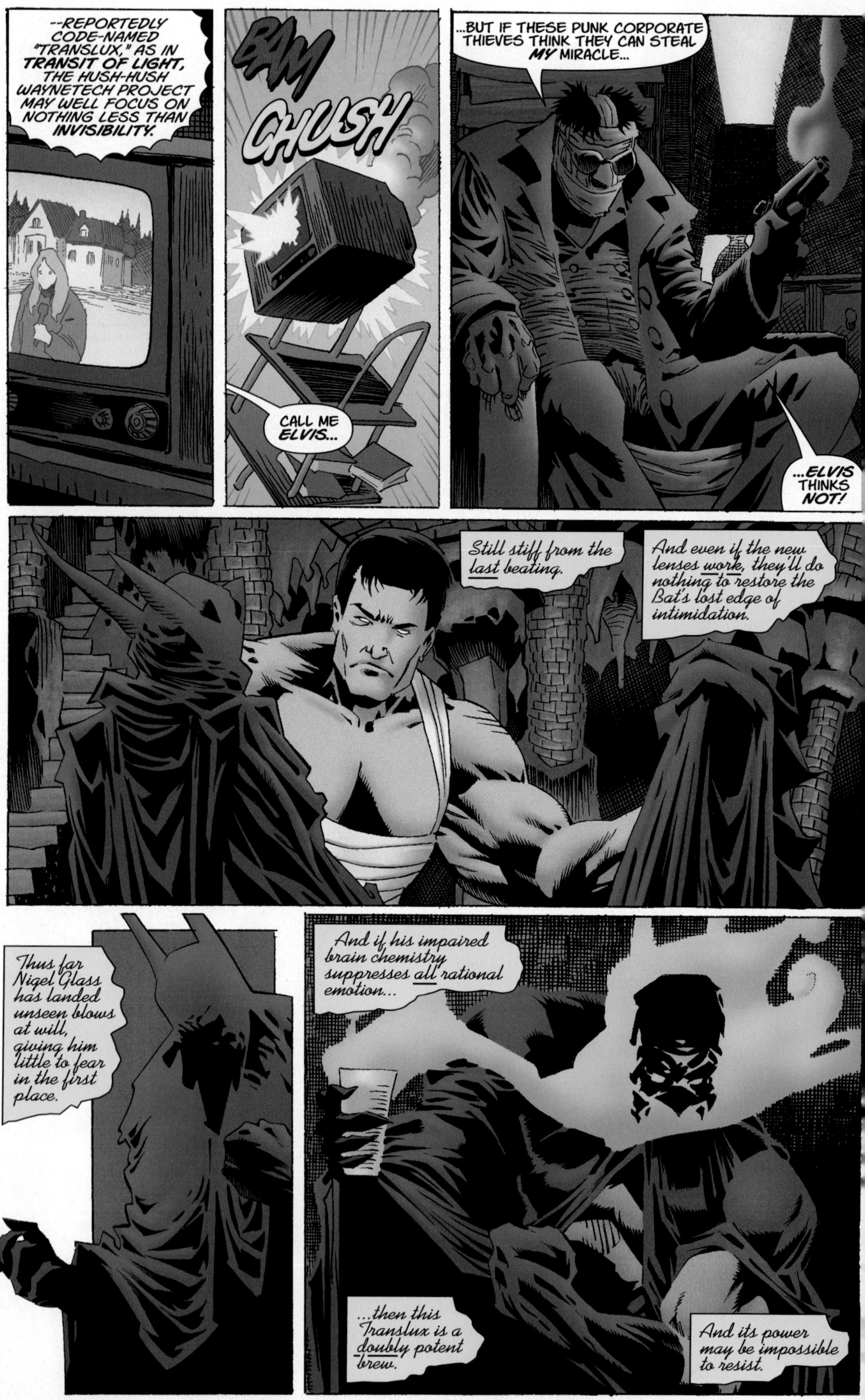
--REPORTEDLY CODE-NAMED "TRANSLUX," AS IN TRANSIT OF LIGHT, THE HUSH-HUSH WAYNETECH PROJECT MAY WELL FOCUS ON NOTHING LESS THAN INVISIBILITY.
BAM
CHUSH
CALL ME ELVIS...
...BUT IF THESE PUNK CORPORATE THIEVES THINK THEY CAN STEAL MY MIRACLE...
...ELVIS THINKS NOT!
Still stiff from the last beating.
And even if the new lenses work, they'll do nothing to restore the Bat's lost edge of intimidation.
Thus far Nigel Glass has landed unseen blows at will, giving him little to fear in the first place.
And if his impaired brain chemistry suppresses all rational emotion...
...then this Translux is a doubly potent brew.
And its power may be impossible to resist.

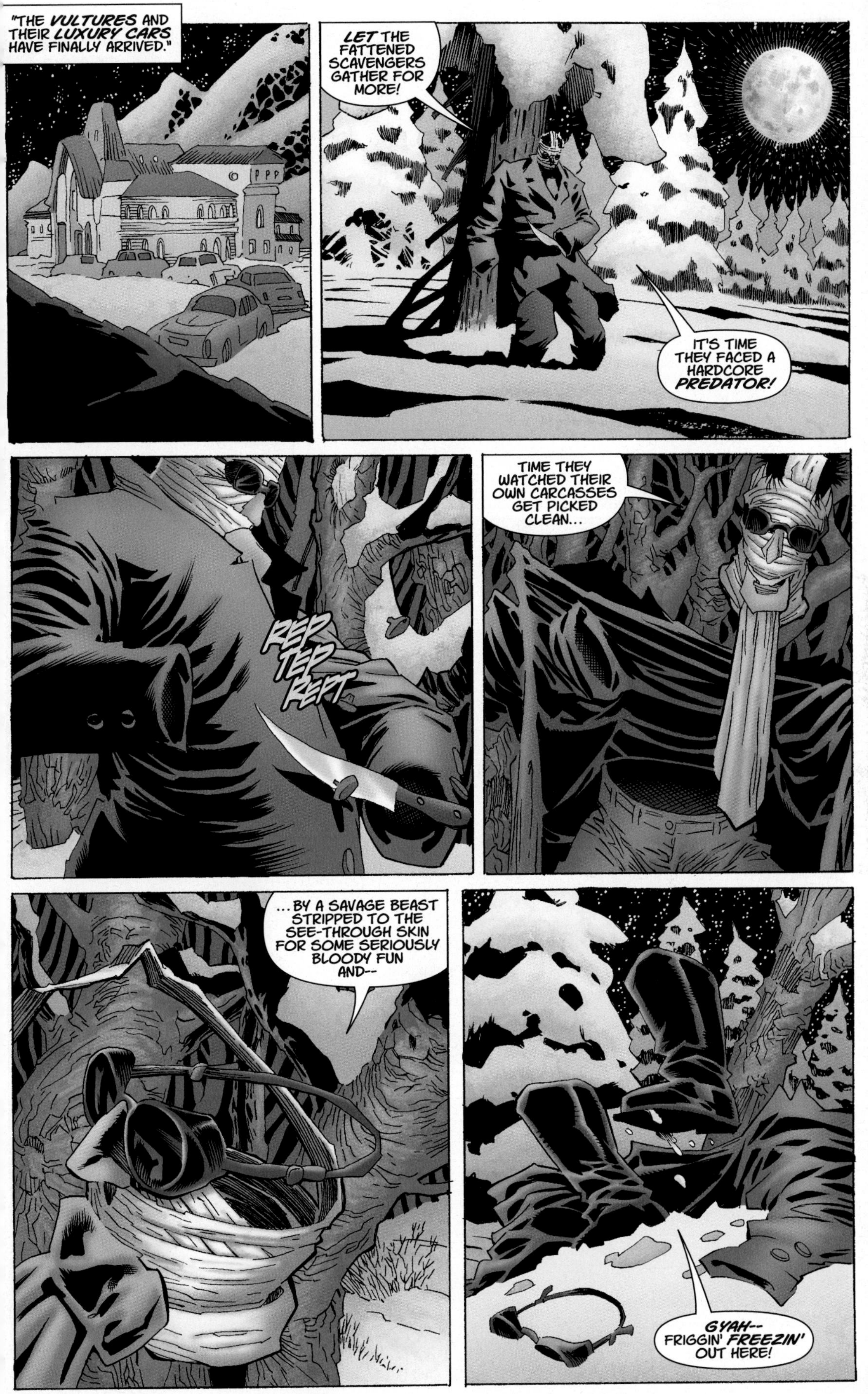
"THE VULTURES AND THEIR LUXURY CARS HAVE FINALLY ARRIVED."
LET THE FATTENED SCAVENGERS GATHER FOR MORE!
IT'S TIME THEY FACED A HARDCORE PREDATOR!
REP TEP REPT
TIME THEY WATCHED THEIR OWN CARCASSES GET PICKED CLEAN...
...BY A SAVAGE BEAST STRIPPED TO THE SEE-THROUGH SKIN FOR SOME SERIOUSLY BLOODY FUN AND--
GYAH-- FRIGGIN' FREEZIN' OUT HERE!

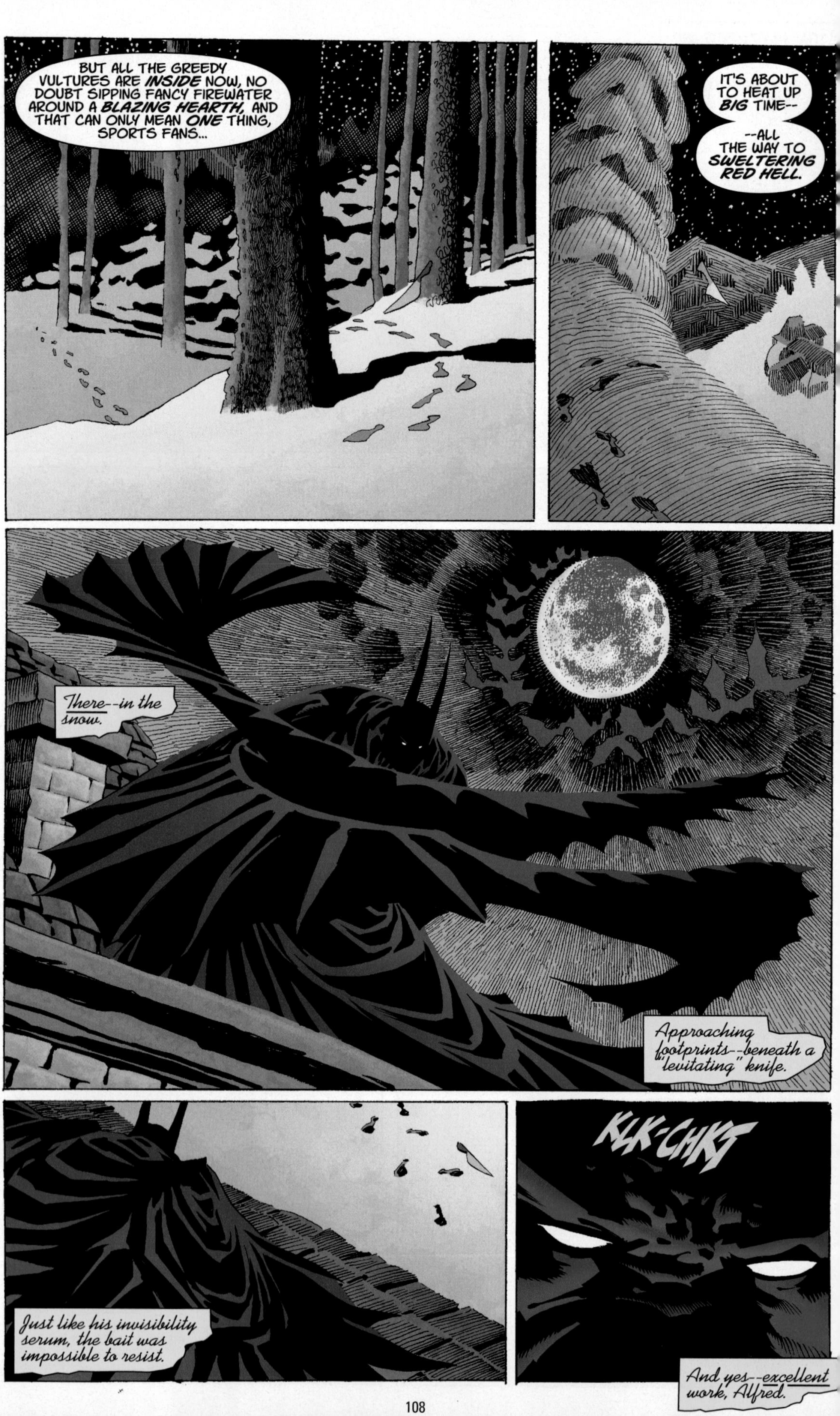
BUT ALL THE GREEDY VULTURES ARE *INSIDE* NOW, NO DOUBT SIPPING FANCY FIREWATER AROUND A *BLAZING HEARTH,* AND THAT CAN ONLY MEAN *ONE* THING, SPORTS FANS...
IT'S ABOUT TO HEAT UP *BIG* TIME--
--ALL THE WAY TO *SWELTERING RED HELL.*
There--in the snow.
Approaching footprints--beneath a "levitating" knife.
Just like his invisibility serum, the bait was impossible to resist.
KLK-CHKT
And yes--excellent work, Alfred.

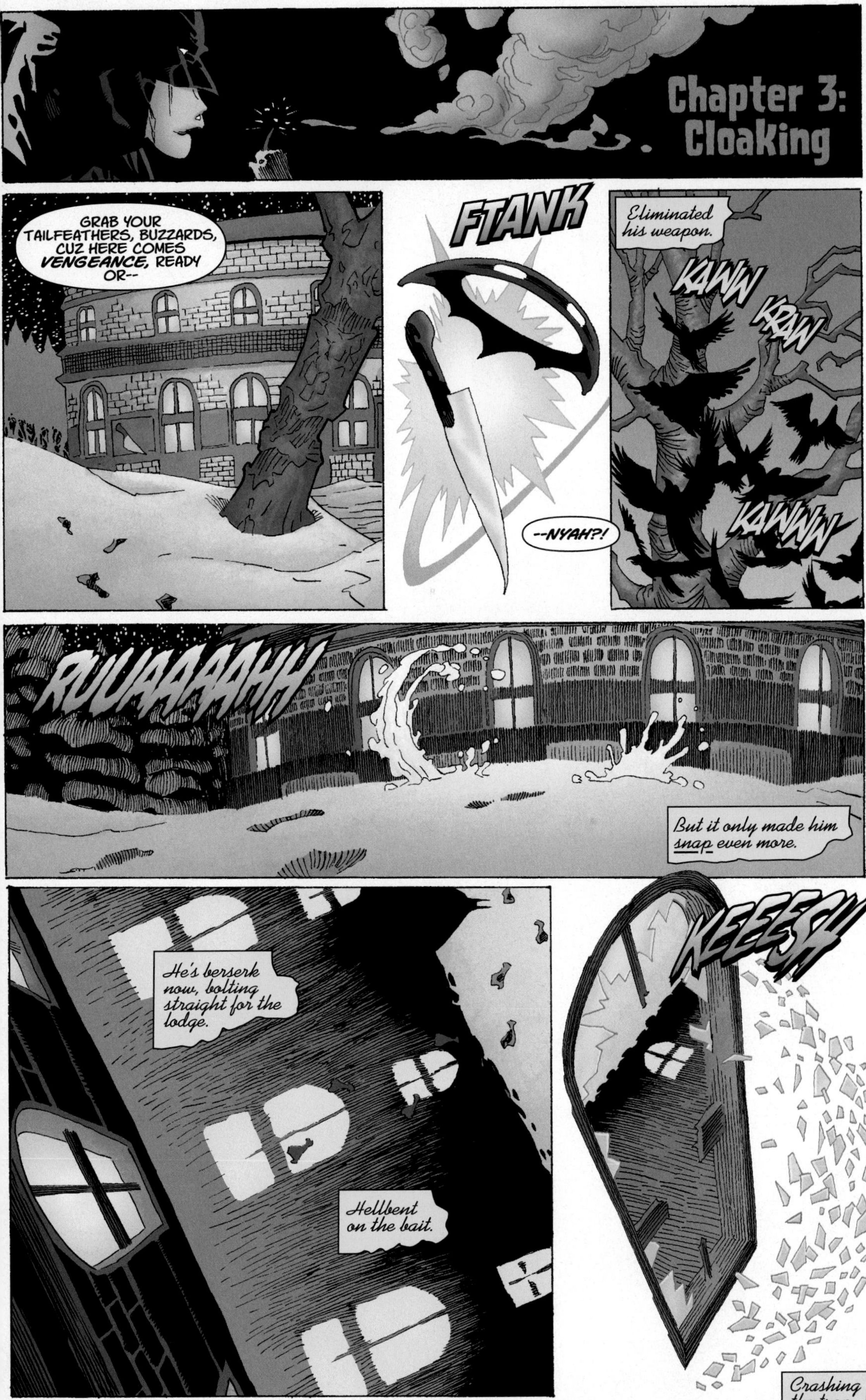
Chapter 3: Cloaking
GRAB YOUR TAILFEATHERS, BUZZARDS, CUZ HERE COMES VENGEANCE, READY OR--
FTANK
--NYAH?!
Eliminated his weapon.
KAWW
KRAW
KAWWW
RUUAAAAAHH
But it only made him snap even more.
He's berserk now, bolting straight for the lodge.
Hellbent on the bait.
KEEESH
Crashing the trap.

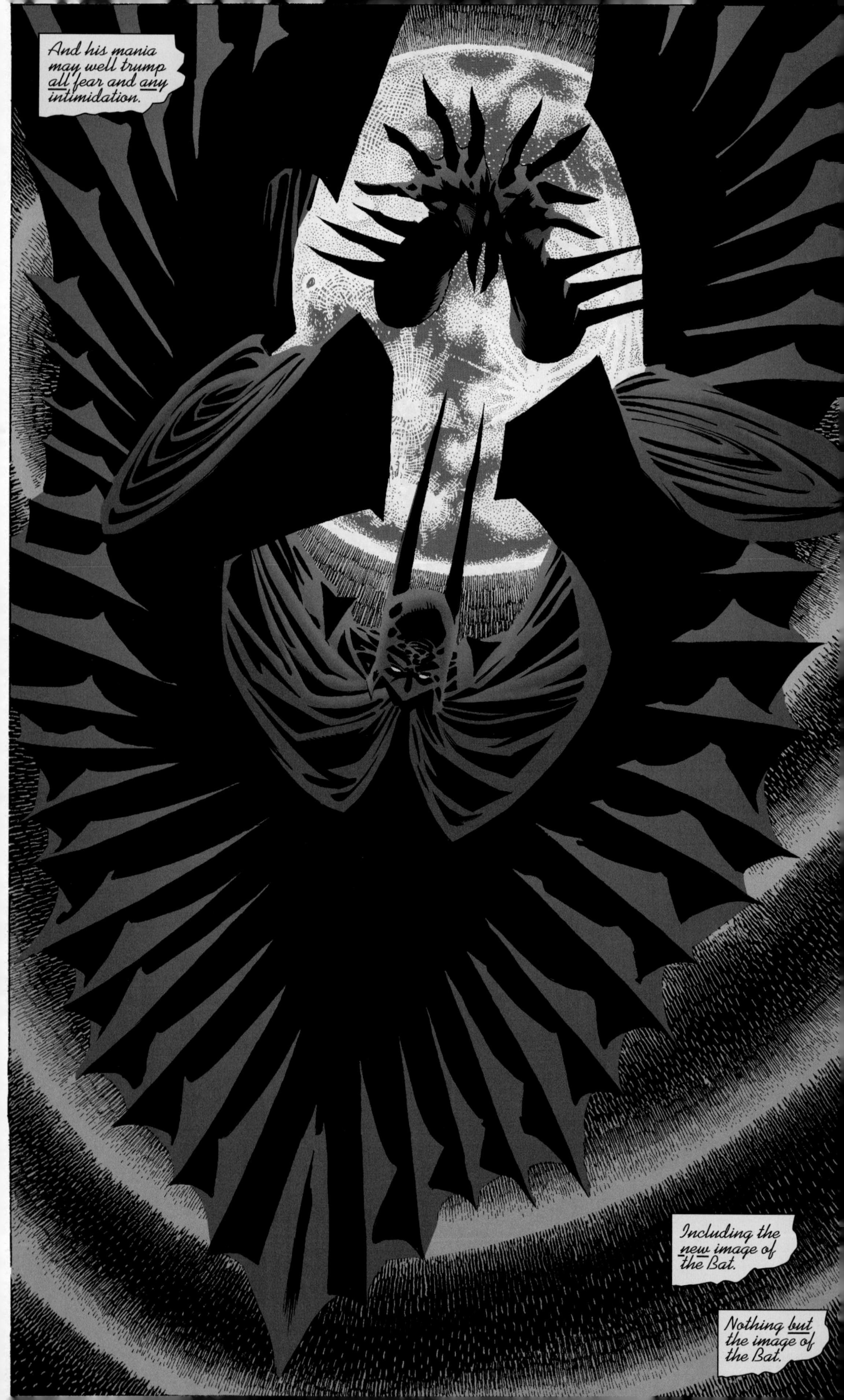
And his mania may well trump all fear and any intimidation.
Including the new image of the Bat.
Nothing but the image of the Bat.

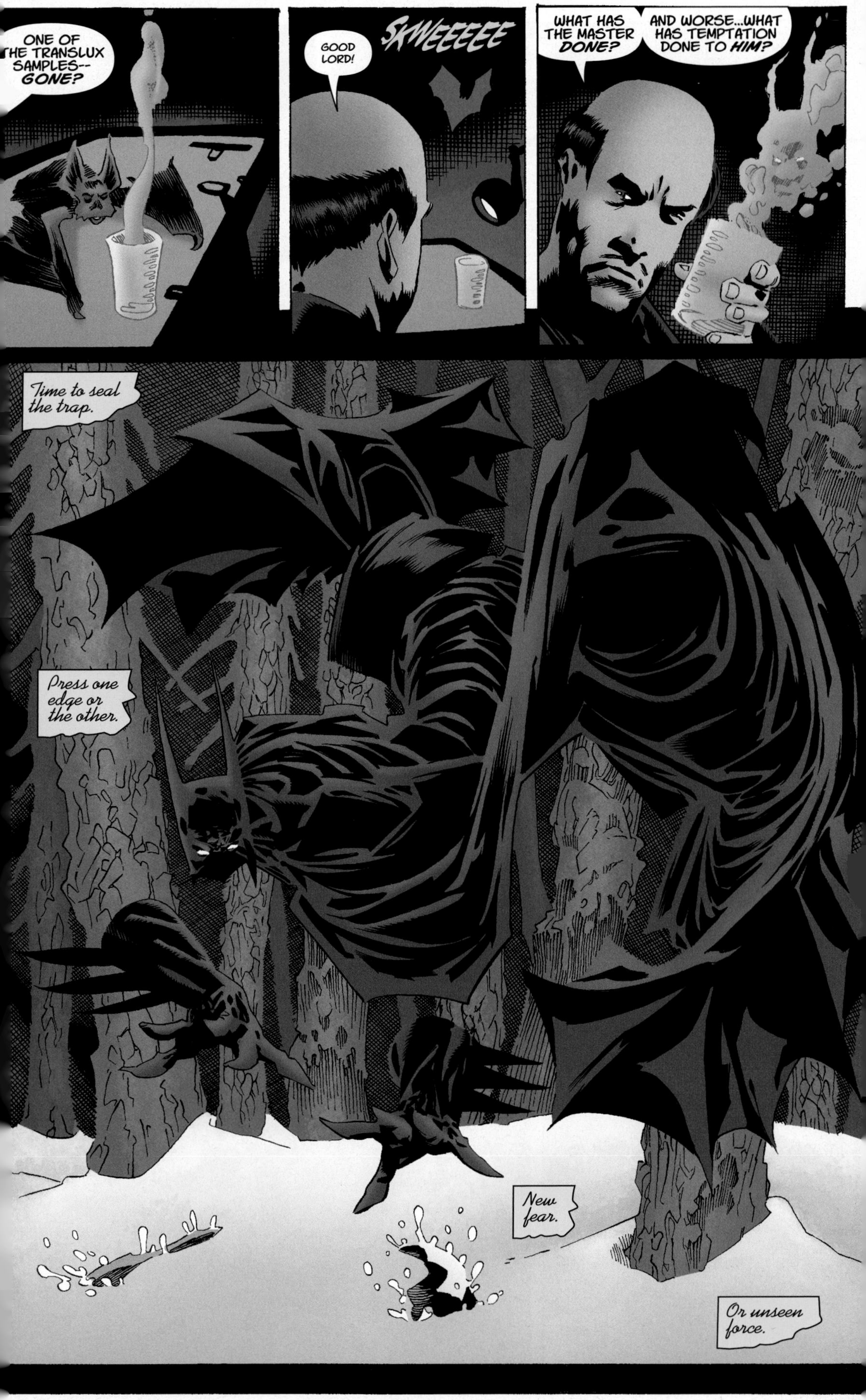
ONE OF THE TRANSLUX SAMPLES-- GONE?
GOOD LORD!
SKWEEEEEE
WHAT HAS THE MASTER DONE?
AND WORSE...WHAT HAS TEMPTATION DONE TO HIM?
Time to seal the trap.
Press one edge or the other.
New fear.
Or unseen force.

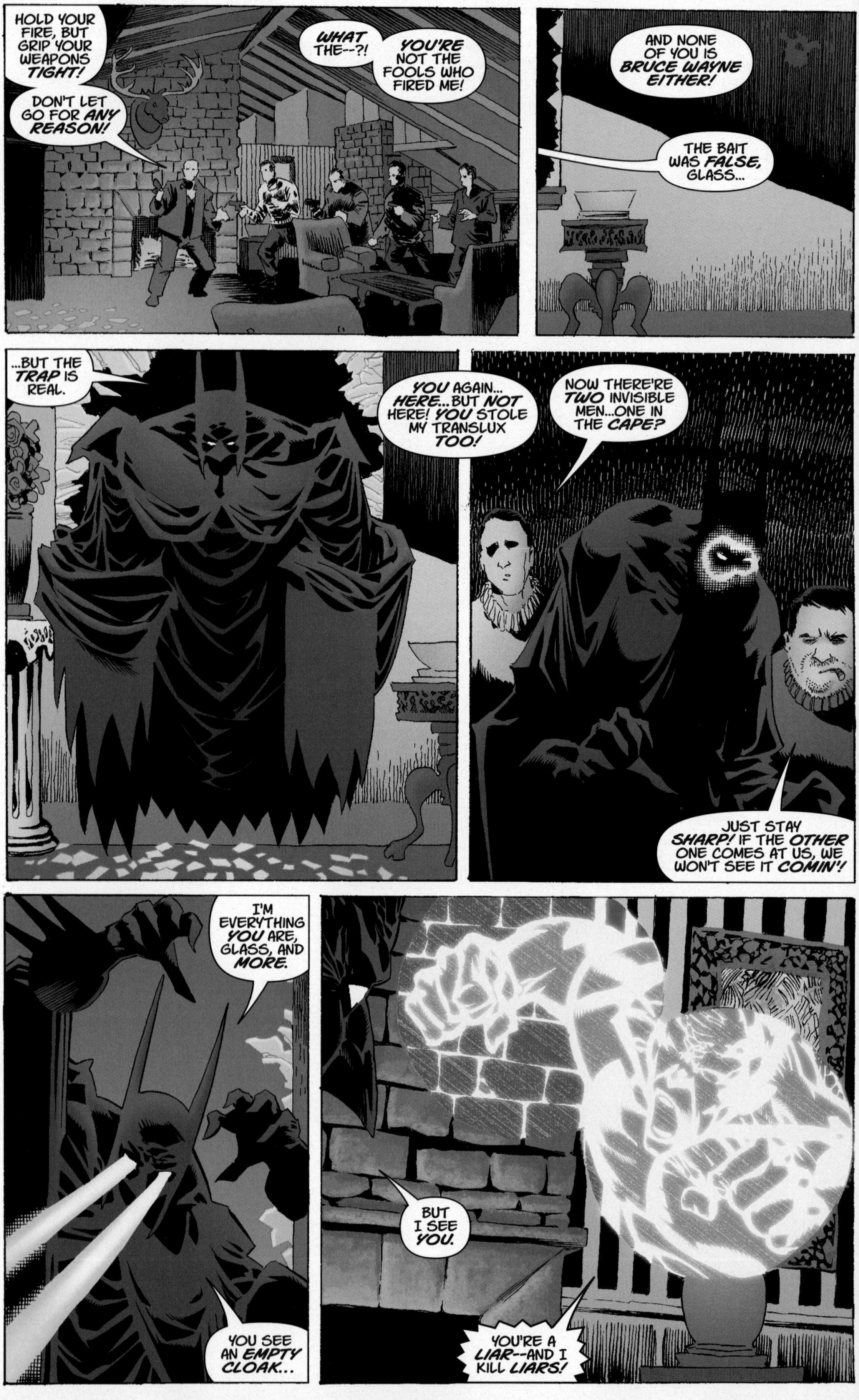
HOLD YOUR FIRE, BUT GRIP YOUR WEAPONS TIGHT!
DON'T LET GO FOR ANY REASON!
WHAT THE--?!
YOU'RE NOT THE FOOLS WHO FIRED ME!
AND NONE OF YOU IS BRUCE WAYNE EITHER!
THE BAIT WAS FALSE, GLASS...
...BUT THE TRAP IS REAL.
YOU AGAIN... HERE...BUT NOT HERE! YOU STOLE MY TRANSLUX TOO!
NOW THERE'RE TWO INVISIBLE MEN...ONE IN THE CAPE?
JUST STAY SHARP! IF THE OTHER ONE COMES AT US, WE WON'T SEE IT COMIN'!
I'M EVERYTHING YOU ARE, GLASS, AND MORE.
YOU SEE AN EMPTY CLOAK...
BUT I SEE YOU.
YOU'RE A LIAR--AND I KILL LIARS!

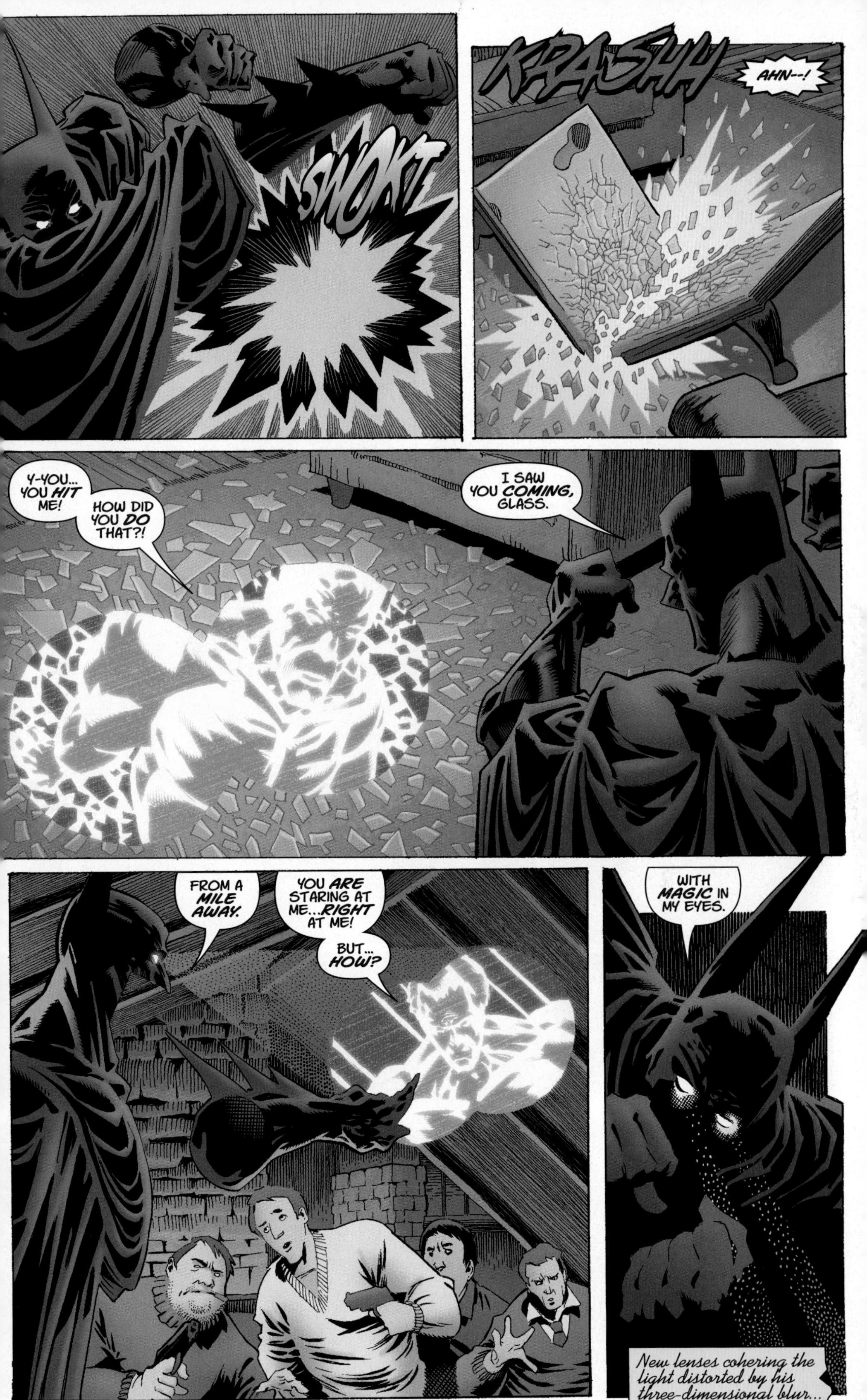
SNOKT!
KRASHH
AHN--!
Y-YOU... YOU HIT ME!
HOW DID YOU DO THAT?!
I SAW YOU COMING, GLASS.
FROM A MILE AWAY.
YOU ARE STARING AT ME...RIGHT AT ME!
BUT... HOW?
WITH MAGIC IN MY EYES.
New lenses cohering the light distorted by his three-dimensional blur...

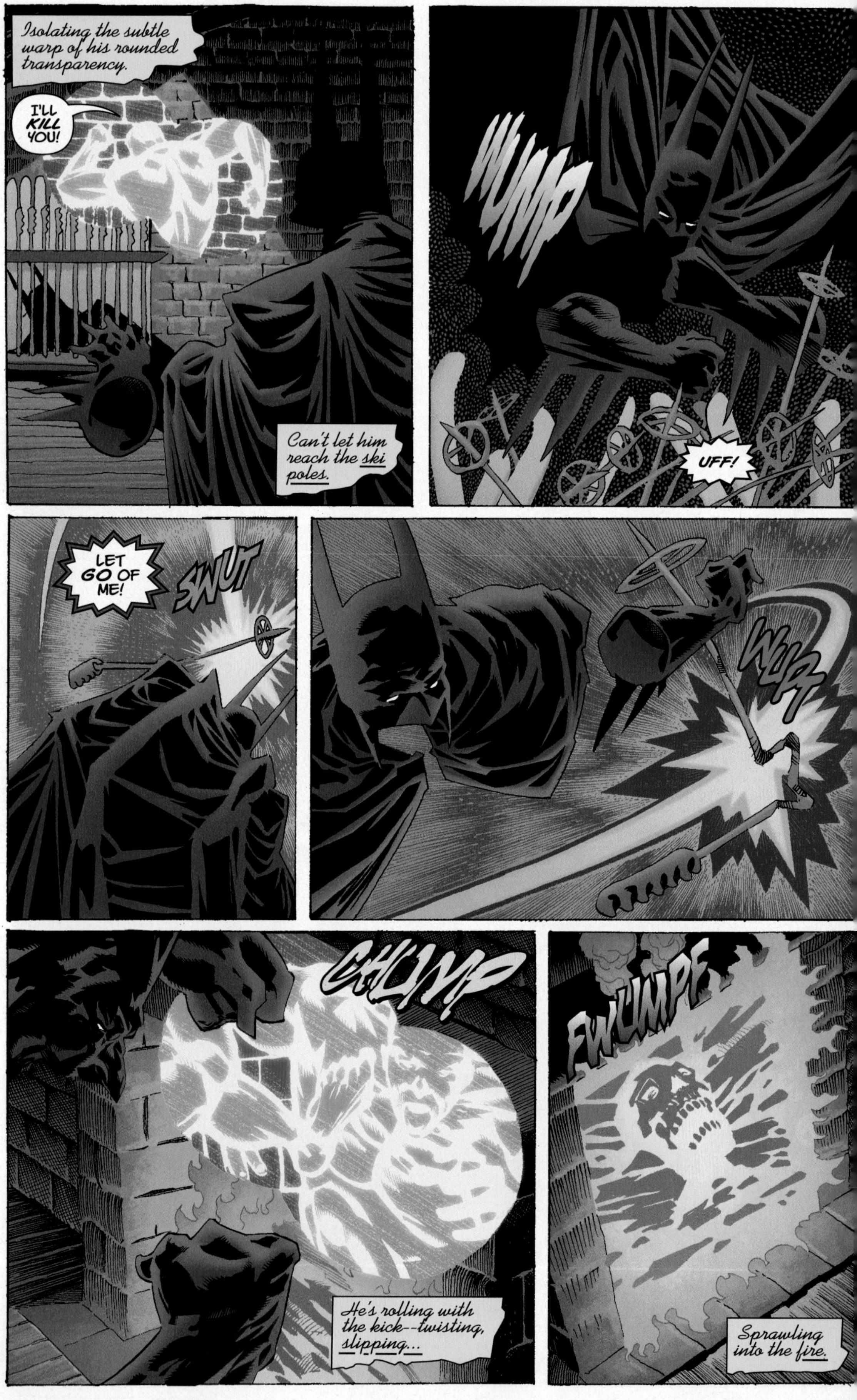

Isolating the subtle warp of his rounded transparency.
I'LL KILL YOU!
Can't let him reach the ski poles.
WUMP
UFF!
LET GO OF ME!
SWUT
WUPT
CHUMP
He's rolling with the kick--twisting, slipping...
FWUMPF
Sprawling into the fire.

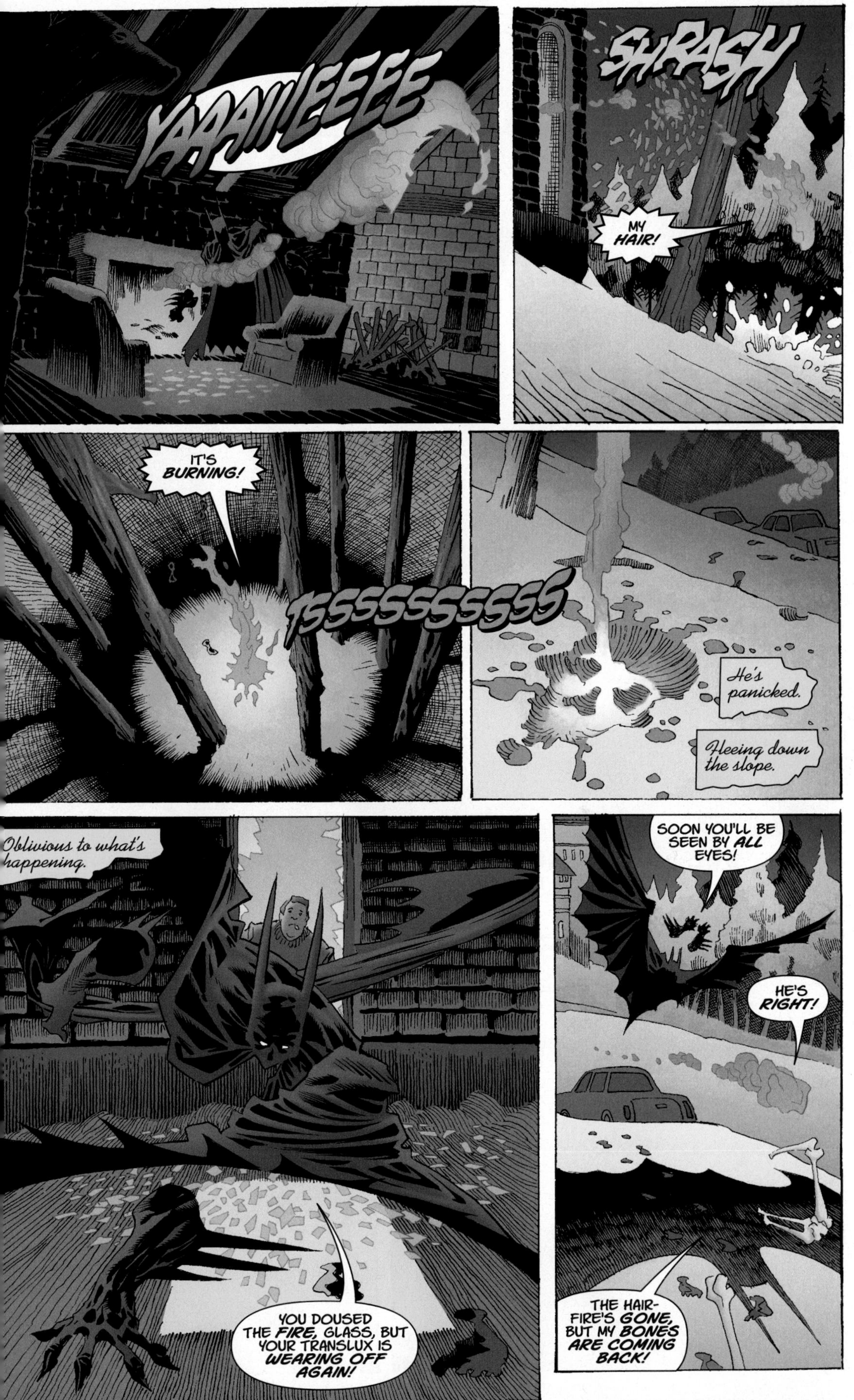
YAAAIIIEEEE
SHRASH
MY HAIR!
IT'S BURNING!
TSSSSSSSSSS
He's panicked.
Fleeing down the slope.
Oblivious to what's happening.
YOU DOUSED THE FIRE, GLASS, BUT YOUR TRANSLUX IS WEARING OFF AGAIN!
SOON YOU'LL BE SEEN BY ALL EYES!
HE'S RIGHT!
THE HAIR-FIRE'S GONE, BUT MY BONES ARE COMING BACK!

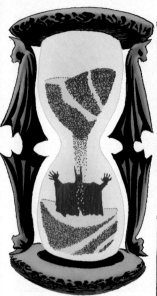

Chapter 4: Expiring

AND A *BALD SKELETON* IS HARD TO MISS!

CAN'T DISAPPEAR FOR MORE THAN AN *HOUR* NOW-- NOT EVEN WITH A *DOUBLE* OVERDOSE!

SOME *MIRACLE.*

STINKING TRANSLUX MIGHT AS WELL BE *WATER* AT THIS POINT!

THEY BOOKED DOWN THE *SLOPE,* COMMISH, *BOTH* OF 'EM!

SO I *SEE.*

YEAH, GOOD THING THE BAT PICKED *SNOWY TURF* FOR THE TRAP...

EVEN IF *THEY* CAN'T BE SEEN, NO WAY TO HIDE THEIR *TRACKS.*

WHICH IS PRECISELY *WHY,* LT. BULLOCK, THIS LODGE WAS *PICKED.*

NEED A *TRIPLE* OVERDOSE FAST-- WITH ALL THE BACKUP TRANSLUX STRANDED IN MY OVERCOAT *ABOVE* THE SKI LODGE...

GOING DOWN IS THE *WRONG WAY,* DAMMIT, BUT HOW DO I TURN BACK WITH THE *BAT* SWOOPING ON MY HEELS?!

AND NOW THERE'S *MORE* OF ME--*FLESH* JUMPING THE *BONES!*

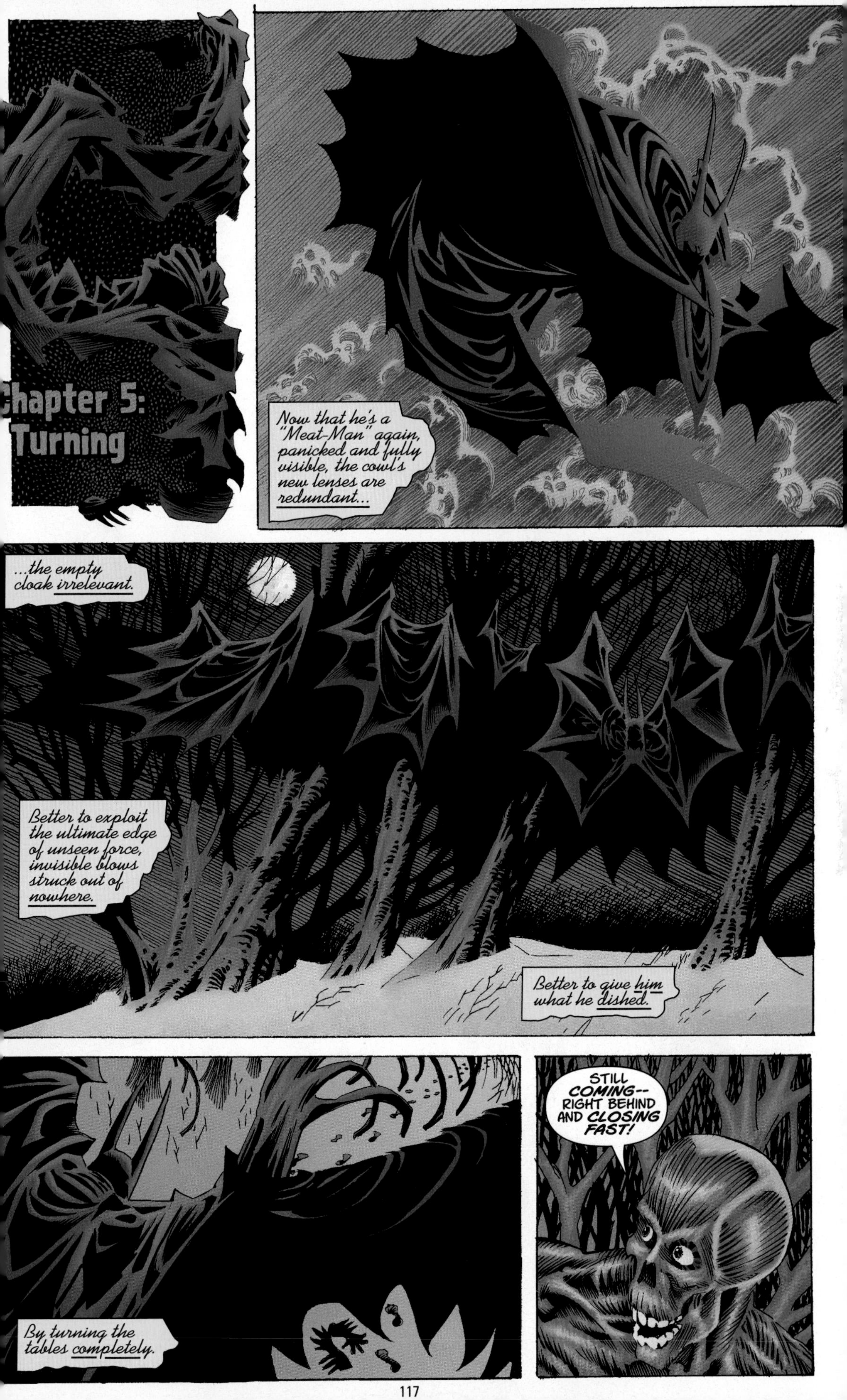
hapter 5:
Turning
Now that he's a "Meat-Man" again, panicked and fully visible, the cowl's new lenses are redundant...
...the empty cloak irrelevant.
Better to exploit the ultimate edge of unseen force, invisible blows struck out of nowhere.
Better to give him what he dished.
By turning the tables completely.
STILL COMING-- RIGHT BEHIND AND CLOSING FAST!

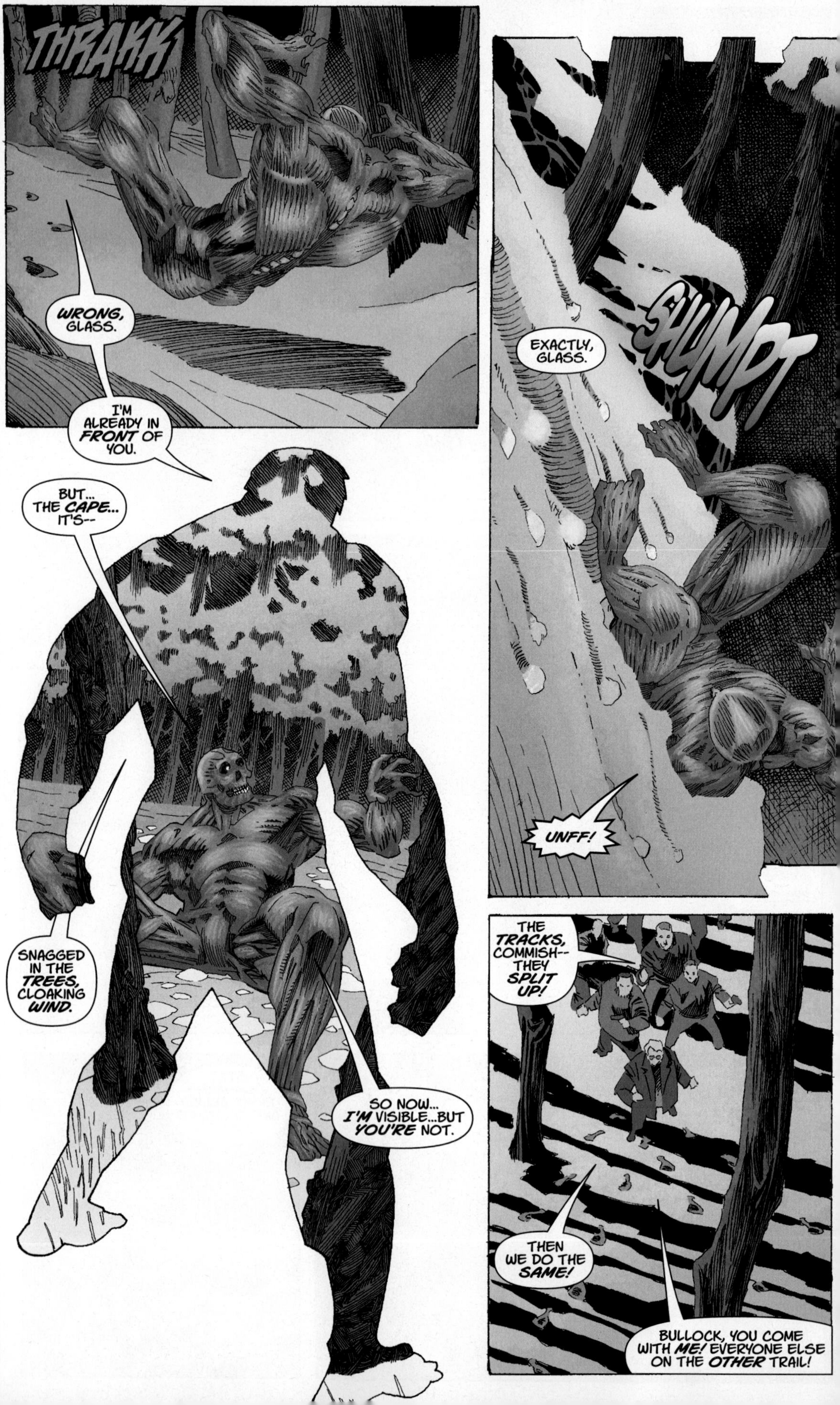
THRAKK
WRONG, GLASS.
I'M ALREADY IN FRONT OF YOU.
BUT... THE CAPE... IT'S--
SNAGGED IN THE TREES, CLOAKING WIND.
SO NOW... I'M VISIBLE...BUT YOU'RE NOT.
EXACTLY, GLASS.
SHUMPT
UNFF!
THE TRACKS, COMMISH-- THEY SPLIT UP!
THEN WE DO THE SAME!
BULLOCK, YOU COME WITH ME! EVERYONE ELSE ON THE OTHER TRAIL!

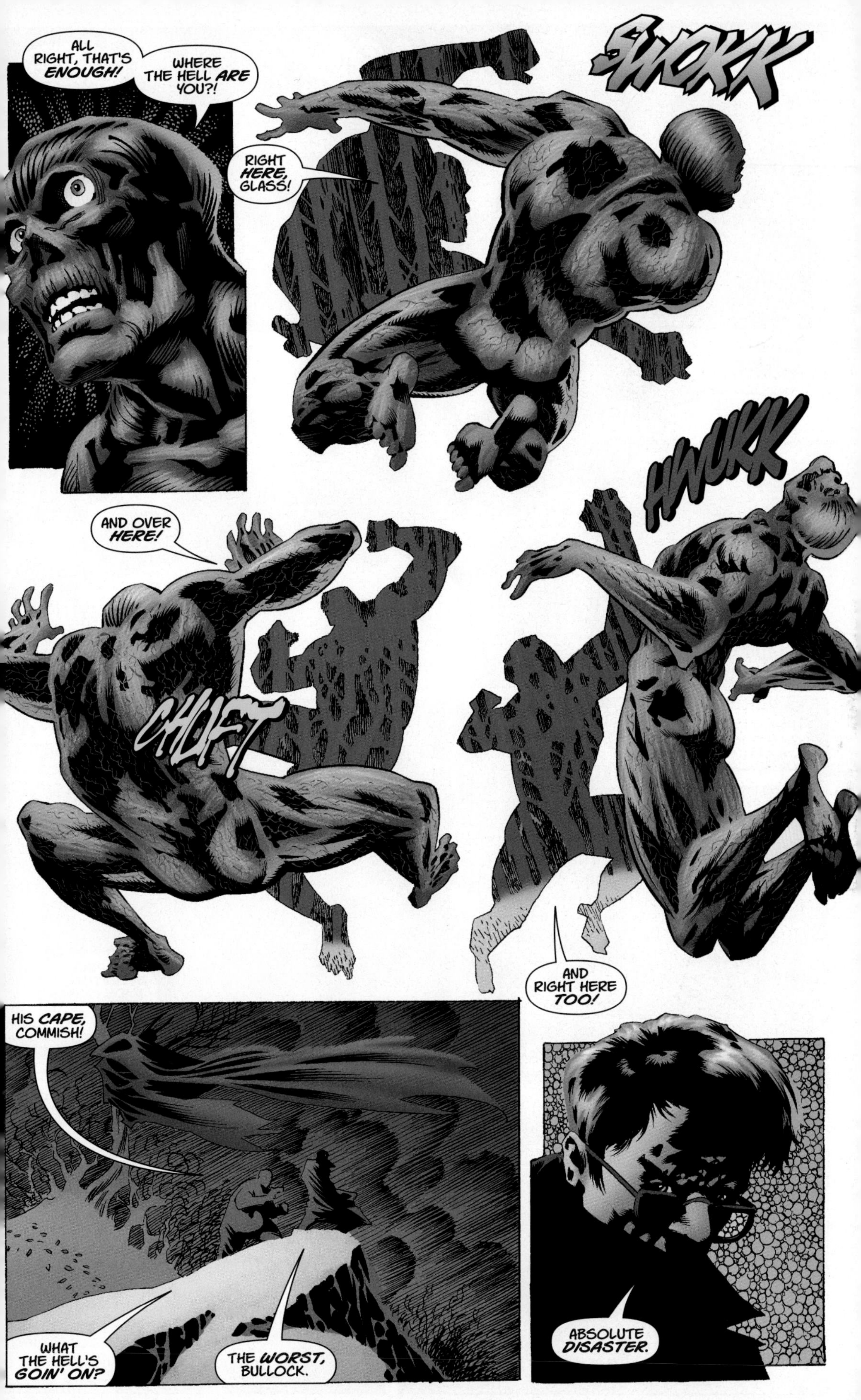

ALL RIGHT, THAT'S ENOUGH!
WHERE THE HELL ARE YOU?!
SWOKK
RIGHT HERE, GLASS!
HWUKK
AND OVER HERE!
CHUFT
AND RIGHT HERE TOO!
HIS CAPE, COMMISH!
WHAT THE HELL'S GOIN' ON?
THE WORST, BULLOCK.
ABSOLUTE DISASTER.

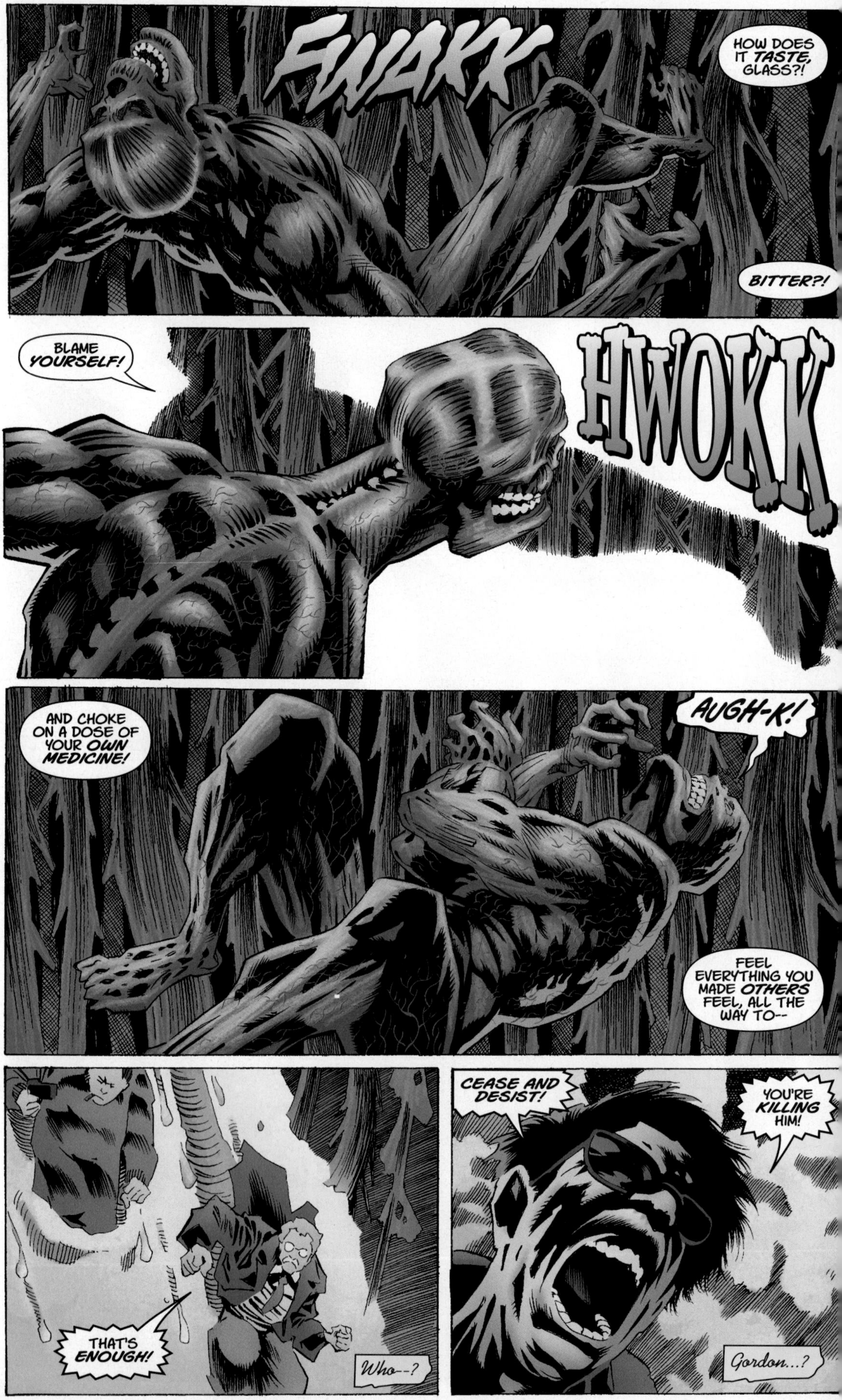
FWAKK
HOW DOES IT TASTE, GLASS?!
BITTER?!
BLAME YOURSELF!
HWOKK
AND CHOKE ON A DOSE OF YOUR OWN MEDICINE!
AUGH-K!
FEEL EVERYTHING YOU MADE OTHERS FEEL, ALL THE WAY TO--
THAT'S ENOUGH!
Who--?
CEASE AND DESIST!
YOU'RE KILLING HIM!
Gordon...?

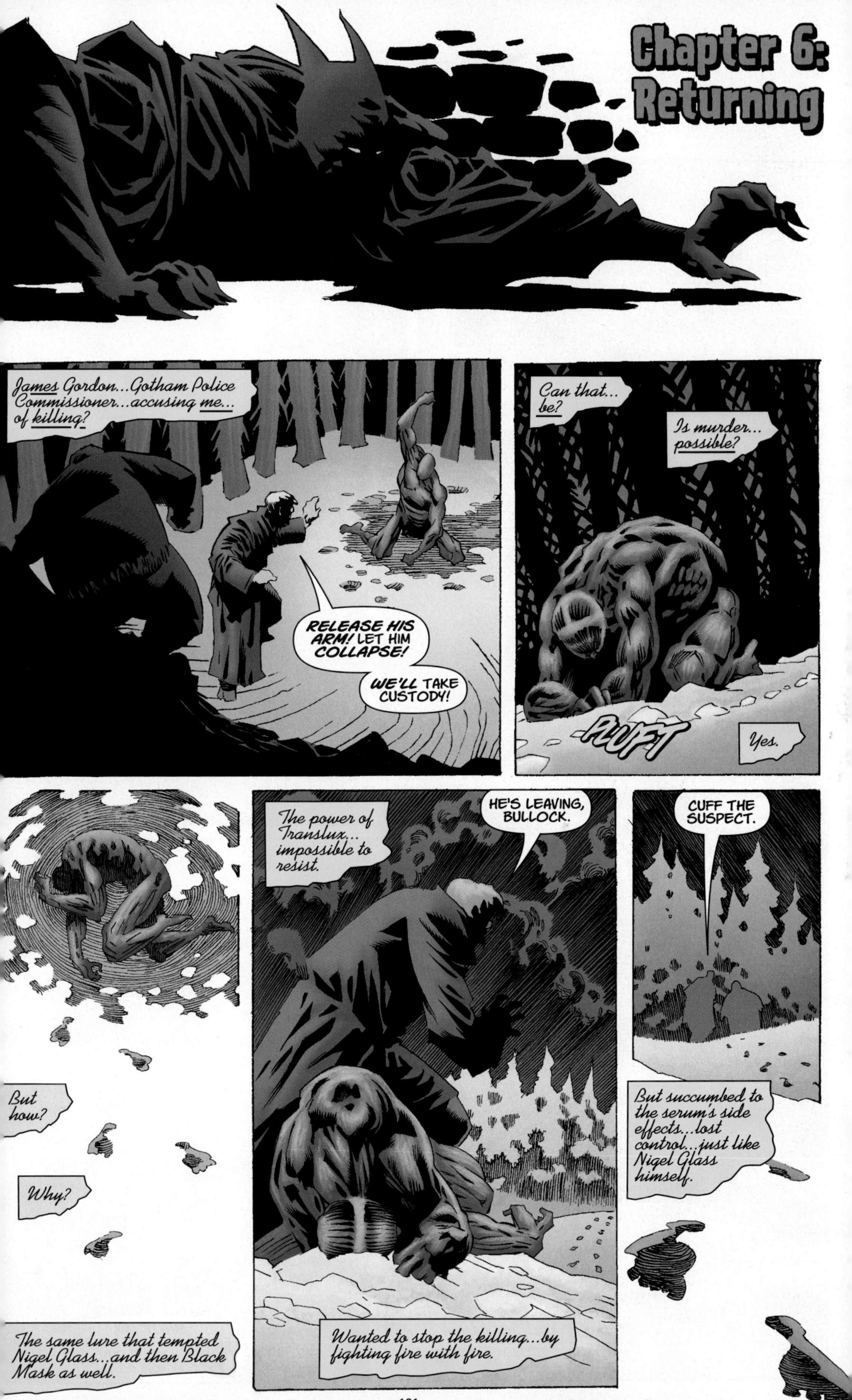
Chapter 6:
Returning
James Gordon...Gotham Police Commissioner...accusing me... of killing?
RELEASE HIS ARM! LET HIM COLLAPSE!
WE'LL TAKE CUSTODY!
Can that... be?
Is murder... possible?
PLUFT
Yes.
But how?
Why?
The same lure that tempted Nigel Glass...and then Black Mask as well.
The power of Translux... impossible to resist.
HE'S LEAVING, BULLOCK.
Wanted to stop the killing...by fighting fire with fire.
CUFF THE SUSPECT.
But succumbed to the serum's side effects...lost control...just like Nigel Glass himself.

THOUGHT I'D SEEN IT ALL, COMMISH--UNTIL *TONIGHT*.

THIS WHOLE CASE, BULLOCK, HAS BEEN ONE HUGE *EYE-OPENER*.

AND ONE THING IS *CRYSTAL CLEAR*.

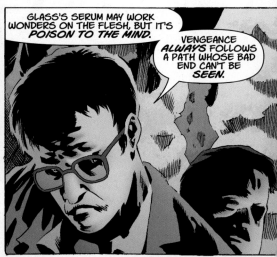

GLASS'S SERUM MAY WORK WONDERS ON THE FLESH, BUT IT'S *POISON TO THE MIND*.

VENGEANCE *ALWAYS* FOLLOWS A PATH WHOSE BAD END CAN'T BE *SEEN*.

Gordon's wrong.

The madness could be seen.

It was obvious.

Just didn't realize brain chemistry could be impaired so fast...nor with a single dose.

But even once was too much.

Enough to chill the soul...and leave it numb.

NIGEL GLASS, YOU'RE UNDER *ARREST*.

YOU HAVE THE RIGHT TO REMAIN--

SHUT UP, FOOL, BEFORE I CHEW THROUGH YOUR RIBS AND *EAT YOUR HEART!*

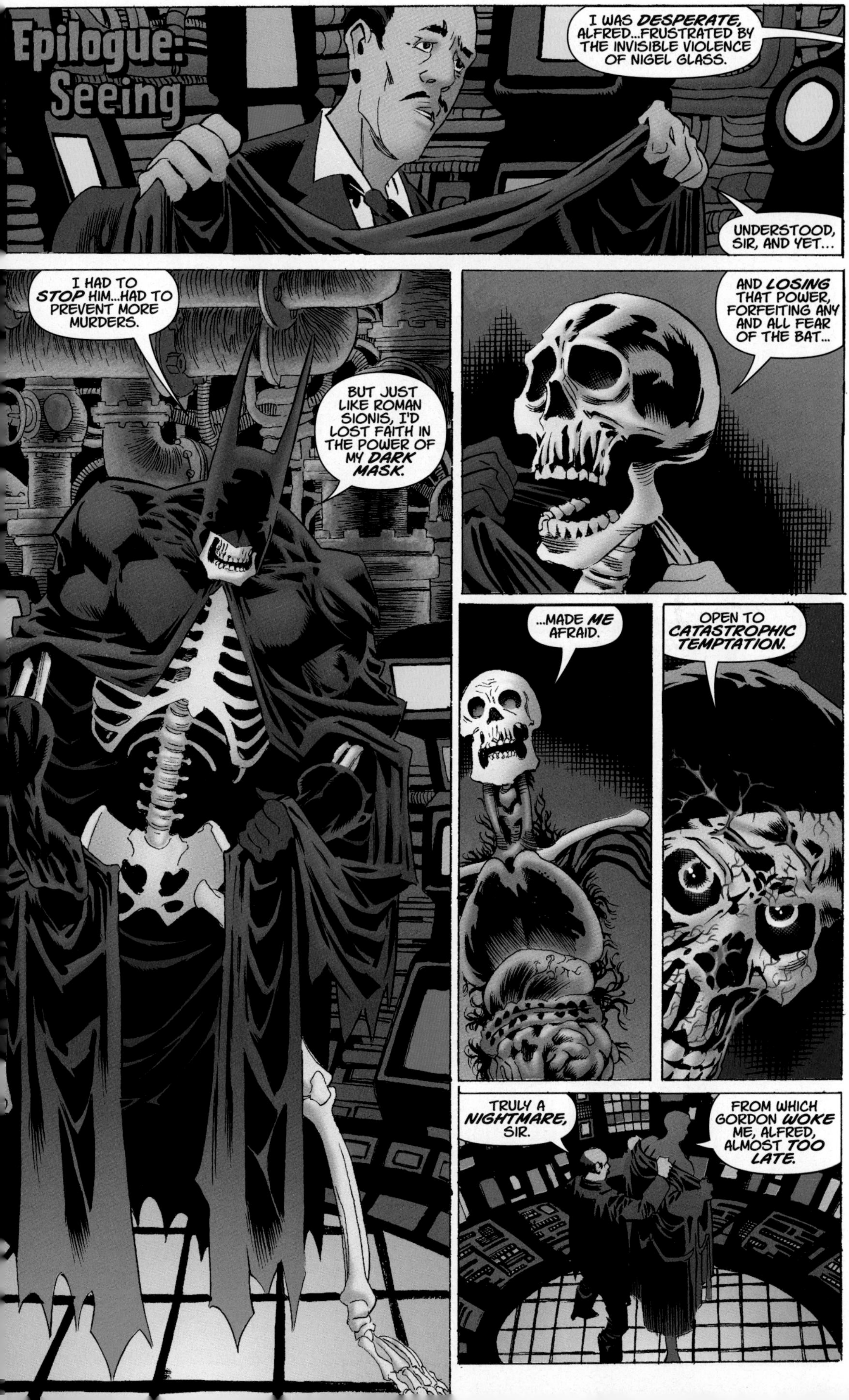

Epilogue: Seeing
I WAS DESPERATE, ALFRED...FRUSTRATED BY THE INVISIBLE VIOLENCE OF NIGEL GLASS.
UNDERSTOOD, SIR, AND YET...
I HAD TO STOP HIM...HAD TO PREVENT MORE MURDERS.
BUT JUST LIKE ROMAN SIONIS, I'D LOST FAITH IN THE POWER OF MY DARK MASK.
AND LOSING THAT POWER, FORFEITING ANY AND ALL FEAR OF THE BAT...
...MADE ME AFRAID.
OPEN TO CATASTROPHIC TEMPTATION.
TRULY A NIGHTMARE, SIR.
FROM WHICH GORDON WOKE ME, ALFRED, ALMOST TOO LATE.

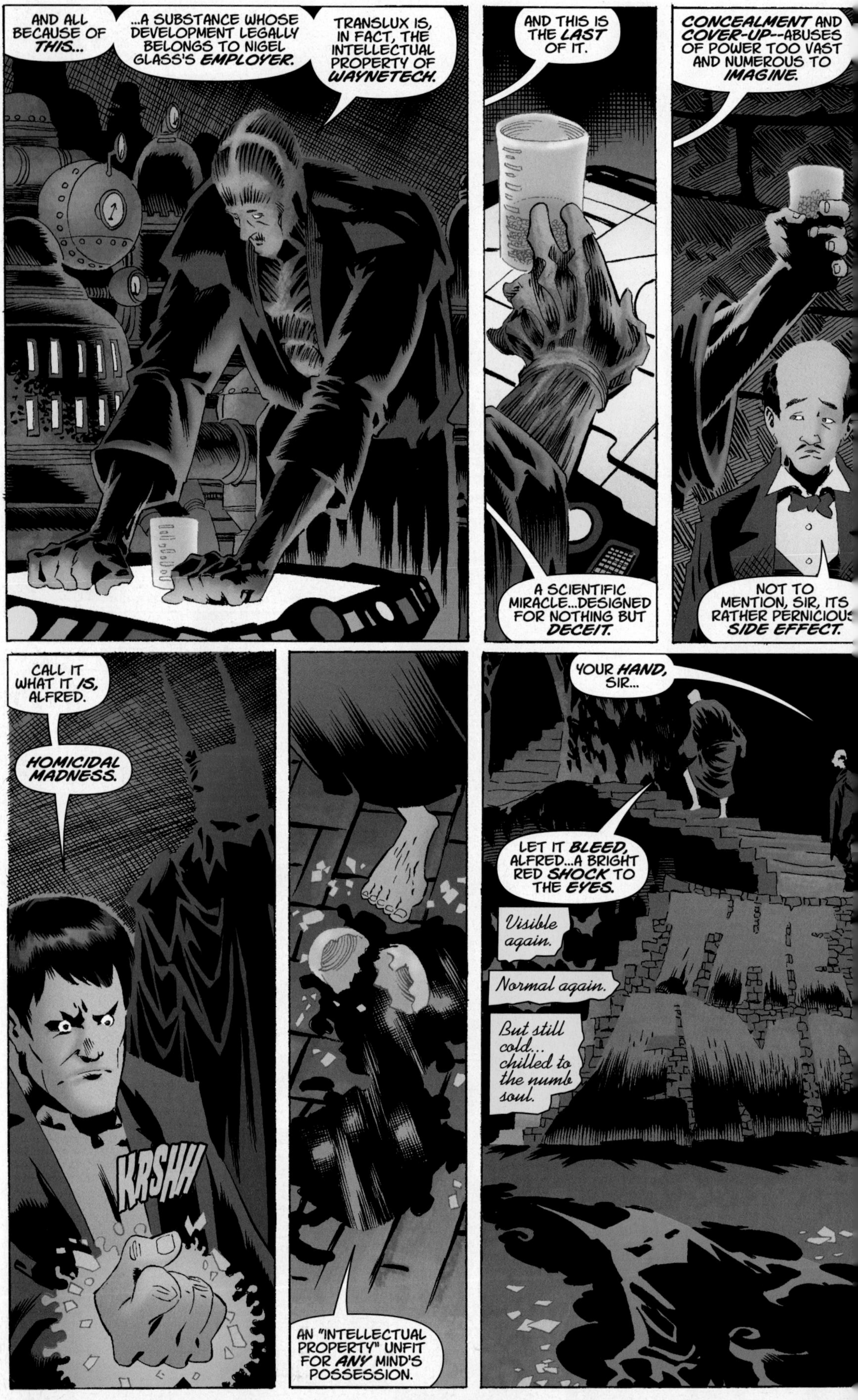
AND ALL BECAUSE OF THIS...
...A SUBSTANCE WHOSE DEVELOPMENT LEGALLY BELONGS TO NIGEL GLASS'S EMPLOYER.
TRANSLUX IS, IN FACT, THE INTELLECTUAL PROPERTY OF WAYNETECH.
AND THIS IS THE LAST OF IT.
A SCIENTIFIC MIRACLE...DESIGNED FOR NOTHING BUT DECEIT.
CONCEALMENT AND COVER-UP--ABUSES OF POWER TOO VAST AND NUMEROUS TO IMAGINE.
NOT TO MENTION, SIR, ITS RATHER PERNICIOUS SIDE EFFECT.
CALL IT WHAT IT IS, ALFRED.
HOMICIDAL MADNESS.
KRSHH
AN "INTELLECTUAL PROPERTY" UNFIT FOR ANY MIND'S POSSESSION.
YOUR HAND, SIR...
LET IT BLEED, ALFRED...A BRIGHT RED SHOCK TO THE EYES.
Visible again.
Normal again.
But still cold... chilled to the numb soul.

MORE CLASSIC TALES OF THE DARK KNIGHT

BATMAN: HUSH
VOLUME ONE

JEPH LOEB
JIM LEE

BATMAN: HUSH
VOLUME TWO

JEPH LOEB
JIM LEE

BATMAN:
THE LONG HALLOWEEN

JEPH LOEB
TIM SALE

BATMAN:
DARK VICTORY

JEPH LOEB
TIM SALE

BATMAN:
HAUNTED KNIGHT

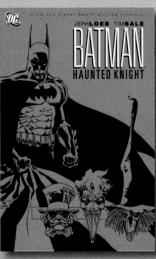

JEPH LOEB
TIM SALE

BATMAN:
YEAR 100

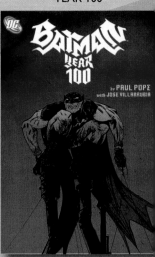

PAUL POPE

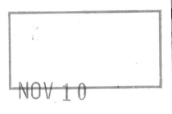